Undoubtedly, the Second World War was one of the darkest periods of history. With untold losses and countless with physical and mental scars, there was little to celebrate except the relief of closure. Yet what happened once the noise of the shelling subsided and the smoke dissipated?

Certainly, late 1940s peacetime Britain was far from easy. Unemployment, power cuts, rationing, national service etc. were difficult to deal with, especially taking into account the physical nature of even some of the most basic tasks. As thoughts turned to recovery of such issues as the economy and unemployment, there was still a need to maintain the Services to such a level that they could provide a peacetime presence in the Rhine area, for example. Of course there were individuals conscripted during the war who were needed for some of the physical rebuilding programmes, the release of whom required national service from the next generation of young men and women. The coal industry needed its men back in the mines, for example. The call up to national service and demobilisation led to a steady stream of young men and women needing either training or an occupation in civvy street. This was at a time when Service numbers needed to be reduced! A difficult balancing act to say the least.

The longer term issues of the day are still casting shadows – even now in the 21st century. For example, some of the concepts in the Education Act of 1944 are still used today and nationalisation of our transport infrastructure continues to be debated. Not forgetting of course that the Welfare State and the National Health Service were founded in the immediate post war years. Although undergoing evolution with time, the basic tenants of their foundation are as relevant today as they always were.

There is one legacy of the Second World War which has mushroomed into a world-wide phenomenon, that of the Paralympic Games. Rehabilitating returning Service personnel with spinal injuries often led to little by way of an active life. The work of Sir Ludwig Guttmann FRS, that of using sport as a means of effecting rehabilitation, has led to treatments beyond expectations.

Dave Rogers set up Danercon Ltd in 2004, having previously worked for a multinational company for 23 years. During his industrial career, Dave spent time working in research and development and in the manufacturing division. His research experience involved product component research, product design and the implementation of process verification equipment.

Dave's manufacturing experience covers the product issues of day to day manufacture, product design as part of a waste reduction effort, as well as leading a process research and development group of some twenty engineers and scientists.

Dave holds a Bachelor and Doctorate degree in Chemistry, Fellowships with the Royal Society of Chemistry, The Royal Photographic Society and the British Institute of Professional Photography (the latter by invitation). He was Visiting Professor at the University of Westminster 2002–2005. Dave is a long term School Governor having recently completed fifteen years as Primary School Governor.

Dave has written or edited thirteen books. Two are war-related which he edited for his father, a third wartime book was co-written by Dave and his father. This is Dave's fourth book for Helion, having previously written *Top Secret. British Boffins in World War One*, *Men Amidst the Madness – British Technology Development in World War Two* and *Destination D-Day – preparations for the invasion of North-West Europe 1944*.

Rebuilding Britain

The Aftermath of the Second World War

David Rogers

Helion & Company Limited

Helion & Company Limited
26 Willow Road
Solihull
West Midlands
B91 1UE
England
Tel. 0121 705 3393
Fax 0121 711 4075
Email: info@helion.co.uk
Website: www.helion.co.uk
Twitter: @helionbooks
Visit our blog http://blog.helion.co.uk/

Published by Helion & Company 2016
Designed and typeset by Farr out Publications, Wokingham, Berkshire
Cover designed by Paul Hewitt, Battlefield Design (www.battlefield-design.co.uk)
Printed by Lightning Source Limited, Milton Keynes, Buckinghamshire

Text © Danercon Ltd 2015
Photographs © As individually credited

ISBN 978-1-910294-45-1

British Library Cataloguing-in-Publication Data.
A catalogue record for this book is available from the British Library.

For details of other military history titles published by Helion & Company Limited contact the above address, or visit our website: http://www.helion.co.uk.

We always welcome receiving book proposals from prospective authors.

Dedicated to my wife Carolyn, without whom my life would be far less enjoyable …

Contents

List of figures   ix
Acknowledgements   xi
Preface   xii

1   Introduction   14
     (a) VE Day   18
     (b) VJ Day   35
     (c) Letters and Telegrams   40

2   Demobilisation   45
     (a) Administration/policies   46
     (b) Benefits/Coupons   56
     (c) Resettlement   61
     (d) Release of Medically trained personnel   68

3   National Service   72
     (a) Administration/Committees   78
     (b) Intake/Training/Qualifications   86
     (c) Exemptions/conscientious objectors   88

4   Education   92
     (a) Administration/Education Act 1944   93
     (b) Communications and training   98
     (c) Wellbeing programmes   102

5   Rationing   107
     (a) Administration   109
     (b) Clothing   116
     (c) Food   121
     (d) Petrol/Domestic fuel   130

6   Nationalisation   136
    (a) Administration   136
    (b) Fuel – Coal/Electricity   140
    (c) Railways/canals   146

7   National Health Service   150
    (a) Admin   150
    (b) Provision of new services   154
    (c) The Paralympic Games   158

8   Welfare State   164
    (a) National Assistance   172
    (b) National Insurance   179

9   Rebuilding works   186
    (a) War Damage Commission/totally destroyed houses   187
    (b) Transport infrastructure   199
    (c) Education Buildings   207
    (d) Bomb Damage to Public or Landmark Buildings   211

Appendices
I   It can now be revealed – Home Forces MOI   226
II   Report on Marshall Aid   234
III   Control of Expenditure after the Defeat in Germany   239
IV   India's Demobilisation Scheme   242
V   Report by the Government Organisation Committee on National Registration 245
VI   Limitation of Suppliers in future rationing schemes   250
VII   Railway (London Plan) Committee 1944. Report to the Minister of
      War Transport 21 January 1946   254
VIII Nationalisation – Transport Bill 1946: Memorandum to the general managers 258

Bibliography   264
Index   266

List of figures

Figure 1.1. A 1940s National Identity Card. (Author's photograph)   14
Figure 1.2. Pre-decimal coins. (Author's photograph)   15
Figure 1.3. Decimal coins and their Wartime equivalent.   16
Figure 1.4. A mechanical calculator. (Author's photograph)   17
Figure 1.5. An armed forces' special voucher. (Author's photograph)   17
Figure 1.6. Number of Underground Coalminers in the Armed Forces.   31
Figure 1.7. An original VJ Day party invitation. (Author's photograph)   36
Figure 1.8. Reconciliation. (Authors photograph)   39
Figure 2.1. Soldier's release book. (Author's photograph)   48
Figure 2.2. Final demobilisation accounts. (Author's photograph)   48
Figure 2.3. Transfer document. (Author's photograph)   49
Figure 2.4. Recall papers. (Author's photograph)   51
Figure 2.5. RAF Service and Release Book (FORM 2520C) detailing the
     authorisation for release and remobilisation instructions. (Author's photograph)   52
Figure 2.6. Class B release data for 1945.   55
Figure 2.7. Coupon uptake in the first 2–3 months.   61
Figure 2.8. Class B releases for men up to 30 April 1946.   63
Figure 3.1. National Service booklet. (Author's photograph)   73
Figure 3.2. National Service Acts.   75
Figure 3.3. National Service Acts explained. (Author's photograph)   76
Figure 3.4. Compulsory medical examination. (Author's photograph)   77
Figure 3.5. Background checks. (Author's photograph)   77
Figure 3.6. Enlistment notice. (Author's photograph)   78
Figure 3.7 Claims for National Service Grants for the first nine months of 1949.   80
Figure 3.8. Potential conscripts.   81
Figure 3.9. Effect on call-up age.   82
Figure 3.10. Effect on raising standards.   82
Figure 3.11. Further reference on National Service.   86
Figure 3.12. Undesirable hostel residents.   91
Figure 4.1. Some National Archives folio references.   94
Figure 4.2. A catering qualification from 1951. (Author's photograph)   105
Figure 5.1. End of rationing in Britain.   108
Figure 5.2. My ration book. (Author's photograph)   109

Figure 5.3. Instructions for using a general ration book. (Author's photograph)   113
Figure 5.4. Bread rations.   114
Figure 5.5. An example of a supplementary clothing coupon book.
    (Author's photograph)   117
Figure 5.6. Clothing coupons issued during and after the War.   118
Figure 5.7. Occupational coupon supplements.   119
Figure 5.8. Seaman's Identity card. (Author's photograph)   120
Figure 5.9. Seaman's clothing coupons. (Author's photograph)   121
Figure 5.10. A part page of food coupons. (Author's photograph)   126
Figure 5.11. Form BS99 – claim form for bread subsidy. (Author's photograph)   127
Figure 5.12. The page of coupons issued to demobilised soldier. (Author's
    photograph)   128
Figure 5.13. Petrol ration book for a small engine car. (Author's photograph)   133
Figure 5.14. Petrol ration book for a large engine car. (Author's photograph)   133
Figure 5.15. Petrol coupons and their gallon amount.   134
Figure 6.1. Some horse numbers from the Horse Stock Record Book.   147
Figure 7.1. Progression in hospitals providing rehabilitation.   159
Figure 7.2. Sir Ludwig Guttmann FRS. (Author's photograph)   160
Figure 7.3. The Paralympic Symbol displayed on Tower Bridge. (Author's
    photograph)   162
Figure 8.1. Some of the immediate post-war Welfare State key Acts.   166
Figure 8.2. Founding members of the Assistance Board.   173
Figure 8.3. A payment card for an Approved Society. (Author's photograph)   181
Figure 8.4. A contribution record card. (Author's photograph)   182
Figure 8.5. Service contributions to National Insurance. (Author's photograph)   185
Figure 9.1. Restoration dedication plaque at St James's Church. (Author's
    photograph)   187
Figure 9.2. North Western Region proposals for 1950.   198
Figure 9.3. London projects.   199
Figure 9.4. Damages to services over a 16 month war period.   200
Figure 9.5. Membership of the Ingles Report.   203
Figure 9.6. School war damage.   208
Figure 9.7. Some land bought by compulsory purchase for use in education.   210
Figure 9.8. Commonwealth gifts to the new House of Commons.   218
Figure 9.9. Colonial gifts to the New House of Commons.   219
Figure 9.10. The area of Whitehall needing work. (Author's photograph)   220
Figure 9.11. A contemporary picture of Coventry Cathedral. (Author's photograph)   225

Acknowledgements

I always have a problem with listing people to thank who have helped me in my research as there is always the opportunity to miss someone. Hopefully if that were to happen I would have the opportunity to correct the mistake well ahead of publication. In this case the person I would most like to thank, my father, died a short while before I started the book. It might seem a little strange to want to thank someone who was not involved in the writing; however, we had many fruitful discussions concerning the paperwork that appears throughout the book. Also my father went through the process of national service, demobilisation and retraining for a job in civilian life, and helped me appreciate some of the complexities of life after the war. I would have been able to muddle through trying to obtain some equivalent paperwork, however, my father's advice last year and his archive enabled the process of piecing together this narrative much easier than it would otherwise have been. He's a hard act to follow.

Of course there are other examples of paperwork issued during the war which appear in the book, some of which was passed down by various members of my close family and others from more distant relatives. To one and all I thank you for helping to make this book contain more personal memories than might otherwise be the case.

As usual the members of staff at the National Archives helped whenever I asked, which was more frequent than perhaps it should have been. Thank you one and all. Similarly the library staff at the Royal Society have continued to be helpful offering advice on various Fellows and their exploits, thank you.

Bill Broadhurst needs a special mention as he proof read the entire manuscript. Those mistakes that are still in this book are, as always, my problem for which I hope the reader will accept an anticipatory apology!

Finally, my family always put up with a lot as I ramble on and on about various anecdotes I find fascinating. They deserve more than thanks.

Preface

I have written a few books about wars. In most cases I have not even considered what happened once the noise, bullets and bombs stopped. How did the front line soldiers cope with the end of what must have seemed their longest nightmare? Furthermore, how did those at home cope with the changes in their family circumstances, perhaps the loss of a close relative, leading to financial deprivation and emotional instability?

The cost of war casts long shadows in all directions. Rebuilding a nation after such trauma is painstaking, requiring years of hard work, a sense of purpose and urgency with many factors requiring attention. I have chosen the end of the Second World War as the exemplar from which to determine some of the many issues involved, partly because some of them are still relevant now some 70 years after the war ended. For example the National Health Service, the Welfare State, the Education Act of 1944, etc.

As one might expect, in some cases there was a balancing act between returning Britain back to a sense of normality on the one hand and ensuring a lasting peace on the other. Whilst some soldiers were being demobilised to help with literally rebuilding work others were conscripted. For example the immediate post-war years saw a British force in the Rhine area of Germany, some of the troops for which were called to National Service after the War ended – including my late father. There was also unemployment at this time adding to the complexities of slowly reducing the overall troop numbers in the Services.

One facet of the immediate post-war era which I had not thought about was the planning for peacetime which took place during the war. As we shall see later, some of the committees meeting to develop a workable demobilisation strategy were active in Whitehall at the same time as an alternative series of committees and soldiers were planning for D-Day! Other examples are also documented.

Some other activities started during the War also continued afterwards. For example there were crews of men clearing bomb sites of debris, which continued after 1945. Some of the rubble was used to create runways for the RAF stations, particularly in the south of England. Another issue which exercised the minds of the post-war government was who owned the rubble? It might seem obvious to us in hindsight, yet less so during the days of wartime. Should you be fortunate enough to own your house and it was bombed, until told otherwise you surely owned the bricks and rubble created by the bomb. Actually it was not that simple for as soon as the government committed to rebuilding these properties, they owned the rubble, or what was left of it.

Another issue facing the Government of the time was the return to civilian use of land or buildings requisitioned for war use. In some cases the land was retained – even now. In other cases, the land created by bombed out buildings was used as temporary accommodation for workers engaged in rebuilding. Other sites were used for prisoner of war camps which were easier to return to public use.

Those who lived through these times talk of rationing, power cuts, nationalisation, etc. It has taken me a while to appreciate the complexities of post-war Britain and the after-effects of wars in general. Hopefully this account, although far from comprehensive (space and time make this difficult for it would need me to replicate many more folios from the National Archives), explores most of the issues involved.

1   Introduction

The post-war years were tough by anyone's standards. Not only were Service personnel returning with unforgettable memories, some carried permanent medical issues needing attention. Many never came home at all. Every man, woman and child was subjected to rationing, some adults were unemployed, travelling was complicated making visits to relatives or looking for work difficult – especially the effects of petrol and food rationing. Add to that constant power outages, rubble to clear and houses to protect/rebuild. Arguably the position was worse than for those old enough to experience the post-First World War years. This is not said lightly for there were many horrors from the First World War. However, aircraft, in their infancy during the First

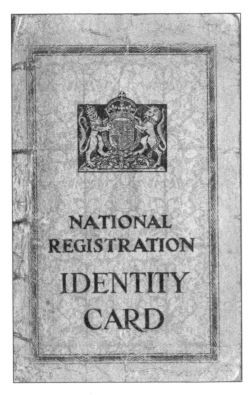

Figure 1.1. A 1940s National Identity
Card. (Author's photograph)

World War, came to the fore in the Second World War and with it the effects of large-scale bombing, leaving many more shattered lives and buildings in mainland Britain than thought possible previously.

Whatever the circumstances, everyone played their part in helping to rebuild Britain – in some cases literally – which was a long and gruelling process. First-hand accounts of these and other issues set the scene for a more detailed exploration from the National Archives of this mammoth task. Anyone who carried a National Identity card from the time, figure 1.1, lived through some of the darkest times of the 20th Century. Ask someone you may know who fits the age profile for their experiences.

Of course rebuilding Britain, in all senses of the word, could only start in earnest once peace was declared. Arguably, the nature of a global conflict complicated the end of the Second World War as had no other war. Peace in Europe was announced and the date chosen as 8 May 1945, and was known as VE Day or Victory in Europe. Victory in Japan, or VJ Day, took place some months later on 15 August 1945.

There was a mixed feeling in Britain at that time. For those who lived through the heavy bombing, VE Day signified a day when there was more safety than previously – even if nothing else changed. Those with relatives in the Services were mindful of the conflicts in the Far East, and for them there was no rest as the uncertainly of war undermined their waking thoughts. Furthermore, as troops and families caught up in the European theatre started to disembark in Britain, the full horror of the European conflict started to become more apparent.

Of course some carried emotional or physical scars for the rest of their lives. As

Figure 1.2. Pre-decimal coins. (Author's photograph)

a teenager in the mid-1960s I had the unfortunate need to visit my elder brother in a hospital in Leeds. This hospital then cared for former service personnel who still suffered the effects of war and who were still in residence in the hospital some twenty years after the end of hostilities. It was a sobering sight and one I will never forget, especially the prosthetic limbs. Technology has come a long way since those dark times. Of course the work of Sir Ludwig Guttmann FRS is of importance here, for without his work at Stoke Mandeville Hospital there would not necessarily be the modern Paralympic Games we now enjoy. More of Sir Ludwig's work appears in chapter 7.

Arguably few at the time knew the full extent of the civil defences during the war. The Ministry of Information compiled an account of some of the means of denial we were to use in the event of an invasion, which was published as a restricted document under the title 'It can now be revealed' after the war ended. This document has been reproduced in its entirety as Appendix I. Some of these initiatives were designed to come into effect in the event of an invasion. Others such as beach defences needed to be removed once the war was over.

Finally, there are later references to the old currency which was in use in the United Kingdom until 15 February 1971. Both my parents, teenagers at the time, thought that the larger differences in coin sizes than those we use currently was useful during the blackout, particularly the threepenny (3d) coin which was twelve-sided. Figure 1.2 shows these coins and figure 1.3 a conversion table of old coins and our now established decimal currency. This will help the younger reader with some of the later chapters which include references to costs of rebuilding for example, which is described in £sd (i.e. pounds, shillings and pence).

Pre-decimal coin	Equivalent Decimal Coin
Farthing	
Half-penny	
Penny	
Threepenny piece (12 sided)	
Six pence	
Shilling	5 pence
Two shillings (florin)	10 pence
Half a crown (two and six pence)	
Crown	
Half Sovereign	
Sovereign	

Figure 1.3. Decimal coins and their Wartime equivalent.

There is no equivalent decimal coin for the pre-decimal pennies as there were 2.4 old pence to one new (decimal) pence. There were 12 pre-decimal pennies to the shilling

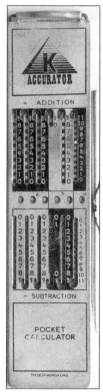

Figure 1.5. An armed forces' special voucher. (Author's photograph)

Figure 1.4. A mechanical
calculator. (Author's photograph)

and 240 pennies to the pound. Simple maths shows us that there were 20 shillings to the pound. Electronic calculators were unheard of for adding and subtracting predecimal currency – in the war years one had to rely on mental maths. By the 1960s one could buy mechanical calculators for adding and subtracting pre-decimal coins, some of which still exist, for example figure 1.4.

Although encouraged to use mental maths, it was still interesting to own a mechanical calculator capable of working out the sums!

Not everyone used our national currency, however. Too young for the start of the war, my father was called up just as war was ending and was sent to Germany as part of the British Army of the Rhine. Whilst there, he used vouchers issued by the Army. Figure 1.5 is an example of a 3d voucher and was valid for use in NAFFI canteens etc. whilst my father was in Germany. He subsequently gave me a new £1 forces voucher which must have been from a considerably later period, suggesting that the practice of issuing vouchers was continued by the Army for some time after the war ended.

Of course the post-war economy was of interest to everyone, not least the Americans who were keen to ensure that the European economy improved after the war and was not in such a state that our thoughts turned to a liaison with Russia. Accordingly the Americans conceived Marshall Aid, Appendix II.

(a) **VE Day**

Whilst war raged in the Far East, and German troops were being defeated, preparations for the celebration of the German surrender started to gather momentum. It was apparent by mid-March 1945 that it was only a matter of time before the end of the war in Europe. As one might expect there were issues to resolve and plans to develop/enact. Amidst all the letters and telegrams sent and received by Allied Governments and senior military figures, there are three aspects of the preparations detailed below which may be of interest, at least in Britain, namely:

a)   Public announcements.
b)   Public celebrations in England.
c)   Ministerial/Government Activities.

Each of these themes will be dealt with separately. Of course some of them overlap, but documenting these separate topics in chronological order of their correspondence is confusing – I tried!

Public announcements

Almost a month prior to the formal announcement of an end to European hostilities, some of the Military and Government leaders discussed the form and timing of a public statement.

> To: War Department
> 13th April 1945
> FWD 19189 SCAF 279
> FWD 19189 Top Secret to for action ADWAR for Combined Chiefs of Staff info AMSSO for British Chiefs of Staff, AFHQ for Alexander from SHAEF Forward signed Eisenhower SCAF 279.
>
> This replies to FACS 180. Present evidence indicates that the Germans intend with every means in their power to prolong resistance to the bitter end in the most inaccessible areas of the continent which their forces now occupy. The possibility of a clear cut cessation of hostilities may therefore be considered unlikely.
>
> Areas in which resistance may be continued after the general linking up of our forces with the Russian Armies; and for which I am likely to be responsible, including the following widely dispersed localities:
>
> A.   Western Austria or National Redoubt.
> B.   North German ports.
> C.   Frisian Islands and Heligoland.
> D.   Western Holland.
> E.   Denmark.
> F.   Norway.
> G.   Channel Islands.
> H.   German pockets in France.

Although resistance in a number of these areas may not be prolonged it is evident that operations against certain of them, notably Norway and Western Austria, may involve considerable forces and also may last for some time.

The declaration of a VE Day will inevitably convey to the people of the United States and of the British Commonwealth that the war in Europe is over and that such hostilities as may continue will amount to nothing more than minor engagements with guerrilla bands. I believe, therefore, that in order to avoid subsequent misunderstandings it is imperative to postpone the declaration of VE Day until it is evident that further months of hostilities on a fairly considerable scale do not lie before us. It may well be that morale in the German outposts will crack as soon as the greater part of Germany has been occupied, but this cannot be proved until the event has happened.

It must be remembered that the storming of the final citadels of Nazi resistance may well call for acts of endurance and heroism on the part of the forces engaged comparable to the peak battles of the war, and I believe that a premature declaration of VE Day might well have a serious adverse effect on the morale of the troops engaged which would in turn affect the operations.

My recommendations are that VE Day should not be announced until the following conditions have been fulfilled:

1. Our forces have joined hands with the Russians in Central Germany over a fairly wide front.
2. Our forces have occupied the key positions in the so called National Redoubt of western Austria, thereby preventing long drawn out operations on a considerable scale.
3. Our forces are in a position to enter Denmark thereby assuring an early assault on Norway.

As to procedure it is my belief that the declaration of VE Day should take the form of a coordinated statement by the Russians, British and United States Governments, the timing of which should be based on the recommendations of SACMED and myself to the Combined Chiefs of Staff.

I fully appreciate the urgent necessity for the early release of forces from this theatre for the prosecution of the war against Japan and this has in fact already begun as we have agreed to the redeployment of a number of units on our troop basis. It will also be possible for us to release progressively essential units from this theatre prior to the cessation of hostilities when the enemy becomes confined to limited areas which I have indicated above. I recommend therefore that the initiation of redeployment should bear no fixed time relationship to the declaration of VE Day but should be timed in accordance with the progress of operations.

Eisenhower

End[1]

Eisenhower was not the only senior figure with these sentiments, for example Field

1   National Archives CAB 122/1278.

Marshall Alexander echoed Eisenhower's comment in a telegram of his own from the Allied Force Headquarters, Caserta Italy on 13 April 1945.

> I am strongly opposed to any announcement of victory in Europe being made until the whole of Germany, Austria and German occupied territory has been overrun and all organised resistance has ceased.
>
> It would be deplorable if victory celebrations took place whilst lives were being lost in operations to eliminate sizable pockets of resistance. Resistance by guerrilla bands will probably continue for some time after organised resistance is over, but this need not hold up the victory announcement.
> Telegram ends.[2]

Further discussions followed:

> The COS have expressed agreement with the view of SACMED that there should be no announcement of victory in Europe 'until the whole of Germany, Austria and German occupied territory has been overrun and all organised resistance has ceased'. If this is the criterion finally adopted by the three Allied Governments the difficulties which might have been created by the Home Secretary's statement on the 12th April will at least be much diminished. But even so, 'all organised resistance has ceased' is capable of varying interpretations and, although it would no doubt cover E-Boat activity, would not necessarily mean that VE Day would not occur before the last U-Boat was rounded up.
>
> In light of the Departmental and Board minutes concerning the present necessity for retaining a complete coastal dim out (and blackout in some local areas), it would seem that some such precaution should be kept in force until it is clear that there will be no more – or at most very few – U-Boats in coastal waters. Otherwise men's lives will be hazarded for the sake of a little extra light for a relatively short period. If the risk is unjustifiable then either:
>
> a)   The Admiralty must press that VE Day should wait until the U-Boat threat has diminished to negligible proportions or vanished OR
>
> b)   If we fail to secure that point, the Home Secretary must be persuaded to state the position clearly that lighting restrictions may have to continue in coastal areas for a time after VE Day. Parliament and the public would surely regard it as a breach of faith if, without any qualification of his statement of the 12th April, he maintained any lighting restrictions after VE Day.
>
> Of these two courses, a) seems far preferable and it is suggested that this should be pursued to the limit before b) is tried. Presumably the best way of pursuing a) would be through the COS and CCS channel. It the CCS accepted such an elaboration of the definition of the pre-conditions for VE Day it would be difficult indeed to challenge.[3]

2   Ibid.
3   Ibid.

Arguably the end of war in Europe needed to be celebrated in a memorable and appropriate manner. For the senior figures in the War Cabinet and Services, there were issues needing clarification before celebrations could proceed. The temptation was to turn on every streetlight and lift the blackout restrictions. Indeed this was mooted at the Cabinet meeting on 27 April 1945.

Dear Archie,

 As you will be the only Service Minister present at the meeting of the War Cabinet this morning which is to consider the arrangements for celebrating the end of hostilities in Europe, I should like to let you know our position in two matters which would be affected by any proposal to fix VE Day.

 The Home Secretary has stated in the House that it is his intention to remove all lighting restrictions not later than the end of hostilities in Europe. I have explained to the Prime Minister and the Home Secretary however that the Admiralty cannot willingly agree to the raising of the blackout and dim out in the five mile coastal strip until the Naval war is over. The Prime Minister's directive on manpower in 1945 states that it is of the utmost importance that releases from the three Services should begin not more than six weeks after the end of the German War. Any substantial releases from the Navy can only take place after a sufficient period has elapsed after the end of the U-Boat war.[4]

Further discussions with our Allies followed:

Re: our immediately preceding telegram.

The following is a text of a draft memorandum to the President and Prime Minister. Begins:

a) Combined Chiefs of Staff have reviewed the question of establishing a VE Day in the light of probable developments in the military situation and have received the views of General Eisenhower and Field Marshal Alexander on the subject. Present evidence indicates that the Germans intend with every means in their power to prolong resistance to the bitter end in the most inaccessible areas of the continent which their forces now occupy. It appears unlikely that there will be a clear-cut cessation of hostilities. Accordingly, we believe that a VE Day can scarcely occur except by public proclamation on our part.

b) Any declaration of VE Day will inevitably be received by the public as an assurance that the war in Europe is over and that such hostilities as may continue will amount to nothing more than minor clashes with guerrilla bands. We therefore believe it most important, in order to avoid subsequent misunderstandings, to postpone declaration of VE Day until it is evident that organised resistance has ceased and that hostilities on any considerable scale are, in fact, over.

4 National Archives ADM 1/17779.

c)   As to procedure, we consider that the declaration of VE Day should be by
     means of a coordinated public statement by the Soviet, British and United
     States Governments, timed in accordance with advice of the Combined
     Chiefs of Staff, based on the recommendation of General Eisenhower and
     Field Marshal Alexander.
Telegram ends.[5]

After further discussions on Friday 27 April 1945, the War Cabinet produced the
following actions:

1.   Agreed in principle that the arrangements set out in the Appendix to this
     minute would be appropriate for the celebration of an armistice or general
     surrender of German forces in all European theatres of war.
2.   Appointed a Committee consisting of:
     a)   The Home Secretary (in the Chair).
     b)   The Minister of Reconstruction, and
     c)   The Minister of Information.
     To settle details of the arrangements outlined in the appendix, and to
consider how these arrangements would have to be modified if the celebrations
were related to an Allied declaration that organised resistance by Germany was
at an end.[6]

The appendix mentioned above is reproduced below:

Summary of main arrangements proposed for VE Day and following days (on
the assumption of an armistice or general surrender of German forces in all
European theatres)

Announcements

1.   Preliminary warning. As soon as it has been decided that an official
     announcement is to be made at a given hour that hostilities in Europe have
     ended, prior notice will be given to HM Governments in the Dominions,
     India and the Colonies.
          The BBC will also inform the public that an important announcement
     will be made by the Prime Minister at the time arranged. Selected factory
     managements will be specially warned in order that any necessary safety
     arrangements may be made.
2.   Parliament, if not sitting, will be specially summoned, on whatever day of
     the week the announcement is to be made.
3.   At the stated hour the Prime Minister, as executive head of the Government,
     will announce on the wireless that hostilities in Europe have ceased.
4.   At the ordinary time for commencement of business the Prime Minister
     will repeat in the House of Commons the announcement previously made

5   National Archives CAB 122/1278.
6   National Archives WORK 21/204.

by him on the wireless. The House of Commons will then adjourn for a Thanksgiving Service in St Margaret's.

5. In the House of Lords a similar announcement will be made by the Leader of the House; and the House will adjourn for a Thanksgiving Service in Westminster Abbey.

6. During the evening of VE Day, His Majesty The King will broadcast to the nation and Empire.

7. On a later day, possibly the day following VE Day, the Prime Minister will make a broadcast speech.

8. It may be convenient that Parliament should stand adjourned on the day following VE Day (this point will be considered in consultation with the authorities of both Houses of Parliament).

9. About one week after VE Day both Houses of Parliament will present Loyal Addresses to His Majesty the King.

    Floodlighting by local authorities and public bodies will be encouraged on VE Day. Restrictions on the illumination of electric advertisements, neon signs and shop window lighting need not be enforced.

As might be expected, Churchill had a view on the matter.

War Cabinet Chiefs of Staff Committee

4th May 1945

General Ismay for the Chiefs of Staff Committee

I am afraid that I am not able to associate myself with the proposed telegram and do not think it will fit the circumstances. We are the principle anti-U-Boat Power in the Atlantic and we do not need to complicate our already tangled difficulties by working up the American Navy Department on the subject.

The cessation of the German War will be followed either by orders, given by some person whom we may deal, to all U-Boats to cease fire and return at once, or, if resistance is maintained in Norway after any coherent Government exists in Germany, they will be pirates. I was about to propose new measures to inform them of the position they will occupy once they ceased to be the instrument of a lawful government. Anyhow, the question of whether the surrender of all Germany is to go unrecognised for an indefinite number of weeks till the German resistance in and from Norway is liquidated, has yet to be decided and it certainly covers the question of the U-Boats.

Winston Churchill 4.5.45.[7]

And on another topic written on the same day and stored in the same folio:

The Prime Minister has minuted (D 130/5) as follows on the minute submitted to him on the 3rd May.

General Ismay for the Chiefs of Staff Committee

7   National Archives CAB 122/1278.

I agree that we should have our share and that liberty may be given to Military Officers on this occasion. I propose that we should have five, namely the three Chiefs of Staff, Field Marshal Alexander and Field Marshal Montgomery. If these names are altered, I should not be able to support the project.

Signed for

Winston Churchill 4.5.45.[8]

General Ismay replied:

Copy of a minute dated 5th May 1945 from General Ismay to the Prime Minister
VE Day – Broadcasts by Commanders-in-Chief

Reference your minute serial no D.130/5, the Chiefs of Staff will willingly give a broadcast message whenever you so desire. They suggest that it would be fitting to give the American Chiefs of Staff the opportunity of associating themselves with their British colleagues on such an occasion. The Chiefs of Staff also entirely agree that Field Marshal Alexander should give a broadcast, supported by the Deputy Supreme Commander and the Naval and Air Commanders, both British and American, in the Mediterranean theatre.

The Chiefs of Staff point out, however, that the project which formed the subject of my minute of 3rd May is confirmed to the North-Western front, and that they feel that it would have an unfortunate effect in America if the senior British Commanders on that front did not take their share.

They therefore recommend that permission should be given to the following to broadcast:

i) Air Chief Marshal Tedder. In his capacity as Deputy Supreme Commander he is well placed to pay a generous tribute to the great work and personality of General Eisenhower. He has prepared a script which CAS thinks excellent.

ii) Field Marshal Montgomery, whose claims are outstanding.

iii) Admiral Burrough. Unless a British Admiral is allowed to broadcast, it is pretty certain that the American Admiral Kirk will do so, and the impression will gain ground in America that it is the American fleet who have been lending all the support to our forces on the Continent. Admiral Burrough is, however, moreover, well known to the Americans owing to the part he played in the North African landings.

iv) Air Marshal Coningham, who has commanded the Tactical Air Force in support of the 21st Army Group.[9]

The following was addressed to Moscow telegram no 2443 of 5 May repeated to Washington and San Francisco.

Personal for Secretary of State

8   Ibid.
9   Ibid.

Please convey the following from Prime Minister to Marshal Stalin dated 5th May.

… President Truman tells me he has sent you a message asking that we should synchronise our announcements about VE Day. I am in full agreement with this.

Best hour for me would be noon today should only take 3 or 4 minutes to announce the victory over Germany. Making allowance for British double summer time this would mean 1pm with you. But it would require President Truman's message to be delivered in Washington at 6am which would hardly be fair either to the President or people of United States. I therefore propose to the American views by fixing on three pm British double summer time which is 4 pm your present clock time. This would enable the President's announcement to be made at 9am Washington time.

Would you let me know as soon as possible whether you agree to this.[10]

The following note from Marshall Stalin confirmed the above action plan, which was enacted a few days later.

Top Secret and Personal
6th May 1945
On 6th May I received your message of 5th May on the subject of time of announcement of victory in Europe and day.

I have no objection to your proposal of 3 o'clock British Summer Time, which corresponds to 4pm Moscow time.

I have also notified President Truman to the same effect.
Signed
Marshal Stalin[11]

Public celebrations

One of the earliest meetings concerned the issue of floodlighting public buildings. There was a powerful symbolism to lighting public buildings with floodlights – especially so after years of blackouts. The first of a series of meetings documenting progress towards the eventual outcome appears below. It is worth noting that these minutes mention a comment by the Home Secretary raising this issue as early as October 1944!

Cease Fire Public Arrangements
27th March 1945
C S Petheran asked me to attend a meeting at the Home Office today, to discuss this matter, which had been reviewed last week by the LP Committee. He thought the Ministry should be represented, as regards the Palace and the Royal Parks.

10 Ibid.
11 Ibid.

There were present C S Petheran and H A Strutt of the Home Office, Air Commodore Lawson and Squadron Leader Whitham of the Air Ministry, R Kelf-Choen of the Ministry of Fuel and Power and myself.

The matter was raised by the Home Secretary last October on the LP Committee but was deferred. It was reviewed last week, 23rd March, and it is expected that the matter will be laid before Cabinet next week.

Norman Brook has written to Strutt with certain suggestions, which had emerged from the meetings of the LP Committee.

Proposals:

There should be floodlighting of the principal public buildings, e.g. Houses of Parliament, and of course Buckingham Palace. Perhaps too, Trafalgar Square, Westminster Abbey, St Paul's and The Tower.

The Ministry of Fuel and Power strongly oppose the restoration of full lighting in the streets. They have no objection to floodlighting.

The Air Ministry would assist with floodlighting, and the War Department and the Admiralty (in the Ports) should be asked to assist.

Starshells, guns and any other noises should be avoided.

No aircraft display.

The arrangements should apply all over the country, but should be in the local control of the Municipalities.

In Government circles there would presumably be some advance in information. The notice to the public might be only one or two days.

Strutt will be preparing a draft of a public announcement.

I could not say what apparatus the Ministry would have for floodlighting, but would see what was available. I know that we had already parted with some to the Defence Departments. I could not offer any suggestions at the moment but I would take note of what had been said.

Flags from existing stocks may be flown, but no large display by the public would be possible, owing to the shortage of material.

Following on from that meeting, lists were generated, one of which is dated 3 April 1945:

Buildings where external floodlights can be arranged in three days and where fittings are available:
a)   Buckingham Palace.
b)   National Gallery.
c)   Big Ben Clock Tower.
d)   St James' Park Bridge over the lake.
e)   Royal Naval College Greenwich.
f)   Ministry of Information Senate House.

Buildings where floodlighting can be arranged in three days provided suitable floodlighting fittings are obtained:
g)   Horse Guards – both fronts.

h)   Admiralty Arch – both sides.
i)   Trafalgar Square – Nelson's Statue.
j)   Somerset House.
k)   Tower of London.
l)   Natural History and V&A Museums.
m) Hampton Court Palace W&S fronts.[12]

The paperwork following this list in the National Archives folio mentioned above also provides checklists of what will be needed and which sites could be made ready at three days' notice. Plans and an enlarged committee were in place by mid-April. Indeed a summary of the agreed actions was written up:

Mr Batch
When you talked to the Minister this morning about arrangements for VE Day it was decided:

1.   That you would prepare a scheme for flying, in two groups, the flag of the British Empire and the flags of the United Nations, in some suitable position where they could be floodlit.
2.   That you would raise, at the Home Office Committee, the question of fireworks.
3.   That you would raise, at the same Committee, what recommendations should be made to provincial towns about floodlighting etc.
4.   That you would see whether a suitable balcony could be built, possibly in the Treasury building facing Parliament Square, or in the Ministry of Health, or the Home Office, facing Whitehall, so that the war leaders of the United Nations might appear before the crowds; and that you would also consider whether a microphone could be installed.
5.   That you would consider whether arrangements could be made to put out all the floodlights at Buckingham Palace, except that spot-lighting the balcony, where the King would appear.

Ewing
16th April 1945.[13]

As is the case even today, important, world-renowned public buildings in the United Kingdom needed The Monarch or Prime Minister's approval. The following documents some of the King's thoughts:

The King has approved:

1.   The floodlighting of Windsor Castle – Round Tower and St George's Chapel.
2.   The focussing of the light on the central Panels of the Palace front when he appears.

---

12   National Archives WORK 21/204.
13   Ibid.

He did not approve the Film Companies' idea of high power floodlights in front of the Palace to enable film to be shot.

The Minister's suggestion that the large King's Birthday standard should be flown has been passed on to the Master of the Household.

The Palace have confirmed that the Royal Standard flies both at night and day when the King is in residence. He will reside at Buckingham Palace on the nights of VE Day and VE+1 Day.

The Dean of St Paul's wants to floodlight the Dome on the following Sunday. I agree with London region that he should be told that this would require approval at a very high level, and that he should be dissuaded from pursuing the suggestion …

Signed

Mr Auriol Barker

3rd May 1945[14]

Some months later (30 November 1945), the cost of hiring the floodlighting fittings from Earls Court Ltd for the VE Day celebrations was reported as £11,500 for engineering services and £500 for surveyors' attendance fees!

Of course even the simple act of flying flags, which has also been a powerful symbol, required some co-ordination.

Flying of Flags

Minister

Following arrangements that have been made in connection with VE Day, it is proposed to issue a general instruction regarding the flying of flags on all occasions on buildings for which the Ministry of Works are responsible (including the Cenotaph) as follows:

1. To ensure that all flags are flown clean, arrangements should be made to replace all flags in use by new or cleaned flags at regular prescribed intervals.[15] Where the Ministry of Works provides the flags but is not responsible for flying them, the Department responsible should similarly be informed that we are prepared to replace the flags at the same intervals as in the case of our own buildings. This will involve maintaining a larger stock of flags.

2. The flags are to be of the largest size compatible with the position in which they are to be flown.

3. All flags are to be of the correct proportions, viz, the length should be twice the breadth. The only exceptions will be certain foreign flags where a particular shape is prescribed.

Do you approve?

R. Auriol Barker

14 National Archives WORK 21/204.
15 Pending further instructions these will be: three months in the case of flags flown daily, annually in the case of flags flown on hoisting days only. In the case of the Cenotaph, new flags should be supplied quarterly and cleaned ones each intervening month.

3rd May 1945[16]

Ministerial/Government Activities

As the threat of further European conflict abated, senior ministers in the Treasury turned their attention to the reduction of our armed forces as soon as possible, in order to reduce the monetary burden of war. The following, written within the Treasury Chambers, was sent to the Prime Minister:

13th April 1945

Prime Minister

During the last few years, when all our resources have been devoted to the prosecution of the war, control of expenditure by the Treasury has been largely superseded by allocation between competing war purposes. With the end of the German war in sight, the Treasury should resume many of the powers of control now delegated to Departments. In this note I submit certain suggestions to this end for which I seek your support and help.

It seems to me that the first essential decision is about the size of each of the Forces, Army, Royal Air Force and Navy, to be deployed in the Far East, and also the total overall number of men to which each of the Services is to be reduced by a target date. I understand that you have in mind a draft directive covering these points.

This directive would provide the foundation for a manpower allocation which would seek to withdraw labour as quickly as feasible from the Supply Departments and to turn it over to civil production. The manpower directive would also provide a framework within which the Treasury can require the Services to work and by which their proposal for expenditure can be tested.

May I give an example? A proposal has recently been submitted by the Air Ministry for various works services in order to enable air transport to be used to lift troops between this country and the Far East, up to a figure of 10,000 per month, in each direction, this air lift being designed to start by 1st October next. Without knowing more of the plans for the campaign in the Far East and the extent of the Services to be deployed, it is difficult for the Treasury to judge whether this scheme is an essential part of our War plans.

On civilian expenditure generally, I am proposing to issue a circular calling on Departments for a) a statement of their wartime activities and b) plans for their reduction. There may be certain fields of expenditure, such as housing, in which allocation will be the appropriate technique. But as from the end of the German war, the general principle will be that Treasury authority will be required for new expenditure. The Treasury will work with Departments while they are preparing these returns so as to promote the maximum manpower and other savings

Expenditure overseas. The Service Departments are still spending very large sums of money overseas, thereby increasing greatly the difficulties of our post-war exchange position. There should be an enquiry into Service expenditure in Ceylon, South Africa, Egypt and the Sudan, Palestine, Iraq, British West Africa, British East Africa and Central Africa, Malta, Cyprus and Persia. Expenditure in these countries as a whole was as high in 1944 as in 1942.

I propose to ask the Service Departments to submit a statement showing the broad headings under which expenditure is still being incurred in these countries and the prospects for reduction in the next six months. If, as I expect, strategic arguments are urged in support of continued expenditure on a substantial scale in these countries, I shall have to ask that cases in dispute should be submitted to you for final adjudication.

Defence Research. There is no machinery for the overall review of the expenditure on defence research or for decision as to the purposes to which this expenditure should be devoted.

I seek your authority for the establishment of a small high level body which can carry out such a review. The detailed scheme will be submitted to you shortly.
JA
Treasury Chambers[17]

The value of such a letter was understood by many departments – even if they could not immediately curtail their expenditure. Appendix III is of a circular published by the Treasury dated 14 May 1945. It outlines some of the difficulties facing economic recovery, some of which will be mentioned in later chapters. It is interesting to note that this circular was written whilst we were still at war with Japan.

On a related theme, the Cabinet was keen for miners called up into the Services during the War be returned to the mines as soon as possible.

War Cabinet
Release of Miners from the Armed Forces
14th April 1945
In accordance with the decision of the War Cabinet on 12th April (WM (45) 42nd Conclusions, conclusion (1), minute 3), officials of the Ministry of Labour and National Service, Ministry of Fuel and Power, and representatives of the Service Departments have met to consider the possibility of arranging, within the principles of the existing scheme of demobilisation, for the return to the mines as soon as possible after the end of the German War, of the largest possible number of experienced miners still in the forces. The Annexed report is submitted by the War Cabinet for the consideration of the Committee of Ministers appointed by the War Cabinet to make recommendations on this subject.
Signed W S Murrie
Offices of the War Cabinet[18]

The annex to the report mentioned above contains the following table, figure 1.6,

17   National Archives T 273/326.
18   National Archives CAB 78/33.

detailing the numbers involved and the Service in which they were serving.

	Age and Service Groups				
	1-17*	18-23	24-36	27 upwards	Totals
Army face workers	6303	5023	3677	5850	20853
Others	1215	1912	2643	4876	10646
Totals	**7518**	**6935**	**6320**	**10726**	**31499**
RAF face workers	250	457	439	1878	3024
Others	64	218	248	1854	2384
Totals	**314**	**675**	**687**	**3732**	**5408**

*   In the case of the Army Groups 1–17 will be released in the first six months from VE Day.

Figure 1.6. Number of Underground Coalminers in the Armed Forces.

Royal Navy: There are very few underground coalminers still left in the Navy. 2,622 have been released out of 2,816 serving on 30th December 1943

At the same time as the Treasury were looking to reduce expenditure, other ministers were seeking to co-ordinate government announcements. The Ministerial Committee on VE Day Arrangements comprised The Rt Hon Herbert Morrison MP (Secretary of State for the Home Department and Minister of Home Security) in the Chair, The Rt Hon Lord Woolton (Minister of Reconstruction), The Rt Hon Brendan Bracken MP (Minister of Information), Sir Edward Bridges (Treasury) and Sir Alexander Maxwell and Mr H A Strutt (Home Office) – at least this was the attendee list for the meeting on Monday 30 April 1945.

The following appears in the minutes:

> The Committee were informed that a meeting of the Official Committee on the Co-ordination of Departmental Measures on the Cessation of Hostilities in Europe had been held on the previous Saturday. A number of points had been raised at that committee on which decisions from Ministers were required. These points were set out in a note which was before this Committee.
>
> This Committee considered first the question whether the Prime Minister's broadcast announcement on VE Day should state the time (i.e., 9pm) at which the King would broadcast later in the day. It was agreed that this should be done.
>
> The Committee then considered the arrangements for the departmental announcements which it would be necessary to make at the end of hostilities. It was agreed, that subject to certain exceptions (i.e. any urgent announcement which the Admiralty might have to make), it would be desirable that departmental announcements should not be made until the Prime Minister had given the broadcast address to the nation which it was proposed that he should give on VE Day+1 or shortly thereafter. It was also agreed that any important announcement

(e.g., the announcement about the revocation of Defence Regulations) should be made to Parliament by the Minister concerned.

The Committee considered draft circulars prepared by the Home Office and the Ministry of Health giving guidance to local authorities about VE Day celebrations …

The Committee approved the terms of a draft announcement about holidays and the maintenance of essential services (a copy of the draft is annexed). The Committee felt that it would be desirable that this announcement should be made by the Prime Minister himself when he announced the end of hostilities.

The Committee agreed that there would be no objection to work being started as soon as necessary in connection with the installation of loudspeakers at suitable points in the West End in order that the crowds in the street might hear the King's broadcast on VE Day. It was suggested that a number of loudspeakers should also be installed at suitable points in the City and East End (e.g., at the Gardiner's Corner, Commercial Road, near Aldgate East tube station).

The Committee also agreed that the Ministry of Health, the Service Departments and the Ministry of Pensions should be asked to ensure that all possible steps should be taken to enable patients in hospitals, particularly Service patients, to hear the King's broadcast.

The Committee considered whether it would be desirable that there should be any preliminary warning of the time at which the Prime Minister would make his announcement on VE Day. It was generally agreed that the Prime Minister would desire to make his announcement at the earliest possible time. There would, however, be no objection to the issue of a preliminary warning an hour or two before the announcement, if the hour at which the announcement was to be made enabled this to be done.[19]

The Committee were informed that the following Parliamentary question had been addressed to the Minister of Health for answer on Thursday 3 May:

To ask the Minister of Health whether he is prepared to give some special allowance to enable the aged people and widows to celebrate VE Day with other workers who are to have holiday with pay

It was explained that the Ministry of Health would have no difficulty in informing local authorities that they could give some extra allowance to recipients of public assistance. This covered only a very small part of the field, however, and if an additional payment were made to public assistance cases it would be necessary for the Government to make a corresponding payment to supplementary pensioners and persons in receipt of unemployment assistance. In the time available it would be impossible to make the necessary administrative arrangements.

19 Ibid.

The Committee agreed that in the circumstances no action should be taken to provide extra payments for pensioners or recipients of public assistance or unemployment assistance.
Offices of the Cabinet
30th April 1945[20]

Mention was made above of the speeches by the King and Sir Winston Churchill. These speeches have been reproduced in many documents from then to now. One magazine which also contained the text of speeches made by their American counterparts, political and military, was the May 1945 edition of the IBM magazine, which was devoted to VE Day news. The following two transcripts are taken from this magazine.

The King, on his VE Day address to the Commonwealth

Today we give thanks to Almighty God for a great deliverance ... Germany, the enemy who drove all Europe into war, has been finally overcome. In the Far East we have yet to deal with the Japanese, a determined and cruel foe. To this we shall turn with the utmost resolve and with all our resources ... In the darkest hours we knew that the enslaved and isolated peoples of Europe looked to us; their hopes were our hopes; their confidence confirmed our faith. We knew that if we failed or faltered, the last remaining barrier against a world-wide tyranny would have fallen in ruins. But we did not falter, and we did not fail. We kept faith with ourselves and with one another; we kept faith and unity with our great Allies. That faith, that unity have carried us to victory through dangers which at times seemed overwhelming.

So let us resolve to bring to the tasks which lie ahead the same high confidence in our mission. Much hard work awaits us, both in the restoration of our own country after the ravages of war and in helping to restore peace and sanity to a shattered world ...

We shall have failed, and the blood of our dearest will have flowed in vain, if the victory which they died to win does not lead to a lasting peace, founded on justice and established in good will.
May 1945.[21]

Churchill's VE Day speech in the House of Commons was also reported in the IBM magazine mentioned above. The extract from which reads:

After years of intense preparations, Germany hurled herself on Poland at the beginning of September 1939, and in pursuance of our guaranty to Poland and in common with the French republic, Great Britain, the British Empire and Commonwealth of Nations, declared war upon this foul aggression.

20   Ibid.
21   National Archives FO 372/4361.

After gallant France had been struck down, we from this island and from our united empire maintained the struggle single-handed for a whole year until we were joined by the military might of Soviet Russia and later by the overwhelming power and resources of the United States of America.

Finally almost the whole world was combined against the evil-doers who are now prostrate before us. Our gratitude to our splendid Allies goes forth from our hearts …

Japan, with all her treachery and greed, remains unsubdued. The injuries she has inflicted against Great Britain, the United States and other countries and her detestable cruelties call for justice and retribution.

We must now devote all our strength and resources to the completion of our task both at home and abroad.

Advance Britain! Long live the cause of freedom! God Save the King.[22]

As one might expect, Churchill also wrote a personal message to the people of the British Empire in the Far East in Japanese control which was set to broadcast immediately after the announcement of VE Day on 7 May 1945.

In the name of His Majesty's Government I bring you great news. The war in Europe is over. It has finished in the complete and overwhelming triumph of the Allies and has today been officially declared at an end by Britain, the United States and Russia, speaking with one voice.

Germany, the ally of Japan, is utterly and finally defeated and has been forced to unconditional surrender, all her armies, fleets and aircraft have been destroyed or captured. All resistance has ceased and Germany is occupied from end to end by the armies of the Allied Nations.

After a gigantic struggle of nearly six years, war has ceased in Europe and all the millions of her people who were enslaved have been liberated from the foul Nazi domination. This means that the time for your liberation is also at hand and it is of you that we are thinking on this day.

The armed might of the British Commonwealth with her Allies against Japan is now free to strike with tremendous and undivided power. You know how much had been accomplished already. There is no slacking in our effort for we know full well that the war is not over until the same freedom has been brought to you.

Be of good cheer and rejoice with us on this day! Let my words and my message penetrate to the remotest villages of your lands. Lift up your hearts for we are coming!

Ends[23]

22   Ibid.
23   National Archives FO 371/46367.

(b) **VJ Day**

As one might imagine the need to co-ordinate the announcements for VJ Day were similar in procedure to those mentioned above for VE Day. Of course VJ Day had further importance as it signified the end of the Second World War, not just the end of hostilities in Europe and therefore had greater impact, not least of which was the reduction in the armed forces and their requirements.

The following telegraphs were sent to the United States outlining in brief arrangements for VJ Day.

> To: BAS Washington
> NDHQ Ottawa
> 1. If official announcement is made that Japanese War has ended civilian employees may be allowed leave at your discretion in consultation with local Naval and Air Force Authorities within the limit of what has been approved for War Department civilians in the United Kingdom which is set out in paragraph 2.
> 2. a) If official announcement that Japanese War has ended is on a working day civilian employees in UK except key personnel will cease work for the rest of the day. The day of the announcement and the working day following will be treated as paid holidays.
> b) If official announcement that Japanese War has ended is on a Sunday the Monday and Tuesday following will be paid holidays.
> 3. Conditions for key personnel retained at work will be as for VE and VE +1 namely as follows:
>   i) Non-industrial overtime grades will be given additional payment at plain time rate for time actually worked after announcement on VJ Day and on the following working day. This will apply on the Monday and Tuesday in the case of 2b) above. Other non-industrial grades will not receive additional pay for the hours worked. Industrial grades will be dealt with under the normal rules regarding pay for work performed on a holiday.
>   ii) As special compensation all employees necessarily retained after VJ announcement will be allowed a day off in lieu with pay for each day which they are retained.[24]

A further telegram followed shortly thereafter:

> To: BAS Washington
> Date: 11th August 1945
> For your information the following arrangements are being made in the UK. VJ Day considered a rest day subject maintenance essential services and NO travel beyond 20 miles. In addition 48 hours special leave as extension privilege leave or given separately. Stressed special leave conditions are equivalent to

---

24 National Archives CAB 122/1181.

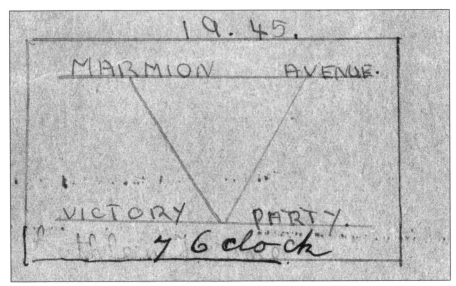

Figure 1.7. An original VJ Day party invitation. (Author's photograph)

two days holiday announcement for civil workers. In mixed civil and military establishments UK civil procedure followed where necessary.
War Office[25]

As one might imagine there were many forms of celebration for VJ Day. Street parties were common. Figure 1.7 is a picture of a surviving invitation to such a party. This invitation is hand cut from recycled cardboard and came to light recently (Spring 2014) when the personal effects of an old soldier, who died late last year, were being catalogued by his family. To have kept this memento for nearly seventy years speaks of the event.

Incidentally the street which hosted this party was knocked down perhaps thirty years after the war and this whole area rebuilt. Nothing remains of the area.

Within a week of VJ Day (in this case through a letter dated 23 August 1945), and with no war to fight, cutbacks in a variety of materials were initiated.

VJ Cancellation or Reduction of Orders
I attach notes of the meeting which I held on the 15th instant to consider the effects of the termination of the War on production arrangements, and the methods by which revised programme figures were to be obtained and the methods by which production should be reduced as quickly as possible in appropriate cases. Also attached is a copy of the circular issued by the Second Secretary (S) and dated 13th August 1945, and a subsequent amendment.

25 Ibid.

In regard to the procedure to be followed in cases where cessation of or reduction in production are brought about, the matter has been further discussed with PAS (S), and the following procedure agreed.

1. In cases where the Ministry of Labour deal with a total labour figure, covering both Ministry of Supply and other requirements (including civilian), there need be no scheduling of labour releases arising from contracts unless the cuts would result in a surplus of labour in the industry as a whole. Thus only where there is a net release of labour after taking into account both the requirements of Government and civilian trade is there any need to follow the scheduling procedure laid down in the circular from the Second Secretary (S).

   a) In all cases other than those covered by (1), the schedule procedure will be followed and, in general, the restricted form of scheduling as set out at appendix a of SS(S) circular will be used by DGES Directorates. Although this appendix is noted as relating to cases where there is a complete stoppage of orders, the full schedule b procedure which normally applied to releases from reduced production will not apply to these cases of DGES production where a diminished rate of output is brought about, with the exception of the cases falling within paragraph 2b below.

   b) The exceptions to 2a which involve the full use of schedule b procedure will only arise in those cases of large production programmes for a type of store which is outside a contractor's normal field of production. As an example of this the case of Jerrycans is cited.

2. After discussion with the Board of Trade and the Ministry of Labour, it has been agreed that the following groups of stores are to be considered as falling under 1) above.[26]

There follows a comprehensive list of materials no longer needed for Service stores from overalls and buttons to boots and shoes, metal badges, crested buttons etc. The cuts continued for months as the various needs of the Services were further reduced.

Ministry of Supply
Memorandum for Production Directors-General
VJ Cancellation of orders

The following amendment to the instructions contained in paragraph 3 (programmed items) of my memorandum dated 13th August 1945 should be noted:

In view of the time which has elapsed since the cessation of hostilities against Japan, it is necessary to revise the procedure to be followed when notifying firms of the cancellation of orders, resulting from complete cuts, see paragraph 3(a) of my memorandum of 13th August 1945. In these cases the sending of telegrams should be discontinued and the following procedure substituted.

26 National Archives AVIA 22/1207.

When lists of contracts to be terminated have been drawn up, in consultation with the Contracts Department, letters to the firms concerned should be prepared by the production department and despatched immediately, and when those letters have been sent out List A should at once be sent to SS12A. The letters should explain that requirements have been reviewed and that no further production of the store in question is now required. The contractor should be informed that a letter from the Contracts Department will follow; meanwhile his co-operation should be requested to ensure that production should stop as soon as possible in order to prevent waste in making stores which are no longer rendered.

Since MOLNS is free to initiate action with the firms concerned as soon as they receive copies of appendix a (or appendix b) it is important that there should be no delay in the despatch of letters by production departments.

Second Secretary

17th October 1945[27]

Reducing production of war related materials in some cases co-incided with the return of some former prisoners of war detained by the Japanese. The full horrors of the Japanese prisoner of war camps only became apparent with time as the surviving soldiers began their return to the West, perhaps following some time in hospitals in the Far East. Some of their stories make for difficult reading. Perhaps this extract from the soldiers incarcerated in Innoshima Camp set the scene.

… as we had numerous accident cases and boils were very common owing to the diet. Also the stack of vitamin pills and such things as thiamine for treatment of beri-beri quickly became exhausted owing to the great number of men suffering from diseases caused by vitamin deficiency. The Nippon authorities also supplied some Japanese medicines. The prisoners contributed monthly to a medical fund for the purchase of medical supplies locally while these lasted. The bulk of this expenditure was on cod liver oil (vitamin A) and on vitamin B tablets, until local supplies became exhausted …

… the medical side of our treatment by the Japanese is one of the most unsatisfactory phases of our life as prisoners of war …

Camp Principles:

The Japanese endeavoured to run the camp on two principles:

1. To maintain military order and discipline.
2. To provide a high percentage of labour at the shipbuilding yard where we were employed.

This worked out that we were treated as military men from the disciplinary point of view when we were at the docks and merely as forced labour in the dockyard. During the military administration (i.e., to December 1943) the guards enforced discipline by punishing offenders against the camp rules themselves. This usually

Figure 1.8. Reconciliation. (Authors photograph)

took the form of slapping, beating and kicking both in the rooms after work and on parade. This seems to be quite the normal method in the Japanese army. When the civilian guards took over, discipline relaxed. They mainly entered our barrack rooms after work and mainly punished us personally. Punishments were usually given by the permanent members of the camp staff for offences both at work and on parade ...

There are many more pages describing the punishment prisoners of war received at this camp, a situation no doubt repeated at other camps across Japan. The war diary records the average weight of prisoners on a monthly basis and was usually between 57 and 60 kilograms – at least during 1944 and 1945.[28]

It is difficult to imagine life in such a camp. It would be surprising if the soldiers or their families ever recovered from such treatment.

As we shall see in chapter 9 during a discussion of the physical rebuilding of Britain, Coventry Cathedral was bombed by the Germans. Rather than rebuild the cathedral on the same site, the authorities decided to leave the remaining walls and rebuild the cathedral on adjacent land. It is a poignant reminder of the conflict. To one side of the bombed out shell there is a statue, figure 1.8.

The plaque beneath it reads:

In 1995, 50 years after the end of the Second World War, this sculpture by Josefina de Vasconcellos has been given by Richard Branson as a token of reconciliation.

28   National Archives AIR 49/384.

An identical statue has been placed on behalf of the people of Coventry in the Peace Garden, Hiroshima, Japan.

Both sculptures remind us that, in the face of destructive forces, human dignity and love will triumph over disaster and bring nations together in respect and peace.

(c) **Letters and Telegrams**

Many people, some more well-known than others, decided to send Sir Winston Churchill a telegram of congratulations. The following were received from the United States.[29]

Greetings well done thou good and faithful servant of all liberty loving people may God give you good health wisdom and integrity for an everlasting world peace. Richard P Barlow

Homage rejoicing and great gratitude. Dame May Whitty

We wish that the energy of the Allied People be used in making a lasting peace. Second shift workers UAWCIO Buick Motor Co

May God Bless your great soul today. Jerry Brooks Lubbock Texas

And the following letter:

Trumble Barton
The American Field Service
French First Army
APO 23 care Postmaster
New York City, New York
Dear Mr Churchill,
I hope that you will forgive the presumption of my writing you at this time, when so many important problems must present themselves on every hand, but I could not help myself from sending this little note to offer my sincere and heartfelt congratulations on the successful Victory achieved by your people, and the gallant part played by you during the last few years.

I went out to Egypt in the early part of 1942, and served under General Ritchie, and later under Field Marshal Montgomery in Africa and Italy. This year I joined the French First Army here in Germany, but you will understand, I hope, if I confess to a sneaking preference for the Eighth and the British, with whom I spent so many happy hours and profitable times. It has always been most heartening to me to observe the way in which the British and American forces have worked together, and I think that you in many ways have been responsible for this accord, for certainly every American has the deepest respect and affection

29   National Archives FO 371/44647 and FO 371/44648.

for your tenacity and courage when things looked so dark and hopeless. I know that I shall always consider it an honour to have served with the British and Colonial men, so very many of whom are now respected and – I trust – lifelong friends.

In conclusion may I ask you to forgive me for the liberty of writing to you on this machine, and also the wretched paper. Both belonged to the Germans, and I have conveniently forgotten how I managed to come into possession of either! Respectfully, and with great admiration.
Trumble Barton

A telegram to Her Majesty the Queen of the Netherlands from His Majesty King George VI, dated 7 May 1945.

At last the day of final and complete deliverance of Your Majesty's country has dawned. Together with my people and, indeed, the whole civilised world, I have followed with increasing anxiety the terrible sufferings of your subjects and their unflinching courage in the face of a merciless enemy. I and my Government are happy to have been hosts to Your Majesty and the Netherlands Government and to have valiant units of the Netherlands Forces who have so distinguished themselves in battle. I send to Your Majesty my sincere wish that the liberation of Your Majesty's colonies in the Far East may soon follow and that under God's providence Your Majesty may long be spared for all your loving subjects in the coming days of recovery and peace.[30]

A day later Queen Wilhelmina replied to King George VI with the following (in the same National Archives folio):

Please accept my heartfelt congratulations on the triumph of your armies and the total and final collapse of the enemy, the due reward of the skill and heroism of your sailors, soldiers and airmen and of the sacrifices and the indomitable spirit of your people who stood undaunted in the darkest hour.

Now that the Netherlands have been wholly liberated I also want to express to you my and my people's abiding gratitude. We owe to the British Commonwealth a debt too great to repay but which we shall never forget.
Wilhelmina

The King also wrote to Her Royal Highness the Grand Duchess of Luxembourg (9 May 1945):

The dark night of oppression which reigned so long over most of Europe and engulfed the Luxembourg nation, has finally been dispelled by the forces of freedom and retribution. The last blows which the common foe was able to strike unhappily brought the severest destruction to your country. But nothing that

30 National Archives FO 372/4358.

the enemy in his blind and brutal ambition could do throughout the war, could quench the ardour of your subjects' patriotism or their devotion to your Royal Household. I rejoice that it has recently been possible for your Royal Highness to return to your faithful country and with my Government and my people I send my most sincere wishes for the continued happiness of Your Royal Highness, your House and your country.

George RI

There are many similar telegrams stored in the National Archives from the King to various national figures. Perhaps this, his telegram to the President of the United States dated 9 May 1945, should serve as the last to be included here.

With the cessation of hostilities on the Continent I hasten to send to you, Mr President, my warmest congratulations on the attainment of victory over our common foe in Europe. In co-ordination with our Russian allies, the British and Americans with our Allied forces advancing from West and South under the supreme command of General of the Army Eisenhower and of Field Marshal Alexander have fulfilled their part in freeing the Continent of Europe from the horrors of German domination.

In the course of the past years and in the face of common danger and grievous losses there has grown up between the peoples of our two countries a comradeship-in-arms of unsurpassed strength. I am confident that this spirit of comradeship will continue not only until Japan has been finally defeated but also in the years to come. It is my earnest prayer that the day of final victory may not be far distant.

George RI

With such a flurry of activity following victory in Europe, unsurprisingly a committee was formed to co-ordinate the messages of congratulation on victory over Japan. This committee held a meeting on 10 August 1945. The following were present:

Sir Arthur Street (Chairman), Mr P N N Synnott (Admiralty), Mr A H Poynton (Colonial Office), Mr M J Dean and Sir James Ross (Air Ministry), Sir Charles Dixon (Dominions Office), Brigadier A H Killick (War Office) and Sir David Monteath (India Office). Mr B Gottlieb (Air Ministry) was in attendance.

It was the general view that the number of messages on this occasion should be kept to a minimum seeing that they would come so closely after the VE Day messages. In particular, there should not be messages from the Admiralty, Army Council and Air Council to the corresponding Dominion and Allied bodies in addition to the messages from the UK Government to the Dominion and Allied Governments. The meeting agreed as follows:

1. **Dominions**. Messages to be sent by the Secretary of State for the Dominions, on behalf of HMG to the Dominion Governments overseas.

2. **India**. A message to be sent to the Viceroy by the Secretary of State for India on behalf of HMG.

3. **Burma**. The Secretary of State for India to send a message on behalf of the Governor.

4. **Colonies**. A general message from HMG to be sent from the Secretary of State for the Colonies to Colonial Governors.

5. **Allies**. It is assumed that messages will be sent by the King. Messages also to be sent on behalf of HMG and to include a reference to the part played by the Armed Forces of the Allied concerned.

6. **Armed Forces**. Messages to be sent by the Board of the Admiralty, Army Council and the Air Council respectively to His Majesty's Naval Forces, Armies and Air Forces.

7. **Government Departments**. It would be appropriate for the Prime Minister to send a VJ message to Civil Servants as on the occasion of Victory in Europe.

8. **Voluntary Bodies**. A paragraph could, with advantage, be included in the Prime Minister's broadcast statement referring to the good work done by the various voluntary bodies.

9. **Local Authorities**. No messages will be sent to local authorities, but it is expected that the Service Departments will receive congratulatory messages from a number of local authorities.

10. **Workers**. The Nation's thanks to the workers by hand and brain could best be conveyed in the Prime Minister's broadcast statement.

11. **Parliamentary motions of thanks to the Armed Forces**. The attention of the drafting authorities to be drawn to the desirability of ensuring that the Motions cover the Dominion, Colonial and Indian Forces as well as the Forces of the United Kingdom.

12. **Merchant Navy and Civilian Air Transport**. The Ministries of War Transport and Civilian Aviation to consider what messages, if any, to be sent.

In discussion later with Sir Alan Lascelles and Sir Edward Bridges, it was provisionally agreed to recommend that His Majesty should send messages as follows:

a) To the three Supreme Commanders covering all the forces under their respective commands but containing a special reference to contingents from the British Commonwealth and Empire.

b) To the liberated territories.

c) To Heads of Allied States.

d) His Majesty's congratulations and thanks to His forces at home and overseas and to His peoples throughout the Commonwealth and Empire would also be expressed in:

e) The King's broadcast and

f) The King's speech on the opening of Parliament.

Drafts of a) to be prepared by the Chiefs of Staff Secretariat, b) by the Colonial Office and c) by the Foreign Office
10th August 1945[31]

Arguably it is fitting to record here the King's message to the American President (on 15 August 1945):

At this historic moment when the surrender of Japan has caused the cessation of hostilities throughout the World I desire to convey to you, Mr President, an expression of my most heartfelt congratulations and of thankfulness that final victory has at last been achieved. These feelings are shared by all my peoples who are proud to have been so closely associated with the armed forces and the people of the United States in the defeat of our enemies. That co-operation which has served us so well in time of war, will, I am convinced, continue in the days of peace to the benefit not only of our two peoples but also of the nations of the World.
George RI.[32]

31   National Archives FO 372/4362.
32   Ibid.

2   Demobilisation

One might think that demobilisation is simply the reverse of calling up fit and able adults into the Service organisations. Unfortunately it does not work like that for there are many issues needing resolution. For example there is a need to consider clothing, conciliation and arbitration tribunals, effect of offences, punishments, etc., on service counting for release (particularly those who found themselves in military prisons during the war), employment, finance and employment taxes, ration coupons, long-term health issues, medical examinations, minimum wages, resettlement, training, vocational guidance and youth, juvenile and disabled persons' training.

Additionally there is a need to consider the possibility of legal measures necessary to provide for recall. Of course the Services are known for their attention to detail and their ability to establish and maintain a system! Demobilisation was no exception.

A letter dated 22 April 1941 is instructive as it sets the scene:

> Dear Sir,
> I am commanded by the Army Council to refer to your letter No. Gen 132 of 22nd January 1941, on the subject of co-operation between the Service Departments and the Ministry of Pensions on those aspects of demobilisation which may affect the Ministry of Pensions.
>
> The Council recognises that the process of demobilisation of the Armed Forces of the Crown will inevitably throw a heavy burden of work on the Ministry, and that plans for demobilisation, which are now being tentatively considered, will need careful co-ordination with your Department.
>
> The Council have set up recently a War Office Committee, under the Chairmanship of the Deputy Under Secretary for War, to give preliminary consideration to questions requiring settlement in connection with demobilisation of the Army so far as they fall within the province of the War Office, and they anticipate that it will be necessary for this Committee, which is about to commence its labours, to act in close liaison with the Inter-Departmental Committee already set up under the Chairmanship of Sir George Chrystal, and upon which the War Office is represented.
>
> It will fall to Sir Frederick Bovenschen's War Office Committee,[1] in effect, to prepare a draft scheme for the demobilisation of the Army, and in the opinion

---

1   Sir Frederick Bovenschen was permanent Under Secretary of state for war at the time.

of the Council it might be preferable to constitute the Inter-Departmental Committee suggested in the last paragraph of your letter ... [2]

(a) Administration/policies

As early as 31 August 1944, the War Cabinet was considering demobilisation and the white paper which led to the Provisional Regulations. At this meeting, the 113th meeting of the War Cabinet, they decided that publication of the scheme for re-allocation of manpower after the end of the war with Germany should stand over until after the summer recess.

The Cabinet minutes for this meeting detailed the following:

Demobilisation
Scheme for re-allocation of manpower
After the end of hostilities with Germany

At their meeting on the 12th July the War Cabinet had before them:

i)   A memorandum by the Minister of Labour and National Service urging that the scheme should be published at the earliest possible moment.

ii)   A memorandum by the Minister of Labour and National Service, to which was attached a revised draft of the White Paper.

The Cabinet first considered the revised draft of the White Paper.

a)   The Minister of Labour and National Service had received a letter from the Parliamentary Secretary strongly urging that a specific referendum should be made in paragraph 11 to release men in Class B for educational purposes.
      The War Cabinet decided that specific reference in this paragraph concerning education would throw the draft out of balance, and would raise the question why a number of other important services were not mentioned ...[3]

It is interesting to note the detailed planning at this level of government concerning demobilisation almost a year before VJ Day. It is worth spending some time looking at some of these regulations for they affected millions of people. Where possible some real paperwork, issued at the time but with the name of the soldier removed, will be used to illustrate the process.

Titled Regulations for Demobilisation of the Army Part 1 (provisional) 194, the draft regulation's opening few paragraphs read (incidentally the document on file in the National Archives deliberately leaves the year of the regulations vague – merely using the three numbers 194 and a blank for part the final year):[4]

---

2   National Archives ADM 116/5533.
3   National Archives WO 32/10564.
4   National Archives WO 32/10559.

Chapter 1

A. Lay-out of Book

100. 'The lay-out' of the book is designed to take the unit CO in sequence through the various steps necessary to implement individual dispersal.

101. This first chapter gives a general picture of the scheme for demobilisation. The chapters following deal in detail with the successive stages of the scheme starting from the preliminary work which has to be done in the unit, thence through the various stages in the dispersal of the individual up to the final disbandment of the unit, the disposal of its equipment and the repatriation of those entitled to return to homes outside the United Kingdom.

102. A brief overview of each chapter is given below:

1.   Chapter 1 – 'The General Picture'. A Brief description of the plan and its principles which are elaborated in the following chapters.

2.   Chapter II – 'The Unit Priority Rolls'. The detail of the preparation of these rolls which the CO of every kind of unit or GHQ 2nd Echelon will have to undertake. These rolls will show, for officers and other ranks separately, the arrangement of the unit by individuals in 'age and service' groups which determine the priority for release to civil life in accordance with instructions laid down in the plan.

3.   Chapter III – 'Procedure for the Demobilisation of Units'. The detail of action required from every type of unit of the Regular and Interim Armies and redundant units, for sorting out their personnel.

4.   Chapter IV – 'Dispersal'. The detail of the process through which an individual will have to pass between leaving the unit and becoming a civilian.

5.   Chapter V – 'Cadres'. Details with the strength, the formation and the disembodiment or disbandment of cadres.

6.   Chapter VI – 'Dispersal of Equipment, Clothing etc.' Deals with the disposal of all equipment and material including documents, funds, etc. as opposed to personnel.

7.   Chapter VII – 'Repatriation'. Gives all detail necessary for the formation for unit to deal with any case in which an individual claims repatriation to a country outside the United Kingdom.

Later in the regulations (paragraph 118e) 'cadre' is defined as:

... a small party of officers and other ranks left in a unit after other personnel have been removed to carry on the administration of the unit up to the time that it is reconstituted, disbanded or disembodied. The use of this word does not imply that this small party is a sufficient framework on which a new unit may be built ...

Paragraph 134 details the priority for release thus:

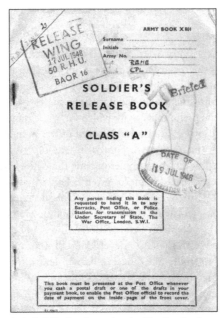

Figure 2.1. Soldier's release book. (Author's photograph)

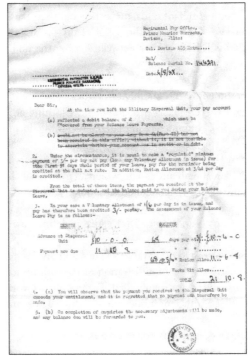

Figure 2.2. Final demobilisation accounts. (Author's photograph)

0160523   Army Form X 202B.

CERTIFICATE OF TRANSFER to the ARMY RESERVE

Army No. ....   Rank ....

Surname (Block letters)...

Christian Name(s) ....

Regt. or Corps ....   R.E.M.E. ....

The transfer of the above-named to the appropriate Class of the Army
Reserve (see note below) is confirmed with effect from ....

*The date to be inserted here will be that following the day on which
Release Leave terminates, including any additional leave to which the
soldier may be entitled by virtue of service overseas.

*Note.—*The appropriate Class of the Army Reserve is as follows:—

(i) Royal Army Reserve—in the case of a regular soldier with reserve
service to complete:

(ii) Army Reserve Class Z (T)—in the case of a man of the
Territorial Army, including those called up for service under the
National Service Acts:

(iii) Army Reserve, Class Z—in the case of all other soldiers not
included in (i) or (ii) above.

Record Office Stamp.

R.E.M.E. RECORDS

LEICESTER

2 8 JUL 1948   Officer i/c ....   R.E.M.E
Date ....   Records.

Warning.—

Any alteration of the particulars given in this certificate may render the
holder liable to prosecution under the Seamen's and Soldiers' False Characters
Act, 1906.

If this certificate is lost or mislaid, no duplicate can be obtained.

Wt. 37285/90 1,000M 12/48 K.H./1550/18 Gp. 38/3
Wt. 40000/210 1,000M 2/40 K.H./1722/32 Gp. 38/2

Figure 2.3. Transfer document. (Author's photograph)

... the basic factors upon which an individual's priority for release will be assessed
will be his age and the length of his service in the present war. The Army will
be arranged in 'Age and Service Groups' combining the two factors. The highest
priority will be composed of those who are both older and have longer service;
on the other hand young men who have served throughout the war will receive
a higher priority than older men who have comparatively little service ... a table
will be issued setting out clearly into which demobilisation group any individual
falls according to his age and service at the time ...

Where appropriate, documents issued at the time will be used to illustrate the
report.

All conscripted Army personnel must have looked forward to the day when they
were demobilised and were handed their own Soldier's Release Book, see figure 2.1.

Paragraph 153 of the regulations makes provision for money:

... for other ranks arrangements will be made for the provision of plain clothes or
money in lieu. A payment in advance will be made for the period of demobilisation
furlough ...

The soldier whose release book appears above also kept a document detailing money
due to him by the Army, figure 2.2.

Of course these soldiers were not completely released from the Services as they were transferred to the Army Reserve, able to be recalled if thought necessary, figure 2.3, paragraph 170.

> ...personnel dispersed on demobilisation, therefore, will, with certain exceptions, not be discharged, but will be relegated to the Reserve, where they will remain until the statutory end of the emergency, when they will be discharged ...

The aforementioned regulations detail the Reserves in the following way (paragraph 172-174).

> ... new (unpaid) classes of the Reserve will be created; Class X of the Royal Army Reserve and Class X(T) of the Territorial Army Reserve. To these classes will be relegated all other rank personnel for whom no appropriate class of Reserve already exists. Class W, Royal Army Reserve and Class W(T) TA Reserve will not be utilised for this purpose.
>
> Personnel of the ATS will be relegated to the Unemployed List.
>
> Certain units will be selected for early remobilisation in the case of emergency. Their equipment will be stored in unit sets in ordnance charge, but the cadre will be dispersed and no personnel retained.
>
> The provision of cadres for the remobilisation of units in an emergency will be the responsibility of the War Office...

Interestingly the soldier whose story we are following above, was initially drafted into the Royal Electrical and Mechanical Engineers (REME), yet if recalled would serve with The Royal Army Service Corps (RASC). This unit was responsible for keeping the British Army supplied with all its provisions except for ammunition, military equipment and weaponry (which were supplied by The Royal Army Ordnance Corps), figure 2.4.

The regulations contained much more information than space and time allow for here. They are available, however, in the National Archives.

The soldiers whose fortunes we followed above was released under class A. Even though the draft regulations mentioned above stated that demobilisation was to be based on age and length of service there was an exception. A further document explained the actual procedure.

> ... the general plan of release by age and length of war service described above will be known as **Class A Release**. It will come into operation as soon as practicable, but a short period will elapse before the releases begin so that the Services may complete their arrangements.
>
> Certain urgent work of reconstruction, mainly building houses, will have to begin at once and the general plan for release by age and length of war service will not of itself provide for the return of men with the required skill and experience in sufficient numbers and quickly enough for this reconstruction work. A limited

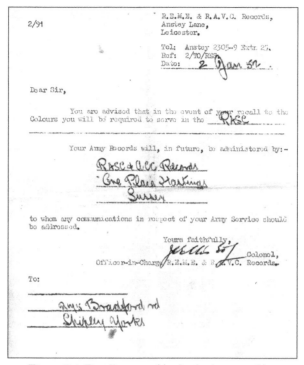

Figure 2.4. Recall papers. (Author's photograph)

number of men will therefore be given the option of transfer to selected industries out of their age and war service order, subject to special conditions; this will be known as **Class B release**...[5]

As one might expect the other Services also prepared for demobilisation. Indeed senior RAF personnel formed the Air Ministry Demobilisation Committee which in turn formed a sub-committee to consider the Machinery of Demobilisation. This sub-committee held its 19th meeting on 21 April 1945 demonstrating how much wartime planning was involved in their preparations. This sub-committee was chaired by Air Vice Marshal J W Cordingley and included many senior officers. Item 2 from the 19th meeting discussed dispersal centres.

... the Chairman stated that there were two points he wished to bring to the notice of the Committee. The War Cabinet had decided:

i) That the 31st May 1945 should be used as the planning date for the cessation of organised resistance in Germany.

ii) The release of RAF personnel as a result of re-allocation of manpower between the Armed Forces and Civilian Employment should be ready to operate not later than six weeks from the 31st May 1945.

5   National Archives ADM 116/5264.

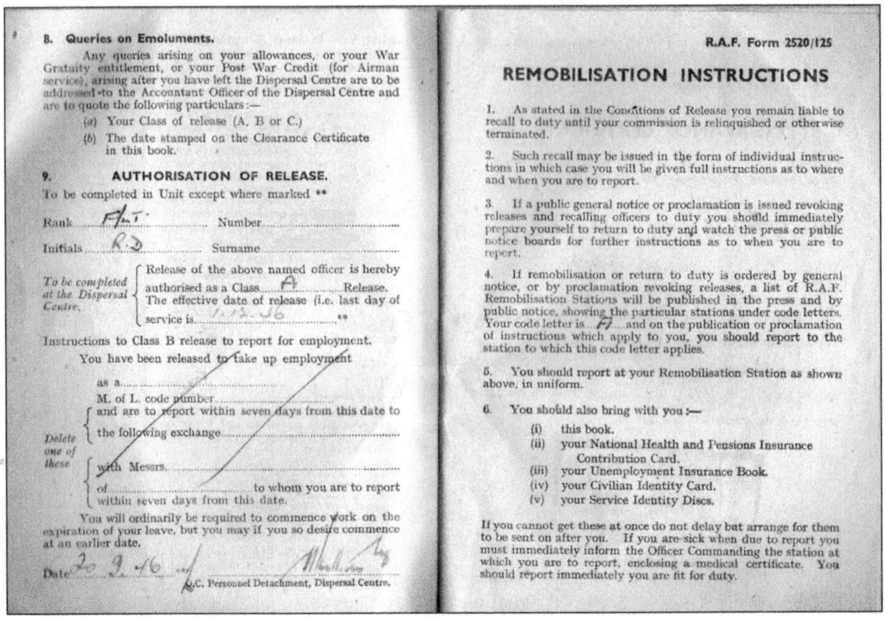

8. **Queries on Emoluments.**

Any queries arising on your allowances, or your War Gratuity entitlement, or your Post War Credit (for Airman service), arising after you have left the Dispersal Centre are to be addressed to the Accountant Officer of the Dispersal Centre and are to quote the following particulars:—

(*a*) Your Class of release (A, B or C.)

(*b*) The date stamped on the Clearance Certificate in this book.

9. **AUTHORISATION OF RELEASE.**

To be completed in Unit except where marked **

Rank F/Lt. Number ....

Initials R.D. Surname ....

To be completed at the Dispersal Centre. Release of the above named officer is hereby authorised as a Class A Release. The effective date of release (i.e. last day of service is 1.12.46 **

Instructions to Class B release to report for employment.

You have been released to take up employment

as a ....

M. of L. code number ....

and are to report within seven days from this date to the following exchange ....

Delete one of these

with Messrs. ....

of .... to whom you are to report within seven days from this date.

You will ordinarily be required to commence work on the expiration of your leave, but you may if you so desire commence at an earlier date.

Date 20.9.46

O.C. Personnel Detachment, Dispersal Centre.

R.A.F. Form 2520/125

REMOBILISATION INSTRUCTIONS

1. As stated in the Conditions of Release you remain liable to recall to duty until your commission is relinquished or otherwise terminated.

2. Such recall may be issued in the form of individual instructions in which case you will be given full instructions as to where and when you are to report.

3. If a public general notice or proclamation is issued revoking releases and recalling officers to duty you should immediately prepare yourself to return to duty and watch the press or public notice boards for further instructions as to when you are to report.

4. If remobilisation or return to duty is ordered by general notice, or by proclamation revoking releases, a list of R.A.F. Remobilisation Stations will be published in the press and by public notice, showing the particular stations under code letters. Your code letter is A and on the publication or proclamation of instructions which apply to you, you should report to the station to which this code letter applies.

5. You should report at your Remobilisation Station as shown above, in uniform.

6. You should also bring with you:—

(i) this book.
(ii) your National Health and Pensions Insurance Contribution Card.
(iii) your Unemployment Insurance Book.
(iv) your Civilian Identity Card.
(v) your Service Identity Discs.

If you cannot get these at once do not delay but arrange for them to be sent on after you. If you are sick when due to report you must immediately inform the Officer Commanding the station at which you are to report, enclosing a medical certificate. You should report immediately you are fit for duty.

Figure 2.5. RAF Service and Release Book (FORM 2520C) detailing the authorisation for release and remobilisation instructions. (Author's photograph)

> The Chairman added that no information was available as to the numbers likely to be released. Air staff plans were not yet available. He said that it was important to know that we are in a position to put the machinery into operation on the target date …[6]

Although the criteria for demobilisation were consistent across the Services, some of the paperwork was different. For example RAF officers were provided with a Royal Air Force Service and Release Book (RAF Form 2520C). Figure 2.5 of this small blue covered booklet detailed the authorisation for release AND remobilisation instructions!

Determining the pay account due to anyone in the armed forces as they were demobilised did have its problems. A few were in military prisons, some had been absent without leave etc. The Demobilisation (Machinery) Committee met on the 13 March 1942 (note the date!), with G Dunn of the Admiralty in the Chair and various officers and civil servants representing the War Office, Air Ministry and Admiralty in attendance.

The following is an abstract of their deliberations.

> The meeting, having considered the conclusions so far reached by the main Committee on the subject, recommends that the term 'Service during the present

6 National Archives AIR 2/8678.

war' should be defined as follows. This definition will have to be edited by each Service in any issued orders, as their technical terms for entry, etc., vary.

1. 'Service in the present war' will commence on whichever of the following dates is the later:
   a) The 2nd September 1939.
   b) The date of entering the Service, or of reporting on being mobilised.

2. The following service will count as 'service in the present war'.
   a) Periods of paid leave.
   b) Time spent in hospital.
   c) Time spent as prisoner of war, or in internment in a neutral country.

3. The following periods will NOT count, except that for reasons of administrative convenience any periods of 28 days or less will be ignored in making the deduction.
   a) Periods of leave without pay.
   b) Periods of release from the Service, for any reason.
   c) Periods of absence without leave.
   d) Periods of imprisonment.
   e) Periods of detention.
   f) Time spent in desertion.

4. Officers may count time served in other ranks that would have counted had they remained in the ranks. Other ranks may count time served as Officer under the same conditions, provided that the Commission (or Warrant) was not terminated for reasons amounting to misconduct.

5. Men who rejoin a Service after discharge may count their former time, if they acknowledge it on rejoining, and if it would have counted had they served continuously; and members of one service may count time spent in another service, which would have counted had they remained in that Service, provided that such Service is acknowledged by them on joining the subsequent service.[7]

With VJ Day the previous month, and all of the concerns ironed out, the Manpower Committee turned their attention to enacting the plans so long in the making. A note by the Minister of Labour and National Service sought clarification on what could be released to the press thus:

I have been considering the terms of the public statement which I shall have to make following the decisions to be taken on the new proposals for releases from the Forces.

In this connection the question arises whether I am at liberty to give the following details:
i) Total strength of the Forces according to Services.
ii) The size of the Armed Forces in various theatres of war by Services.
iii) The programme intake for each Service for the current half year.

7   National Archives ADM 1/16621.

iv)   The releases proposed up to the end of 1945 and up to 30th June 1946 by Services, and
v)   Details of the transport and shipping facilities.

I have had requests for this information from various sources. On 23rd August Mr Churchill asked me in the House of Commons 'whether figures can be given showing the ration strength of the Armed Forces at the present time and, if possible, the theatres in which they are serving' ...
GAI
Ministry of Labour and National Service
26th September 1945[8]

The stage was set, and demobilisation started. Officers commanding military disembarkation camp units were to ensure that Class A release personnel were medically examined before discharge,[9] and those demobilised personnel thought able for teacher training were identified[10].

There was also a need to ensure adequate training for recently remobilised personnel. For example:

... the Croft Committee in their report on education in the demobilisation period recommend:
i)   That the BBC should be requested to make provision for army education broadcast programmes during the demobilisation period, and
ii)   That urgent negotiations should be opened for the purchase of 5,000 receivers.

With regard to ii), we have, as you know, ordered 2,500 specially selected sets, and these are already under production.

In view of the obvious importance of broadcasting, both in the Education Scheme and as a powerful factor contributing to morale the AG decided himself to discuss with Mr Haley, the Director-General of the BBC, the possibilities of obtaining substantial assistance from the Corporation. The DG of the BBC promised the fullest co-operation, and as a result of their discussion a small committee was set up ... [11]

As with any large operation, the organisational elements of demobilisation improved with time. The immediate need was the release of Class B personnel so that they could help with the physical rebuilding of each and every community (see chapter 9 for further details). In a letter dated 19 December 1945 Class B release figures were documented as being:[12]

8   National Archives PREM 8/75.
9   National Archives WO 32/9762.
10 National Archives WO 32/10561.
11 National Archives WO 32/10461.
12 National Archives PREM 8/77.

Service	18th June to 31st Aug	1st Sept to 15th Sept	16th Sept to 30th Sept	1st Oct to 15th Oct	16th Oct to 31st Oct	1st Nov to 15th Nov	16th Nov to 31st Nov
Navy	300	129	447	420	485	365	416
Army	2,915	2,294	4,008	6,088	9,510	10,740	10,285
RAF	2,195	885	1,117	1,631	2,712	2,341	5,158

Figure 2.6. Class B release data for 1945.

Unfortunately there was a problem with strategy, or at least there was an issue needing resolution for the release of Class B service personnel. The Rt. Hon. Clement Attlee CH MP outlined the problem in a letter to the Prime Minister thus (stored in the same National Archive folio as above):

13th September 1945
My Dear Prime Minister,
The preparation of housing plans is at present being held up principally by one factor. I have endeavoured to explain this more than once to the Cabinet but unfortunately without much success. The point is this: unless we are able to secure the rapid release from service with the Forces of Local Government Housing Staffs and General Administrative Staffs, I can foresee that we shall have many building workers idle this winter owing to the fact that plans on which they are to be set to work will not be ready. I am compelled day by day to inform local authorities that their applications for the release of individuals of this type have been rejected by the Service Departments, and this is making my relations with local authorities on Housing questions ever more difficult.

I feel that I must now bring the matter to a head. I suggest that you should insist that the Service Departments should release named individuals sponsored by the Ministry of Health for this purpose. At present, when I have decided that a man is urgently needed for Housing work by a local authority it is quite possible, and frequently happens, that some Commanding Officer decides that he is more urgently needed in the Forces.

The matter is now an issue between me and the Services, though I cannot say that they are ultimately to blame since the responsibility must rest with the Cabinet. But it is pointless for me to use language in public to the effect that housing must be pushed on like a military operation if the Service Departments, who have now no military operations to worry them, are going to set their claims above my own.

Please give this your immediate and personal attention as it is a matter of the greatest possible importance to the whole of my work here.
Yours sincerely,
The Rt. Hon. Clement Attlee.[13]

13   Ibid.

(b) **Benefits/Coupons**

Final demobilisation accounts, mentioned earlier (see figure 2.2 on page 48), detailed the pay for a REME corporal on demobilisation. As one might imagine, these figures were calculated by a standard formula, the background for which could be traced to World War One.

Assessment of War Gratuities

June 1943
Introduction

After informal discussions between the War Office and the Air Ministry it is considered desirable to review the proposed method of assessment of war gratuities. Although the question whether any war gratuity is to be issued at the end of the War (and if so, on what scale) has been left for decision by the Government of the day, in light of circumstances then existing, it is essential that the method of assessment of any such gratuity should be determined beforehand, and the machinery prepared in advance to enable payment to be made (if authorised). The method of assessment at present holding the field war proposed by an interdepartmental committee (the Walker Committee) which was set up in 1922, and was approved by the Treasury. It is questionable whether this approved scheme is practicable for any of the three Services and it is desirable to consider alternative schemes of a simpler character.

Walker Committee

An interdepartmental committee, under the chairmanship of Sir Charles Walker was appointed in 1922 to consider (*inter alia*) the gratuity to be given to temporary officers, etc., in any future emergency. Extracts from their report are attached as appendix a. Briefly their conclusion was that, as regards officers, gratuities on the Great War scale would be unduly generous with the then existing rates of pay, and the method of calculation gave rise to the greatest difficulties and inequalities; they accordingly recommended that the gratuity should be based upon a percentage of total pay drawn during the emergency, the majority recommendation being 15%, with the Treasury representative favouring 10% as being sufficient. The gratuity would be subject to a maximum equivalent to an average of £150 (or £100 if the percentage were 10%) a year for the period of service, and a minimum of one year's gratuity not exceeding £150 (or £100), or in the case of service of less than four months, a minimum of four month's gratuity.

In the case of other ranks, the Committee recommended a similar percentage assessment of gratuity, the limits to be a maximum equivalent to an average of £30 (or £20) a year, and the minimum fixed in the same way as that for officers.

The gratuity was to be calculated on ordinary rates of pay, and in the case of officers or men on special rates (e.g., with Colonial forces) would be based upon the British rates of the rank held.

This scheme was approved in principle by the Treasury before the war and actual percentages on which the gratuity was to be based were left in abeyance for decision at the beginning of any future emergency.

At the beginning of the war, however, it was decided that the question of whether any war gratuity should be granted after the war should be left for a decision by the Government of the day in light of the circumstances then existing.

Air Ministry Proposals

It is understood from informal discussions that neither the Air Ministry nor the Admiralty would be in a position to implement the Walker formula, and that major modifications of it would be necessary before they could proceed. The Air Ministry have therefore tentatively proposed for consideration an alternative formula for other ranks to give a gratuity equal to:

The actual monthly rate of pay at the Armistice date, multiplied by the number of months of service, multiplied by a percentage (to be fixed).

They intend that the percentage to be taken shall be such as would give a total cost (for the service as a whole) roughly equal to the cost of the Walker Scheme, and suggest 7½% as a suitable figure in comparison with the Walker 10%.

They find less substantial difficulty in the way of application of the Walker Scheme to officers, but are in favour of the simplification scheme extending to officers, not necessarily with the same percentage figure.

War Office proposals

The War Office view is that assessment on the Walker basis is practical for most Army other ranks provided that before payment of gratuities becomes necessary time was allowed to dispose gradually of the accumulated arrears assessment of the amount of pay issued to date … [14]

The above statement is difficult to understand for those less familiar with the terminology. Later in the document the War Office re-stated their scheme thus:

… a flat rate of gratuity (preferably a daily rate) to be fixed for each service rank. The gratuity issuable to be equal to the number of days' service during the war in each rank held multiplied by the gratuity appropriate to that rank …

The daily rates would be flat rates for each rank throughout the whole war period and would be the same for tradesmen and non-tradesmen; they would not take the variations in pay according to service or of additional pay, they should be the same for corresponding ranks in each service … In principle the rates should be fixed in advance so as to give an average gratuity approximating to the Walker 10% but they would not be announced, and would therefore be capable of modification up or down the same way as the Walker percentage was liable to modification on the decision of the Government of the day … [15]

Whilst this formula was being revised and example ranks worked through the modified formula, others were considering other aspects of demobilisation (stored as above in the National Archives). Incidentally, the issue of a war gratuity was also

---

14   National Archives ADM 116/5324.
15   Ibid.

documented in this memorandum:

War Cabinet
22nd November 1944
Memorandum by the Chancellor of the Exchequer

Men released from the Armed Forces are already to receive eight weeks' resettlement leave of full pay and allowances, with an additional period of paid leave for men with service overseas. Civilian clothes will be issued to the value of about £12 at retail prices, and men who have served in the ranks will have the service post-war credit which has been accruing since January 1942. Provision is made for reinstatement, for further education or training, for the completion of apprenticeships, and for resettlement grants up to £150 for those wishing to restart in business on their own account. The cost of the release benefits and post-war credits alone will approach £500 millions. It has been announced that in addition a war gratuity will be granted and the amount of this gratuity now requires to be settled.

I have discussed this question with the Service Ministers and the Secretary of State for India, and we have reached agreement on the general principles to be followed. We propose that the gratuity should take the form of a lump sum for each complete month's war service on full pay, the monthly rate being determined by the highest rank held for six months. (Service in the ranks and commissioned service would be reckoned separately and the results added together in the case of men with both kinds of service) ... .

Even at this stage there were still issues, as the document goes on to state:

... I have not, however, been able to reach agreement with my colleagues on the basic monthly rates for other ranks and for officers, respectively. The measure of difference between us is illustrated in the two sets of rates given in the appendix. The scale proposed by the Service Ministers (notwithstanding that it represents a substantial modification of the original proposals made by the Service Departments) involves expenditure which is likely to fall far short of £300 millions. My proposal would represent a substantial saving, but would still cost well over £200 millions. The gratuities after the last war cost something over £150 millions ...

It seems as if – even during the war – there was an attempt to cut costs on demobilisation. However, the memorandum goes on to state:

... the Service Ministers acknowledge that, whichever basis for gratuity is adopted, the total provision made for ex-Service men, including the gratuity, will not only be adequate but generous ...

Issuing demobilisation clothing, mentioned above, was the subject of an Army

Council Instruction which was issued on 5 December 1945.

Amendments

Release – Additional Clothing Coupons

1. Soldiers discharged or released from army service to civil life on or after 18th June 1945, who have completed more than one month's paid service exclusive of any period of leave granted pending discharge but who do not qualify for the released soldier's outfit of civilian clothes are entitled to 63 extra civilian clothing coupons from the civil authorities, except in the following circumstances:

a) When disqualification is due to their having already received an outfit of civilian clothes from Service sources on the occasion of a previous discharge or temporary release since 15th October 1944 (i.e., having received the new scale of civilian outfit).

b) When, through disqualification for any reason from receiving the free civilian outfit, they are permitted to obtain on payment of civilian clothing from Service sources under ACI 682 of 1954, para 22.

Those who have not completed one month's service will receive no supplementary coupons on leaving the Service nor any coupons in lieu of civilian outfit not issued in kind. On return to civil life they will be entitled to their current maintenance ration.

ATS auxiliaries who are not entitled to the cash allowance of £12.10s and 0d for civilian clothes on discharge or release from the Service to civil life are entitled to 56 coupons subject to the conditions laid down in paragraph 1 above. The coupons will be issued by OsC military dispersal units in the case of auxiliary release under Class A and by the O i/c ATS records if discharged or released under any other category … [16]

This Army Council Instruction created a small industry, simply caused by the large numbers of garments involved.

Demobilisation Clothing

11th May 1945

I attended Sir Cecil Weir's meeting today. The Services were represented, including the Admiralty and the RAF, and he had his many Directors with him.

The object of the meeting was primarily to agree with the War Office what was their requirement for demobilisation clothing, a requirement which DGES proposed to meet if possible even if he has to tell the Board of Trade that it will take the bulk of their civilian capacity. He is very anxious to go before Lyttelton with a united front on this issue.

A long discussion took place on the make-up of the Services requirements, out of which some information on the rates of demobilisation emerged. As a matter of interest these were:

Army   300,000 per month

16   National Archives BT 64/1939.

RAF   40,000 per month for the first six months, 21,000 per month thereafter

Admiralty 10,000 per month for the first six months, 20,000 per month thereafter

The needs of all the Services are still for three million outfits by the end of June 1946 and the phasing can only be indicated at the present time by the rates of demobilisation given above. The present production plan is for 1,750,000 outfits by December 1945 and to achieve the balance of 1,300,000 by June 1946, the rate of production would have to be raised from the existing level of 25,000 per week to something like 45,000 per week by September of this year. That as Weir said is going to set them a headache all the way.

However, he seemed determined to achieve it and looks forward confidently to an increase in the labour strength of the clothing trade following releases of labour from munitions industries.

Planned production of shoes seems adequate at 1.3 million by June 1945, two million by Dec 1945 and three million by June 1946. Raincoats may lag behind but nobody considers this will present serious difficulty ... [17]

The demobilisation clothing supply situation was completely reversed by 13 March 1946, at least for shirt making:

Demobilisation Clothing
Shirt Sub-Committee
13th March 1946

... Mr Reeve stated that the completion of the present contracts would be the end of the major part of the programme for shirt demobilisation. Only a little over 700,000 shirts remained to be placed, and after consultation with the Commandant, Branston, it had been tentatively agreed not to place this quantity automatically as extensions to existing contracts, but to reserve it to meet sizing problems as they arise. (He explained that the present contracts were due to finish at the end of June, but that, in point of fact, they would not do so because for one reason or another, chiefly delay in receipt of materials, contractors were running into arrear.)

The Ministry was concerned with the problem of easing the blow to shirt makers when the programme finished, and had discussed the matter informally with the Board of Trade. As they saw it, the Ministry has a liability towards those firms who had given good service to the Government, and who might find themselves in difficulties when Government contracts declined, because of their inability to obtain sufficient supplies of civilian materials ... [18]

Two years later the situation had changed.

17   National Archives AVIA 22/465.
18   Ibid.

Minute 79

7th June 1948

On 1st June 1948 consequent upon an Announcement in the House, the distribution of 'Additional Coupons for Demobilisation' was resumed and the Services were so informed on the same day. It was also decided that the qualified would include those who proceeded on Release, Discharge or Retired, terminal leave from (inclusive) 1st July 1946 to 31st December 1947 and who served to Age and Service Groups – about 1.8 million – since the distribution now petering out to the end, (which was announced in the House on 13th April 1948 as to the last), included applicants who went on terminal leave up to 30th June 1946. The 4th August 1948 was the obvious date for opening the distribution as being the first convenient day (after the Bank Holiday and when the bulk of the distribution of Food Books from Ministry Food Offices had been fully cleared off), and was accordingly announced.

It was then necessary to review the existing procedure for these distributions with a view:

a) To eliminate serious weaknesses found by experience in the current distribution now ending.

b) To solve any new problems not previously met.[19]

The uptake of clothing coupons was significant, figure 2.7.

26 supplementary clothing coupons for ex-service personnel (SC/V/2) Comparison of issues made during the first 2–3 months of each distribution			
Distribution	No of persons eligible	No of applications in the first 2–3 months	Percent issued
First (25.11.46-1.11.47)	1.5 million	1.25 million (25.11.46–31.1.47)	83%
Second (3.11.47-31.5.48)	1.9 million	1.5 million (3.11.47–31.1.48)	79%
Third (4.8.48–31.3.49)	1.8 million*	0.8 million (4.8.48–30.10.48)	44%

* Those who did not apply during the second distribution (approximately 0.25 million) could also apply during the third distribution.

Figure 2.7. Coupon uptake in the first 2–3 months.

(c) Resettlement

The Minister of Labour and National Service made the following statement in the House of Commons on 29 June 1944.

... The Government have decided that a special service, under the control of the Ministry of Labour and National Service, shall be set up for this purpose. I am accordingly making plans to establish Resettlement Advice Offices, as an

19 National Archives BT 64/1500.

extension of the existing service given by this Department in all parts of the country. The function of these offices will be to give advice and information to all men and women released from the Forces or from other forms of war service, and to render every possible assistance to them in dealing with their resettlement problems. By providing these centres, at which such persons may seek assistance whatever their requirements may be, we intend not only to help them to solve their difficulties, but also to save them avoidable journeys and inquiries. The work of these offices will be dovetailed in with that of my outside Welfare Officers and will be co-ordinated with that of the voluntary organisations ... [20]

Those released under Class B, must have had mixed feelings about this announcement. Elsewhere in the same National Archives folio is an appendix to a report which documents the effect of release benefits on Class B releases thus:

The difference between Class A and Class B releases are:
a)   The man released in Class B gets five weeks less pay.
b)   The man released in Class B is not free to choose his own job.
      The second of these differences is of the very essence of the Class B scheme and would have to be retained even if the financial benefits were the same for both Class B and Class A. It is not, however, possible to say what proportion of the men who refused Class B because of the release conditions or because they did not want to be tied down in obtaining employment. There is, however, reason to think that more important than the release conditions was the attractiveness or otherwise of the particular occupation concerned. The Army have figures for many occupations showing the percentage of offers accepted to offers made. These show that, taking into account the estimated acceptances on offers outstanding, 56% of offers made have been or will be accepted, i.e., more than one man in two accepts the offer ...

The following table shows an analysis by industries and services up to 30 April 1946 for Class B releases, and is shown here to demonstrate the occupations these men were offered under Class B.

Category	Programme	Releases			
		Navy	Army	Air Force	Total
Building and civil engineering	120,000[a]	8,473	75,910	24,337	108,720
Building materials	21,000	1,024	10,684	2,708	14,416
Coalmining	15,000[b]	74	4,687	475	5,236
Agriculture	18,000[c]	251	12,743	2,414	15,408
Railways	5,000	182	3,700	797	4,679
Food	6,720	201	2,910	583	3,694

20   National Archives LAB 12/680.

Category	Programme	Releases			
		Navy	Army	Air Force	Total
Cotton	14,700[d]	65	2,622	588	3,275
Wool		60	2,849	640	3,549
School Teachers	13,200[e]	377	4,948	3,142	8,467
Police	As many as possible	1,533	5,088	2,218	8,839
Fire and Police recruits	14,000[f]	33	213	-	246
Students	6,100	467	2,988	714	4,169
Specialists	17,500	1,210	8,102	3,653	12,965
Others (including cases not yet analysed)	35,512[g]	1,132	11,390	5,327	17,849
Total (excluding police)	286,732	15,082	148,834	47,596	211,512

[a] increased since 30th April to 134,000; [b] reduced since 30th April to 9,500; [c] programme aims at releasing all agricultural workers with more than 12 month's service. Releases are expected to reach 20,000; [d] reduced since 30th April to 14,200; [e] reduced since 30th April to 14,200; [f] reduced since 30th April to 10,900; [g] now adjusted to 35,812

Figure 2.8. Class B releases for men up to 30 April 1946.

Resettlement of service personnel took place in both directions, i.e., those Service personnel who were born in the United Kingdom who chose to live abroad on demobilisation, and those born abroad who chose to settle in the UK.

Throughout the War, India continued to be part of the British Empire, gaining independence in 1948. It is understandable, therefore, that some soldiers were members of the Volunteer Forces commissioned in the Indian Army. Their benefits on release were discussed in various documents, for example:

In reply to an enquiry, India Office have been informed that where an officer in the Indian Army has had previous full-time mobilised war service with one of the Far Eastern Volunteer Forces, a proportion of his release benefits appropriate to the period of his Volunteer Service, would be accepted as a charge against the funds of the Colonial Government concerned. It was explained, however, that the proportionate cost to Colonial funds could be calculated only at the rate applicable to the rank held by the officer during his Volunteer Service, irrespective of whether he attained a higher qualifying rank during his service in the Indian Army.

India Office now point out that it is the agreed policy between that Department and the Service Departments, in cases where terminal benefits are paid by the last employing authority with subsequent financial adjustment for service under another authority for Service in the British and Indian forces to be aggregated and for release benefits, including war service gratuity and overseas service leave, to be paid at the rate appropriate to the highest qualifying rank held during the whole of the officer's war service … [21]

Interestingly, India's demobilisation scheme took the British Forces into account, Appendix IV.

The situation in South Africa is worth mentioning. The following are a series of questions asked of the Minister of the Interior – his replies are in bold:

1. How many a) aliens and b) British subjects from other countries who have not yet become Union nationals are presently in the Union?
   Reply:
   a) **Up to date 66,412 aliens have applied for registration in terms of the Aliens Registration Act No 26 of 1939. This figure includes visitors who may have left the Union, but does not include Aliens who have been exempted from registration. It is not possible to give the number of Aliens in the Union at any given date as the number changes from day to day owing to departures and new arrivals.**
   b) **As the acquisition of Union nationality is automatic in the case of British subjects and depends on the intention of the individuals, it is impossible to determine how many British subjects there are in the Union who have not yet acquired Union nationality.**
2. Whether members of British Forces from outside the Union who are at present within the Union, will have to wait two years, or a longer or shorter period after their discharge from the army, before they will automatically become Union nationals?
   Reply:
   Members of the British Forces from outside the Union and at present in the Union, who are natural born British subjects must wait the required two years after their discharge in the Union before they will automatically acquire Union nationality, provided that on discharge they signify their intention to reside in the Union permanently.
3. Whether the Government intends introducing legislation to compel all persons who entered the Union from other countries in connection with or during the present war, to obtain permits for permanent residence in the Union?
   Reply:
   Aliens, including naturalised British subjects who entered the Union in connection with, or during the present war must comply with the requirements of the Aliens Act No 1 of 1937, if they wish to remain in the Union. Natural born British subjects must comply with the requirements of the Immigrants Regulation Act No 22 of 1913 on entering the Union
4. How many a) aliens and b) British subjects from other countries, who came to the Union since 4th September 1939, have already applied for permanent

---

21   National Archives CO 968/189.

residence in the Union or have intimated to the Government in some other manner that they wish to reside permanently in the Union?
Reply:
a) and b) **In view of the time and labour involved I must ask the Hon. Member not to press for the information.**[22]

Interestingly by chance I met a lady whose parents emigrated to South Africa after the War as they could not find jobs in England. This lady has since moved back into the country following the deaths of her parents. The numbers confirm that many people chose to live in South Africa after the War, some of whom are still living there.

Soldiers discharged abroad who chose to live in the country in which they served and from which they were discharged are documented for many countries. The following, however, demonstrates that it was sometimes difficult to be discharged.

6th September 1944
To: Hon. The Colonial Secretary
I acknowledge your S151/42/F of the 8th September 1944.

Discharge Procedure – Cyprus Regiment
Discharge of the Cyprus Regiment personnel during wartime is only authorised under the following categories:
a) Having been improperly enlisted.
b) Soldiers under age.
c) Unsuitable for military service.
   These paragraphs refer chiefly to cases which came to light during the period of training at Polymedia, and the soldiers discharged have had hardly any military service. The latter case is only applicable to a soldier who, during his first two months of training, proves to be unsuitable. No soldier falling under any of these categories, in my opinion, would be entitled to any bonus or gratuity.
d) Compassionate grounds.
   These cases are few and are only authorised in extreme cases. Discharge in these cases is in no way the fault of the soldier, and it is considered that some form of gratuity or bonus should be payable at the cessation of hostilities.
e) Having been convicted by the civil power for felony.
f) Having been sentenced to penal servitude by Court Marshal or civil power.
g) For misconduct.
h) Having been sentenced before discharge with ignominy.
i) Service no longer required.
   The majority of discharges from the Cyprus Regiment up-to-date are under one of these categories. The soldiers are definitely of bad character, and by this have forfeited any gratuity or bonus which may be payable to good character soldiers at the cessation of hostilities.

22 National Archives DO 35/1133.

j)   Soldiers granted a commission.
     It would appear that any gratuity or bonus at ORs' rates would be applicable for anyone under this category during the period he served in the ranks.
k)   Soldiers over 60 years of age.
     Any person discharged under this paragraph will naturally be considered for a gratuity or bonus.
l)   Permanently unfit for any form of military service.
     Discharges under this category fall under two headings.
     i)   Those who have been rendered unfit by military service.
     ii) Those who have been rendered unfit for a reason not attributable to military service.
     In respect of the first case, they would be pensionable, and the amount payable to them is decided upon by the Pensions Committee in the United Kingdom.
     Personnel under the second category should, in my opinion, be eligible to a gratuity or bonus. They have been accepted for service in the Forces, having been examined by a Medical Officer and marked 'fit', and their discharge from the Army before the cessation of hostilities is not due to any fault of their own.
m)   To pension.[23]

In some cases, those born abroad, including Polish airmen and French soldiers, chose to stay in Britain at the end of the War, for example.

> Turnstile House
> High Holborn
> London WC1
> 15th Jul 1942

To A I Tudor
Home Office
Aliens Department
Box 2
Bournemouth
Dear Tudor,
Referring to our recent discussion in Bournemouth, I am sorry I have been rather a long time in putting down on paper the suggestions which I then made to you about the discharge of Polish Air Force personnel. I have, however, been in communication with the Polish Depot, Blackpool, and I do not think there will be any difficulty in working my proposals from the Air Force side if they are acceptable to you.
     As I pointed out, the procedure under the Aliens Order 1920 was really intended for civilians arriving in this country and not for members of the armed forces who may have been here for upwards of two years. Every person who joins

23   National Archives FCO 141/2800.

one of the Allied Air Forces is vetted for security before he is allowed to join. That vetting is done by my Branch with the assistance of MI5 and of the Security Bureaux of the allied authorities concerned. I think I am right in saying we take greater precautions than the other services because it is felt that there are greater opportunities for subversive activities and sabotage in the Air Force than there are, for example, in the Army. I would suggest therefore that there is not the same necessity for the Immigration Officers' personal examination of a man awaiting discharge from the Air Force as there is in other cases …

… where a man is to be employed in industry he is brought to Blackpool pending completion of the proceedings and, therefore, the permission to land could be handed to him at the Polish Depot there and the two conditions upon which the permission is granted explained to him at the same time. The same procedure could apply to walking medical cases. If the man is unfit to travel, an Air Force officer could visit the man in hospital to hand over to him the permission to land and at the same time he could impound the man's identity card and obtain local police registration. He could also arrange for the man's uniform, if any, to be returned to Blackpool for clearance … [24]

Towards the end of the War there was also a need to demobilise some French forces stationed in Britain.

To:
The Under Secretary of State
Home Office
Aliens Department
10 Old Bailey
London EC4
1st August 1945

Sir,
The discharge of the French forces stationed in Great Britain has started. Several servicemen have asked if it is possible for them to be demobilised here and therefore to work and live in Great Britain.

I have informed them that they must prepare their files and send them to you for a decision.

On the whole, you will only receive the dossiers of French servicemen who appear to us as serious, who have a technical or university knowledge, speak English and married to British women.

I think that the following points should be considered when examining the requests for a permit to stay.
a) The agreement of the 16th May 1928 between the French and British authorities is still in force.

24 Ibid.

b)   The letter from the Foreign Office to the French Embassy in the procedure of discharge from the 1st December 1944.

I would be grateful if you would apply those instructions leniently. There would only be 100 to 150 cases and this number is rather small if one takes into consideration the Frenchmen who went to war in 1939, who were in England and who will not come back, also on the other hand the high number of British subjects in France who have been allowed to stay and work.

Yours faithfully

Le Gérant du Consulat Général.[25]

(d) Release of Medically trained personnel
Doctors

The Demobilisation Committee of the Central Medical War Committee was active during the war – at least they were holding meetings as early as 11 June 1943. The minutes documented the need for the Demobilisation Committee thus:

> ... resolved: that a special committee be appointed to consider all questions relating to the post-war demobilisation of medical officers in the services and cognate matters. The following minute documented that the Demobilisation Committee be constituted as followed ... [26]

Further in the minutes, actually item 4, the work of the committee was outlined in more detail:

> Considered: reference to the Committee as set out in item 1 of the agenda and in connection forthwith, following confidential letter dated 22nd April 1943, from the Ministry of Health:-
>
> ... I am directed by the Minister of Health to inform you that, as part of a plan which has been prepared by an official committee for the consideration of the Government, it is proposed that, subject to the exigencies of the Services, demobilisation shall in general proceed in groups based on a combination of age and length of service in the present war. All persons above an age (say 50) to be fixed by the Government before commencement of demobilisation, would be placed in the first group. The enclosed table is an illustration, and nothing more than an illustration, of the principles on which the groups might be formed. It is also proposed that a special priority should be given in a limited number of cases, e.g.:
>
> a)   Individuals or industrial groups and occupations vitally needed for reconstruction.
>
> b)   Returned prisoners of war and internees.
>
> c)   Those qualifying on grounds of extreme compassion for domestic or business hardship.

25   National Archives HO 213/1829.
26   National Archives MH 79/547.

d)   Married women.

And further that within demobilisation groups priority should be given by Commanding Officers so as to include industrial groups and occupational classes of importance to industry, individuals with guarantee of employment, and married men.

In the case of Officers it is recognised that a decision whether they should be retained with the forces or demobilised depends on rather different considerations than in the case of other ranks, but in determining priorities amongst those who are to be demobilised it is proposed that the above plan should be followed as far as possible. It is further proposed that, subject to the over-riding needs of the Services, medical and dental officers should as far as possible be given the priority to which their age, length of service and other circumstances would entitle them under the general scheme of demobilisation, but that the Service Departments should consult with the Government Departments and representative professional bodies concerned so that special priority of demobilisation can be freely given to individuals whose early demobilisation would be in the national interest.

I am, therefore, to request that your Committee will take into consideration the arrangements proposed above and submit proposals in due course for giving priority of demobilisation, within the general framework of those arrangements, to individual practitioners whose release from the Forces should be specially expedited in the interests of the medical needs of the civilian population ...[27]

Later the Committee Secretary wrote a note concerning demobilisation which starts:

... the general plan approved by the Committee at its meeting on 11th June regarding the demobilisation of the profession was that – leaving aside certain priority groups – the primary consideration for demobilisation should be that of civil need, including the needs of hospitals, public health and other essential medical services, regard also being had to age and length of service ... thus the tentative proposals of the Committee constitute a material departure from the plan outlined in the Minister's letter ... [28]

Many letters and committee meetings followed this initial statement. Towards the end of December 1944, the Central Medical War Committee plans consolidated and a statement was published in the *British Medical Journal*. A letter was also issued which started:

... you will note that the first medical officers to return from the Forces after the end of the war with Germany will be those due for release according to the age-service formula, among whom men of 50 or over and married women will have special priority. When a start has been made with the release of these officers (Class A) consideration will be given to the transfer from the Forces,

27   Ibid.
28   Ibid.

out of their turn, of a strictly limited number of medical practitioners whose return is considered necessary on the grounds of urgent civil need (Class B). The arrangement for release at the present time will continue to operate for the purpose of individual Class B transfers; recommendations will be made to the Service Departments by this Committee after consideration of applications submitted by the Local Medical War Committees ... [29]

Nurses

The future of nursing within the framework of the armed forces was the subject of much thought, not least because of the proposed National Health Service.

Ministry of Health
Whitehall
7th February 1945
To Local Authorities
Joint Boards of Tuberculosis and Joint Sanatoria Boards
Joint Hospital Boards
Voluntary Hospitals
Local Emergency Organisations

Sir

Civil Nursing Reserve
Position on termination of hostilities in Europe

1. I am directed by the Minister of Health to state that he has had under consideration the position of the Civil Nursing Reserve on termination of hostilities in Europe, and has consulted the Civil Nursing Reserve Advisory Council in the matter. The Council expressed the opinion that, as there is still likely to be an acute shortage of nurses after hostilities in Europe cease, the Reserve should remain in being and recruitment of all grades to the Reserve should continue.

2. The Minister, after consultation with the Minister of Labour and National Service, has decided to accept the advice of the Council. He recognises that the termination of hostilities in Europe will not diminish the total number of nurses required for the civilian health services, including hospitals in the Emergency Hospital Scheme. Although some saving of staff will be made possible by the concentration of the casualty services, there will undoubtedly be demands for additional nursing staff to reduce working hours where these have been unavoidably long, and to replace wastages as well as to make up for existing deficiencies ... [30]

29 Ibid.
30 National Archives MH 55/2023.

Pharmacists

In a letter from the Secretary of the Central Pharmaceutical War Committee (CPWC) dated 11 November 1943 to F Bliss of the Ministry of Health concerning demobilisation, the Secretary asked:

> ... we want if possible to secure that any scheme of ours should dovetail into the general scheme and I should be grateful if you could ask the War Office or the Minister of Labour if Stewart (the Secretary of the Demobilisation Committee of the CPWC) can be put in touch with whoever is the appropriate person so that they can have a talk about the situation ... [31]

There was a move the following February to clarify the position:

> ... the demobilisation of pharmacists, dispensing and pharmaceutical students must be co-ordinated with the general scheme for the release of men from the Forces and as information is not yet available on national plans, it is impossible at this stage to suggest more than an outline of the procedure and considerations which may affect future policy ... representations should, therefore, be made that the release of pharmacists and dispensers should be effected on the recommendation of the Central Pharmaceutical War Committee, i.e., the enlistment machine would be reversed ... [32]

The final thoughts of the procedure appeared in a memorandum. Paragraph 3 and 4 dealt with special releases, the latter being reproduced below:

> Applications for special release should be initiated only by:
> 1.   The District Pharmaceutical War Committee.
> 2.   The man concerned, or
> 3.   His employer.
>   No application for release should be decided by a District Committee who should be required to submit all applications received by them, with their comments if any, to the Central Committee.
>   Applications for special release received by the Central Committee will normally be referred to the District Committee in the area concerned and the recommendation of that Committee reviewed by the Central Committee whose recommendation will be forwarded to the Ministry of Health ...

31   National Archives MH 79/552.
32   Ibid.

3   National Service

Anticipating a possible war with Germany, the British Parliament, with Neville Chamberlain as Prime Minister, approved the Military Training Act in May of 1939. This act applied to single men aged 20 to 22 who were required to undertake six months' military training. Some 240,000 registered for service which was known as conscription or national service. On 3 September 1939, the day Britain declared war on Germany, Parliament immediately passed the National Service (Armed Forces) Act which was more wide-ranging.[1]

In this act ALL males between the ages of 18 and 41 were required to register for service. Key industries such as baking, engineering, farming and medicine were exempted. Conscientious objectors had to appear before a tribunal and, where the case for objection was dismissed, the individual had to serve in the forces in a non-combatant job. Whilst greatly increasing the numbers serving in the forces, it was not until the second National Services Act of December 1941 that parliament further widened the scope of national service to include unmarried women and all childless widows between 20 and 30. Furthermore, men were now required to undertake some form of National Service until they were 60, including military service for those under 51.

The main reason for introducing these further changes was to address the shortfall of those volunteering for civilian defence and police work, and for women in the auxiliary units of the armed forces.

National Service covered the full range of options available to men and women of all ages – not just fit young men who wanted to join or were conscripted into the Services. A full and detailed guide to all of the options for National Service was produced in 1939, figure 3.1. The intent was to provide 'a guide to the ways in which the people of this country may give service'.

With a message from the Prime Minister and a foreword from the Lord Privy Seal, the Right Hon Sir John Anderson MP, this was a comprehensive booklet. Sir John's foreword set the scene thus:

> ... men and women all over the country are today eager to fit themselves voluntarily for National Service. Some have already decided what service they can

1   British Parliament website, *About Parliament – Living Heritage* <http://www.parliament.uk/about/living-heritage/transformingsociety/private-lives/yourcountry/overview/conscriptionww2/>. (Accessed June 2014).

Figure 3.1. National Service booklet. (Author's photograph)

best give and are fitting themselves by training to give it. Others are wondering how they can be most useful, and I hope that they will find the answer in this guide.

The call is to peace and not to war. We have no thought of aggression; our one wish is to live at peace with all peoples. But if this wish is to be fulfilled we must be up and doing. We must make ourselves strong so that our influence for peace may be real, and we must make ourselves safe so that others cannot be tempted to thoughts of aggression against us.

It is for the Government to make clear what service the country needs and in what forms it can be given, and that is the object of this Guide. It is for you to judge what service you can best give, and the Guide will help you decide.

Arrangements are being made to help those who, after reading the Guide, feel that they need further advice. Very soon National Service Committees will be at work for this purpose throughout the United Kingdom and meantime the Local Offices of the Ministry of Labour will be glad to give assistance. National Assistance can take many forms ...

The contents of this guide list:

    1.   Civilian Services.
       a)   Air Raid Precautions.

b)   Police.

c)   Fire Service.

d)   Nursing and First Aid.

e)   Other Civilian Services including: hospital supply workers.

2.   The Armed Forces.

a)   The Royal Navy – regular service, reserves and auxiliaries.

b)   The Army – regular service, reserves and auxiliaries.

c)   The Royal Air Force – regular service, reserves and auxiliaries.

3.   Other Registers included:

a)   Medical practitioners.

b)   Professional, Scientific and Technical.

Car owners were needed for various duties in connection with hospital work, in particular for the evacuation of light cases to their homes in the event of air attacks. Page 23 of the guide documents the evacuation of children from dangerous areas:

> ... the Government's plans for removing children in an emergency from the dangers of air attacks in crowded cities to districts of greater relative safety would make an unprecedented call on the services of women. These plans for saving child life make it necessary to find homes for children, and any householder in these districts who has spare accommodation could do no more useful service in the national interest than undertake their care and maintenance ...

Living in North West London today (in 2014) there are still some people who were evacuated from the East End of London to towns and villages in Buckinghamshire. Some of them moved back to their childhood villages and towns in later life, obtaining jobs in London boroughs once the Metropolitan Line allowed access to the area. This cannot have been unique to my part of London. Now in his 80s, there is one person who still vividly remembers with dread being put on a train and not seeing his parents for the remainder of the war. At least he was evacuated with his brother which was some consolation.

On the other side of the coin, as it were, there is a former head teacher in my London borough who was a student teacher at the outbreak of War (he celebrated his 92nd birthday in 2014). One of his tasks on the outbreak of war was to knock on the doors of families whose children attended the school he worked in, asking if the parents wanted their children to be evacuated. This particular individual was conscripted into the Air Force during the War and returned to teaching on demobilisation.

The professional, scientific and technical communities were to be included in a Central Bureau for men and women with appropriate qualifications who were prepared to undertake work of a specialist character in the event of an emergency. The guide explained (on page 46):

... the Bureau would in wartime be used by Government Departments to meet their needs for additional scientific, technical and professional staff, and will be available to assist industrial concerns in a similar way ...

Some of these scientific and technical exploits are documented elsewhere.[2]

As one might imagine, there was a need to co-ordinate activities and ensure that the men and women were placed in the correct occupations for their age and skills. For the most part, young men were sent to war and women and children too old for school yet too young to be called to arms backfilled the occupations left by those called up to the Services.

Of course national service was not unique to the Second World War. Within its living heritage webpages, the British Parliament website documents all the relevant National Services Acts of the 21st century, figure 3.2.[3]

Year	Purpose of the Acts
1914	Aliens Restriction Act: foreign nationals to register with the police and the Defence of the Realm Act gives wide discretionary powers to the government to assist with internal security and the war effort
1915	Munitions of War Act illegalises strike action in munitions factories
1916	Military Service Act imposes conscription on all men aged between 18 and 41 and the British Summer Time Act allows longer working days
1918	Military Service (No 2) Act raises the conscription age limit to 51
1939	Military Training Act: limited conscription for single men aged 20-22
1939	Emergency Powers (Defence) Act gives the government extensive discretionary powers to issue controls and regulations over many aspects of social and economic life
1939	National Service (Armed Forces) Act imposes conscription on all males aged between 18 and 41
1941	National Service Act: all men up to the age of 60 eligible for National Service and some women liable for conscription
1947	National Service Act imposes National Service on all males aged between 17 and 21
1960	End of National Service

Figure 3.2. National Service Acts.

It would be a daunting task for anyone not familiar with the law to understand the implications of the 1939 and 1942 Acts. Fortunately, a leaflet was produced which set out the position for men, see figures 3.3, 3.4 and 3.5.

As one might expect, the first stage in the enlistment process was to attend a

2   Rogers, David, *Men Amidst the Madness: British Technology Development in World War II*, (Solihull: Helion and Company, 2014).
3   British Parliament, *About Parliament* <http://www.parliament.uk/about/living-heritage/transforming society/private-lives/yourcountry/key-dates-/1914-1960/>. (Accessed June 2014).

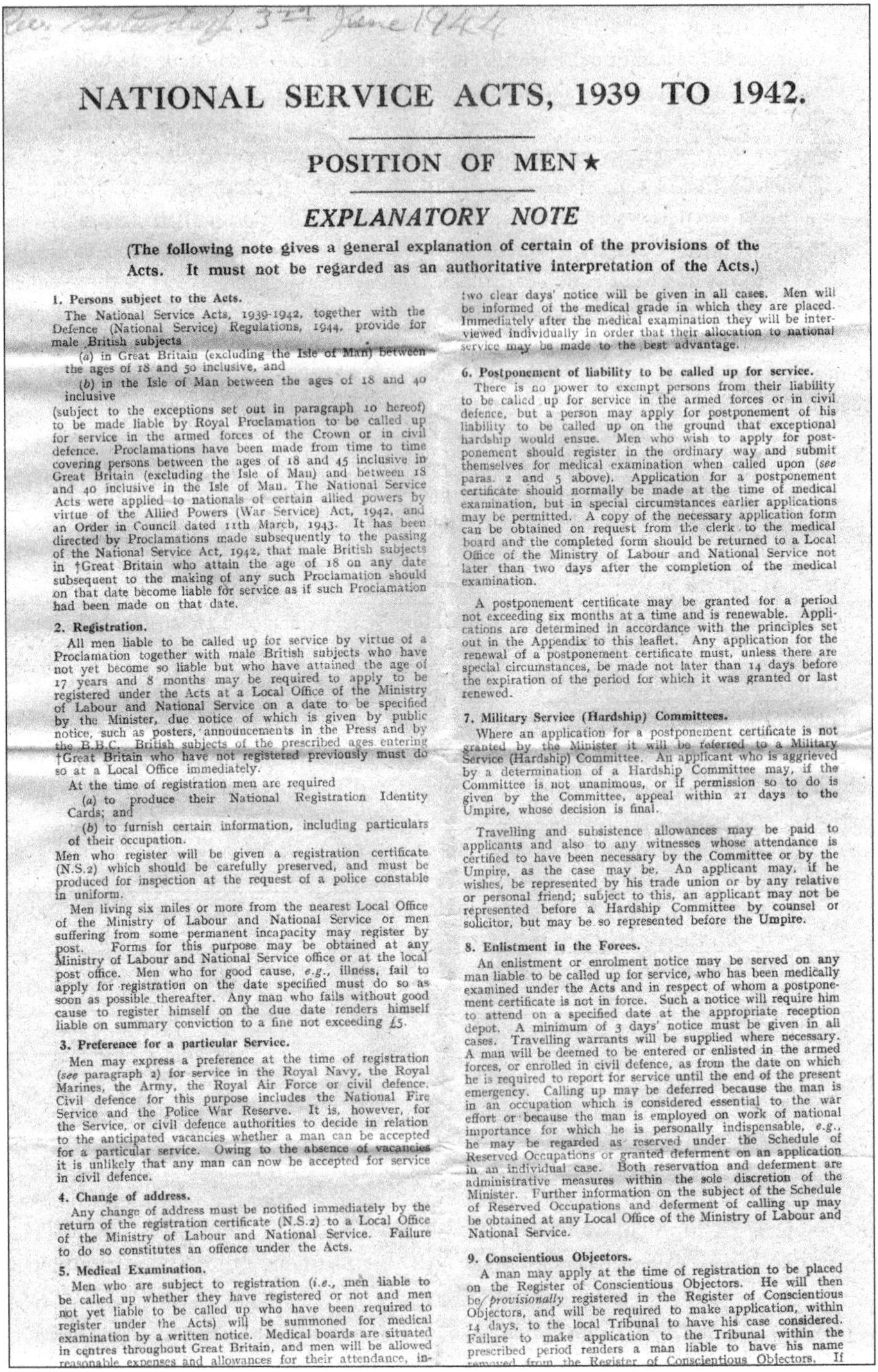

Rec. Salford 3rd June 1944

NATIONAL SERVICE ACTS, 1939 TO 1942.

POSITION OF MEN ★

EXPLANATORY NOTE

(The following note gives a general explanation of certain of the provisions of the Acts. It must not be regarded as an authoritative interpretation of the Acts.)

1. Persons subject to the Acts.

The National Service Acts, 1939-1942, together with the Defence (National Service) Regulations, 1944, provide for male British subjects

(a) in Great Britain (excluding the Isle of Man) between the ages of 18 and 50 inclusive, and

(b) in the Isle of Man between the ages of 18 and 40 inclusive

(subject to the exceptions set out in paragraph 10 hereof) to be made liable by Royal Proclamation to be called up for service in the armed forces of the Crown or in civil defence. Proclamations have been made from time to time covering persons between the ages of 18 and 45 inclusive in Great Britain (excluding the Isle of Man) and between 18 and 40 inclusive in the Isle of Man. The National Service Acts were applied to nationals of certain allied powers by virtue of the Allied Powers (War Service) Act, 1942, and an Order in Council dated 11th March, 1943. It has been directed by Proclamations made subsequently to the passing of the National Service Act, 1942, that male British subjects in †Great Britain who attain the age of 18 on any date subsequent to the making of any such Proclamation should on that date become liable for service as if such Proclamation had been made on that date.

2. Registration.

All men liable to be called up for service by virtue of a Proclamation together with male British subjects who have not yet become so liable but who have attained the age of 17 years and 8 months may be required to apply to be registered under the Acts at a Local Office of the Ministry of Labour and National Service on a date to be specified by the Minister, due notice of which is given by public notice, such as posters, announcements in the Press and by the B.B.C. British subjects of the prescribed ages entering †Great Britain who have not registered previously must do so at a Local Office immediately.

At the time of registration men are required

(a) to produce their National Registration Identity Cards; and

(b) to furnish certain information, including particulars of their occupation.

Men who register will be given a registration certificate (N.S.2) which should be carefully preserved, and must be produced for inspection at the request of a police constable in uniform.

Men living six miles or more from the nearest Local Office of the Ministry of Labour and National Service or men suffering from some permanent incapacity may register by post. Forms for this purpose may be obtained at any Ministry of Labour and National Service office or at the local post office. Men who for good cause, e.g., illness, fail to apply for registration on the date specified must do so as soon as possible thereafter. Any man who fails without good cause to register himself on the due date renders himself liable on summary conviction to a fine not exceeding £5.

3. Preference for a particular Service.

Men may express a preference at the time of registration (see paragraph 2) for service in the Royal Navy, the Royal Marines, the Army, the Royal Air Force or civil defence. Civil defence for this purpose includes the National Fire Service and the Police War Reserve. It is, however, for the Service, or civil defence authorities to decide in relation to the anticipated vacancies whether a man can be accepted for a particular service. Owing to the absence of vacancies it is unlikely that any man can now be accepted for service in civil defence.

4. Change of address.

Any change of address must be notified immediately by the return of the registration certificate (N.S.2) to a Local Office of the Ministry of Labour and National Service. Failure to do so constitutes an offence under the Acts.

5. Medical Examination.

Men who are subject to registration (i.e., men liable to be called up whether they have registered or not and men not yet liable to be called up who have been required to register under the Acts) will be summoned for medical examination by a written notice. Medical boards are situated in centres throughout Great Britain, and men will be allowed reasonable expenses and allowances for their attendance, in-two clear days' notice will be given in all cases. Men will be informed of the medical grade in which they are placed. Immediately after the medical examination they will be interviewed individually in order that their allocation to national service may be made to the best advantage.

6. Postponement of liability to be called up for service.

There is no power to exempt persons from their liability to be called up for service in the armed forces or in civil defence, but a person may apply for postponement of his liability to be called up on the ground that exceptional hardship would ensue. Men who wish to apply for postponement should register in the ordinary way and submit themselves for medical examination when called upon (see paras. 2 and 5 above). Application for a postponement certificate should normally be made at the time of medical examination, but in special circumstances earlier applications may be permitted. A copy of the necessary application form can be obtained on request from the clerk to the medical board and the completed form should be returned to a Local Office of the Ministry of Labour and National Service not later than two days after the completion of the medical examination.

A postponement certificate may be granted for a period not exceeding six months at a time and is renewable. Applications are determined in accordance with the principles set out in the Appendix to this leaflet. Any application for the renewal of a postponement certificate must, unless there are special circumstances, be made not later than 14 days before the expiration of the period for which it was granted or last renewed.

7. Military Service (Hardship) Committees.

Where an application for a postponement certificate is not granted by the Minister it will be referred to a Military Service (Hardship) Committee. An applicant who is aggrieved by a determination of a Hardship Committee may, if the Committee is not unanimous, or if permission so to do is given by the Committee, appeal within 21 days to the Umpire, whose decision is final.

Travelling and subsistence allowances may be paid to applicants and also to any witnesses whose attendance is certified to have been necessary by the Committee or by the Umpire, as the case may be. An applicant may, if he wishes, be represented by his trade union or by any relative or personal friend; subject to this, an applicant may not be represented before a Hardship Committee by counsel or solicitor, but may be so represented before the Umpire.

8. Enlistment in the Forces.

An enlistment or enrolment notice may be served on any man liable to be called up for service, who has been medically examined under the Acts and in respect of whom a postponement certificate is not in force. Such a notice will require him to attend on a specified date at the appropriate reception depot. A minimum of 3 days' notice must be given in all cases. Travelling warrants will be supplied where necessary. A man will be deemed to be entered or enlisted in the armed forces, or enrolled in civil defence, as from the date on which he is required to report for service until the end of the present emergency. Calling up may be deferred because the man is in an occupation which is considered essential to the war effort or because the man is employed on work of national importance for which he is personally indispensable, e.g., he may be regarded as reserved under the Schedule of Reserved Occupations or granted deferment on an application in an individual case. Both reservation and deferment are administrative measures within the sole discretion of the Minister. Further information on the subject of the Schedule of Reserved Occupations and deferment of calling up may be obtained at any Local Office of the Ministry of Labour and National Service.

9. Conscientious Objectors.

A man may apply at the time of registration to be placed on the Register of Conscientious Objectors. He will then be provisionally registered in the Register of Conscientious Objectors, and will be required to make application, within 14 days, to the local Tribunal to have his case considered. Failure to make application to the Tribunal within the prescribed period renders a man liable to have his name removed from the Register of Conscientious Objectors. If

Figure 3.3. National Service Acts explained. (Author's photograph)

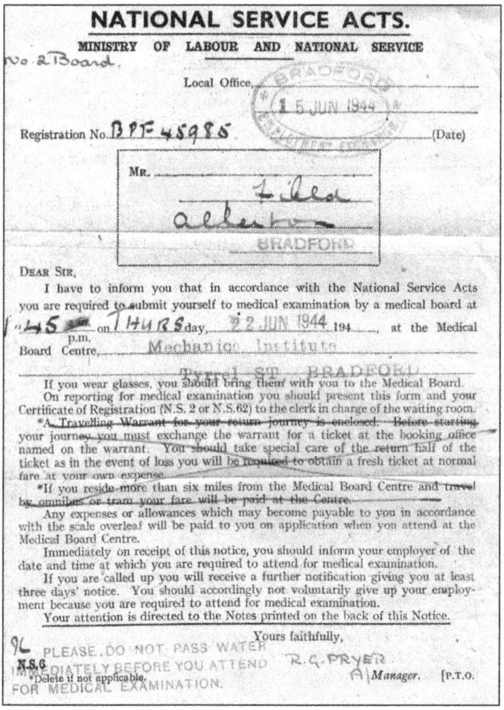

NATIONAL SERVICE ACTS.

MINISTRY OF LABOUR AND NATIONAL SERVICE

No. 2 Board.

Local Office, BRADFORD

15 JUN 1944

Registration No. BPF 45985 (Date)

MR. Fred Allerton
BRADFORD

DEAR SIR,

I have to inform you that in accordance with the National Service Acts you are required to submit yourself to medical examination by a medical board at 1.45 p.m. on Thursday, 22 JUN 1944 194 , at the Medical Board Centre, Mechanics Institute Tyrrel ST BRADFORD

If you wear glasses, you should bring them with you to the Medical Board.

On reporting for medical examination you should present this form and your Certificate of Registration (N.S. 2 or N.S.62) to the clerk in charge of the waiting room.

~~*A Travelling Warrant for your return journey is enclosed. Before starting your journey you must exchange the warrant for a ticket at the booking office named on the warrant. You should take special care of the return half of the ticket as in the event of loss you will be required to obtain a fresh ticket at normal fare at your own expense.~~

~~*If you reside more than six miles from the Medical Board Centre and travel by omnibus or tram your fare will be paid at the Centre.~~

Any expenses or allowances which may become payable to you in accordance with the scale overleaf will be paid to you on application when you attend at the Medical Board Centre.

Immediately on receipt of this notice, you should inform your employer of the date and time at which you are required to attend for medical examination.

If you are called up you will receive a further notification giving you at least three days' notice. You should accordingly not voluntarily give up your employment because you are required to attend for medical examination.

Your attention is directed to the Notes printed on the back of this Notice.

Yours faithfully,

R. G. FRYER

A/Manager.

PLEASE DO NOT PASS WATER IMMEDIATELY BEFORE YOU ATTEND FOR MEDICAL EXAMINATION.

N.S.6

*Delete if not applicable. [P.T.O.

Figure 3.4. Compulsory medical examination. (Author's photograph)

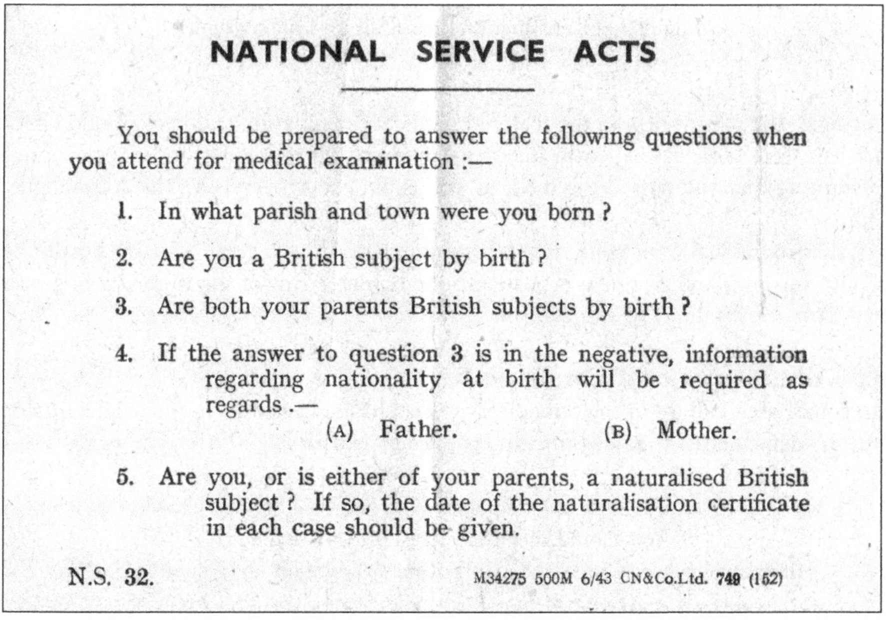

NATIONAL SERVICE ACTS

You should be prepared to answer the following questions when you attend for medical examination :—

1. In what parish and town were you born ?
2. Are you a British subject by birth ?
3. Are both your parents British subjects by birth ?
4. If the answer to question 3 is in the negative, information regarding nationality at birth will be required as regards .—
   (A) Father. (B) Mother.
5. Are you, or is either of your parents, a naturalised British subject ? If so, the date of the naturalisation certificate in each case should be given.

N.S. 32. M34275 500M 6/43 CN&Co.Ltd. 749 (152)

Figure 3.5. Background checks. (Author's photograph)

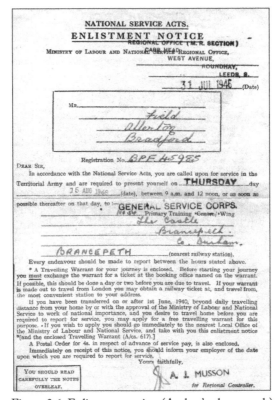

Figure 3.6. Enlistment notice. (Author's photograph)

medical. The man to whom the featured medical examination and background check notices were sent was called to his medical when still too young to be conscripted. Assuming that you passed the medical, you could expect to receive the above, figure 3.6.

This individual was conscripted into the REME after the end of hostilities. Following basic training he was posted to the British Army of the Rhine serving near the dams blown up by 617 Squadron.

(a) Administration/Committees

In some cases, call up to the armed services could have resulted in financial hardship for the dependents. The Government produced a leaflet:

Notice to men called up under the National Services Acts
You should keep this form for future reference
Allowances to wives and dependents of men serving in His Majesty's Forces

... applications for war service grants – see paragraph 3 – can be made at the same time as application for marriage of dependants allowances, or at any time afterwards ...

... War Service Grants may be payable in addition to Service Pay and Allowances. The maximum amount of such grant is £3 a week. These grants are in no sense a charity, but are just as much the due of those called up under the National Service Acts, as any other part of the pay and allowances given by the State.

War Service grants are paid weekly and in the case of a married man with children, the intention is to provide the family, while he is serving, with not less than 22s a week for each unit of the household – a child under 14 counts as a half unit – for living expenses after paying rent or interest on mortgage rates, insurance, etc. If earnings in civil life gave the family a higher standard of living than 22s a unit, a larger grant may be payable ... [4]

Some years later (23 December 1948 to be precise), an Air Ministry Order announced the introduction of National Service Grants and Progressive elimination of Dependents Allowance, Special Dependents Allowance and War Service Grants. Until that happened there needed to be a series of checks and administrative procedures to cope with the various grants on offer.

The Treasury considered this proposal with the following outcome (filed in the National Archives as above):

1st June 1949
To: S S Burridge
Air Ministry

Dear Burridge,
This letter is to place on record the Treasury acceptance of the final report of the Inter-Departmental Working Party on the Review of Dependent's Allowances and War Service Grants.

If the Service Departments, the Ministry of Pensions and the National Assistance Board also accept the report, we are prepared to agree to its being fully implemented without reference to the DWPP Working Sub-Committee.

I am sending copies to Bovenizer, Dancyger, Pavey, Kendrick and Miss Collins.
Yours sincerely,
A H Clough

The final meeting of the Interdepartmental Committee on Post-War pay, allowances and pensions was held the previous month. The minutes of this meeting document that from the 1 January 1949 the National Service grants were to be administered and paid by the Ministry of Pensions on behalf of the Service Departments, and the abolition

4   National Archives AST 7/1098.

from that date, so far as new grants were concerned of the old scheme of dependents allowance, special dependents allowance, War Service grants and emergency grants.

The first meeting of the Standing Committee on National Service Grants was held later in the year on 7 November 1949 at the Ministry of Pensions. The Chair was the previously mentioned Mr Dancyger who worked at the Ministry of Pensions.

Month (in 1949)	Royal Navy			Army			RAF		
	Claim	Award	Rej	Claim	Award	Rej	Claim	Award	Rej
Jan	14	4	10	303	86	201	286	65	190
Feb	60	10	36	477	134	328	193	62	141
Mar	58	22	44	740	233	529	263	65	217
Apr	61	15	51	839	189	602	312	79	241
May	40	5	35	959	271	683	297	65	240
June	50	10	31	741	220	522	290	68	205
July	69	13	45	820	229	584	292	71	223
Aug	28	12	20	816	207	493	246	62	154
Sept	63	25	34	843	278	553	263	96	177
Total	443	116	306	6538	1847	4495	2442	633	1788

Figure 3.7 Claims for National Service Grants for the first nine months of 1949.[5]

Revamping Service Grants was not the only administrative issue needing resolution. For example the emergency powers brought into force during the war allowed for the creation of National Registration. This register was continued for several years after war ended, but was eventually the subject of discussion. A Cabinet document records the announcement as:

Note for the Record

National Registration

I understand that Mr A Johnston is the Chairman of the Interdepartmental Working Party which is coordinating departmental preparations for the abolition of National Registration which it is intended to announce on 14th February next. Abolition will be affected by Order in Council so that no Parliamentary time will be involved beyond that required for making the announcement.
8th January 1952

The details behind the decision are documented as Appendix V.

Whilst the discussions of the financial issues of compensation for conscription continued, there was a continuing discussion of the numbers to be conscripted. One of the issues was the need to conscript new intakes of service personnel whilst also

5   Ibid.

keeping the overall cost under control, for example:

National Service Intake
1.   The numbers of national service men available for call-up (including the numbers due to expire of deferments) are estimated as follows:

Year	Numbers
1948	171,000*
1949	193,000
1950	226,000
1951	229,000
1952	240,000
1953	240,000

* Plus 20,000-25,000 from 1947

Figure 3.8. Potential conscripts.

The problem is how to limit the intake to about 150,000 a year.

2.   Any scheme must, if possible:
    1.   Preserve the principle of the universality of call-up.
    2.   Be sufficiently flexible to meet the changing circumstances of the present uncertain times.
    3.   Must be manifestly just as between man and man.
3.   The only measures which fulfil these requirements are:
    1.   Slowing down registration (thus raising the age of call-up).
    2.   Raising the medical and educational standards.
    I suggest that a combination of these methods is easily the best and most practicable and likely to raise the least difficulties.
4.   The effect of the decision already taken to omit in 1948 the first of the quarterly registrations, via the March registration, is that men who would have registered in March will not do so until June, thus they and all who follow them will register three months later than they would have done and their age of call-up will be raised by three months. The result of omitting the March 1948 registration will be that the number available for call-up during 1948 will be about 131,000 (plus 20,000–30,000 from 1947).
5.   If in each succeeding year there are only three registrations instead of four, the numbers available for call-up and the minimum call-up ages will be as follows:

Year	Numbers available	Call-up age
1948	131,000*	18 years and 3 months
1949	153,000	18 years and 6 months
1950	190,000	18 years and 9 months
1951	195,000	19 years and 0 months
1952	206,000	19 years and 3 months
1953	206,000	19 years and 6 months

* Plus 20,000-25,000 from 1947

Figure 3.9. Effect on call-up age.

6.   Raising the standards would further reduce the annual intake by about one-eighth, taking account only of medical standards (the effect of raising educational standards has still to be considered). I suggest however that the raising of standards should be combined with the slowing down of registrations only when it becomes necessary, and this on the above estimates would not be until 1950. By raising the standards in 1950, figures given in paragraph 5 for 1950 to 1953 become:

Year	Numbers available
1950	166,000
1951	170,000
1952	180,000
1953	180,000

Figure 3.10. Effect on raising standards.

This indicated that after omitting one registration from 1948 onwards and raising the standards from 1950 the numbers of available from 1950 would still exceed the 150,000 required. The numbers becoming available, however, can be varied as necessary by so arranging the dates of registration and the raising of the age of call-up as to yield the required result. Also, if the additional numbers should be required in any year, it would be possible to keep the call-up age stable by reverting to four registrations in a year. Maximum flexibility is thus preserved.

7.   So long as no more than about 150,000 a year are needed, the effect of this system is to raise the call-up age progressively, not at all a bad thing. It will seem that the measures proposed take care of the position until at least the end of 1953, by which time the call-up age would not in any event have reached beyond 20½. Under the Military Training Act, 1939, men were called up between the ages of 20 and 21. This is on the whole a better age of call-up than 18 and would probably have been adopted in the National Service Act, 1947, had it not been

for the fact that it would have resulted in a sudden cessation of recruitment for two years.

8. I would emphasise that the slowing down of registration and raising the age of call-up does not result in any piling up of men in the military recruiting machine; it only means that if and when compulsory military service comes to an end, a certain number of men who would otherwise have entered the machine will not do so because they will not have reached the stipulated age.

9. Apart from preserving universal military service, being flexible and just, the above proposals do not involve an amendment of the National Services Act, 1947, do not add to the difficulties of the Services, are easy to carry out and are advantageous to industry. I would, therefore, urge their adoption.

10. Finally, I feel I must point out that the total number of volunteers that the Services are likely to get is unlikely to exceed 450,000 (and this I regard as an optimistic figure), the acceptance by the Services of only 150,000 national service men each year means that the total size of the Forces will not exceed 600,000 and may well be below this figure.[6]

An extract from the minutes of the 22nd meeting of the Defence Committee held on 25 November 1949 has this to say on the subject of Service cuts:

> ... the Committee first considered the possibility of reducing the expenditure on defence by making some changes in National Service; by the reduction of the size of the forces in Tripolitania; and by reducing the scale of the provision for Naval equipment.

National Service
The Lord President of the Council said that he realised from the arguments put forward in DO(49)70 that it was impossible to make a radical change in the system of National Service such as he has mentioned in DO(49)69 – for the present at any rate we could not afford to abolish the period of service with the colours altogether and substitute for it a system of part-time service in the Territorial and Auxiliary forces. He wondered however whether it might not be possible to save some money by reducing the proportion of National Servicemen serving with the colours, perhaps insisting instead on some longer liability for reserve service.

The Minister of Defence and The Chiefs of Staff did not feel that any such change was practicable in present circumstances. To carry out their current responsibilities the Services were at present absorbing the whole of the available intake – regular recruiting was falling off in an alarming fashion. Moreover the importance of national service as the means of providing reserves for war should not be overlooked.

The Committee accepted this view and agreed that there could be no question at present at any rate, of making any radical change in the system of

6   National Archives LAB 25/208.

National Service. The right course was to continue the present system, restricting the intake as necessary by raising the normal age of call-up by the omission of quarterly registrations, as proposed in DO(49)74. Under these arrangements the age of call-up would not exceed 18years 9 months by 1952. There could be no question of introducing a ballot.

Tripolitania

The Foreign Secretary said that for political reasons he was particularly anxious to withdraw all British forces from Tripolitania as soon as possible. If the French should have trouble with the Arabs, there would be less chance of our becoming embroiled if there were no British troops in the vicinity of the Fozzan or Tunisia. Further, it was embarrassing for him to have to justify the presence of British troops in this territory – so many people drew the conclusion that they were there because we intended to seize it …

The provision for Naval equipment

The Prime Minister said that in the matter of equipment it was clear that first priority should be given to the Royal Air Force and to radar and the air raid warning system. Other re-equipment programmes would have to be scrutinised more closely and in particular he wondered whether the imminence of the naval threat had not been overestimated and there was not room for some further reduction in the provision proposed for naval equipment … [7]

The ever changing economy, political situation and armed forces numbers determined the need for changes to the National Services legislation on an ongoing basis until the mid-1950s. It seemed that even before a bill became law there was a need to consider the next amendments to National Service. For example, even before the Act of 1947, a committee was formed to bring amendments to the regulations to Parliament concerning the regulations for 1949:

Ministry of Labour and
National Service
St James' Square
London

28th November 1946
To: Clark Turner
     Ministry of Health
     Caxton House

Dear Clark Turner,

We have to get instructions to the Parliamentary Council as soon as possible for the drafting of the National Service (Armed Forces) Bill which is to be taken this Session, under which men will be called up for service as from 1st January 1949.

7   National Archives WO 32/12242.

I am writing to you because it is necessary to consider the position of doctors and dentists in relation to the upper age-limit for call-up which will be specified in the Bill.

The men, other than doctors and dentists, who will be liable for call-up will be those who have attained the age of 18 and who have not attained the age of 25 (there will be special provision for lowering the age to 17½ for men who wish to be called up at that time). It is clear that doctors and dentists are unlikely to be qualified and sufficiently experienced for call-up before attaining the age of 25, and we therefore propose to provide in the Bill for calling up male registered medical practitioners and registered dentists who have attained the age of 25 and who have not attained the age of 30. The reason for raising the lower as well as the upper age-limit is to avoid subjecting doctors and dentists to a longer range of liability than other men – actually the above limit provides for them a shorter range ... [8]

The bill was wider than just doctors and dentists, however. The purpose of the legislation was covered in a document of Instructions to Parliamentary Council thus:

1. The object of the proposed legislation is to establish a scheme of compulsory service in the Armed Forces of the Crown to come into force on 1st January 1949. At the present time men are called up for service in these forces under the provisions of the National Service Act 1939 to 1946. These Acts although not technically of a temporary character will lose their effectiveness at the end of the present emergency which will be on a date to be appointed by His Majesty's Order-in-Council (Section 21(1) of the National Service (Armed Forces) Act 1939), since under the National Services Acts persons can be enlisted until the end of the present emergency only.

2. It is desired that the proposed legislation should follow in the main the principles laid down in the National Services Acts. There will be, however, two main differences, namely:
   i)   The Bill is to apply to men only, and not to women, and
   ii) In addition to the liability to give the whole time service for a period in the armed forces there should be imposed on the completion of this whole time service a liability to serve in the Territorial Army or other reserve service of the branch of the armed forces concerned.

3. It is essential that persons who complete their whole time service should have rights of reinstatement in their pre-service civil employment similar to those provided for now leaving the Services by the Reinstatement in Civil Employment Act 1944, and that some appropriate provision should also be made in regard to the civil employment of persons who are, from time to time, called up for training in the reserve service.

4. The new legislation is to come into force on the 1st January 1949, and as from that date the National Service Acts 1939 to 1942 should be repealed (but

see paragraph 42). It is possible, however, that the National Service (Release of Conscientious Objectors) Act 1946, will have to remain in force after that date suitably amended to cover the point raised in paragraph 41 of these Instructions.
5. Some minor amendments will also be necessary to the Reinstatement in Civil Employment Act 1944.

Persons liable to be registered for service in the armed forces

6. It is desired that there should be maintained by the Minister of Labour and National Service a register to be called the 'Military Service Register' of persons liable to be called up for whole time service in the armed forces.

7. All male British subjects resident and for the time being in Great Britain (other than exempt persons – see paragraph 13) should be made liable to register in this Register on attaining the age of 17 years and 8 months or immediately they enter Great Britain. The Minister should be empowered to make regulations prescribing the place, time and manner at and in which registrations are to be made and the particulars relating to himself which the person registering should furnish on such registration. These particulars should include a statement by the person registering as to whether he would prefer the army, navy or air force ... [9]

This document is just one of a number in the National Archives documenting changes in the National Service regulations as the threat of war receded. Some of the other amendments can be found in the following table.

Content	National Archives folio
National Service Bill 1954: proposals for the amendment of the National Service Acts 1948-50	LAB 6/678
National Service Bill to consolidate the National Service Acts 1939 to 1947	MH 79/621
National Service: extension of National Service Scheme for a further five years; reserve liability for National Servicemen and Class 2 and G Reservists; Navy, Army and Air Force Reserves Bill	PREM 11/935

Figure 3.11. Further reference on National Service.

(b) Intake/Training/Qualifications

More so than during the war years, intake into the services for post-war National Service included trying to match training and ability to service occupations. Indeed a document was produced outlining the seasonal variation in mental abilities of National Service men.

9   Ibid.

Qualifications of National Service Personnel

1. Objective

To show the significance of seasonal variation in abilities of National Service intake. To provide a means of measuring this variation so that representative samples may be taken and estimates made of the ability of National Service personnel entering at any particular date or throughout the year as a whole. To assist in selection, allocation and training policy and practice in the RAF.

2. Background

The young men of Great Britain, when they become liable for military service under the National Service (1948) Act, on their 18th birthday, attend a local recruitment centre for registration and interview. They are called up shortly after registration unless they apply for deferment. The number doing so has gradually risen and is probably now approaching 50 percent of the total at the present time.

3. Those who defer fall into two main groups:

a) Students who want to complete a course of fulltime study.

b) Apprentices who want to complete apprenticeships (often combined with evening study courses).

4. Student deferment begins from the man's birthday and usually ends with the ending of the current academic year. Apprentice deferment also begins with the 18th birthday, but is usually for more than a year, since industrial apprenticeships commonly cover five years beginning at age 16. In some industries apprenticeship begins at the New Year, or after summer holidays, and terminates at the year's end or at about mid-summer. In others there is no particular customary date …

5. National Service intake to the RAF during the period reviewed was at the rate of approximately 4,000 men per calendar month. Intake consists of:

i) Graduates granted commissions, medical or dental or proceeding direct to Officer Training Units on entry.

ii) Men accepted for training as aircrew on entry, without revision of their National Service engagement.

iii) Others, about 90% of the total, with whom this enquiry is mainly concerned.

Group iii) is again divisible into three groups:

a) Men whose educational achievement qualifies them for consideration for commissioned rank (taken in at the rate of about 10,000 a year).

b) Men who have completed civil industrial apprenticeships (about the same number as group a) with some overlap).

c) The remainder, taken in at a rate of about 20,000 a year.

6. Personnel in groups iii) a), b) and c) were tested by Personnel Selection Units at Schools of Recruit Training in the fifth week after entry, with a view to ground trade allocation as airmen, or selection for commissioned rank. Records of the distribution of scores on ten tests despatched weekly from each SRT, have been used for this investigation.

7. Certain changes occurring in the general situation during the year under review affected National Service intake. As from September 1st 1950, the new

period of National Service was increased from 1½ to 2 years, and a new pay code was introduced throughout the Services. The pay of regulars was raised, and also the pay of National Service men during their added months of service ...

10. Average scores on all tests are much higher in the autumn months than during the remainder of the year, among NS men tested at Schools of Recruit Training.

11. The educational quality of the NS intake, like its test achievement, varies by the seasons of the year, and is higher in autumn.

12. Apprentice weekly entry has not yet been analysed in regard to quality of achievement on tests, but it is noticeable that the results of mechanical aptitude tests rise sharply – much more than other tests – at New Year and after the Technical College courses close. This is probably due to the entry of large numbers of well-trained apprentices around these dates.

13. The effect of the observed seasonal variation is that personnel qualified to be considered for commissioned rank and as highly skilled tradesmen are available in much greater numbers among men entering between July and December than among men entering between January and June. This statement refers to that 90% of NS intake from whom those granted commissions as University graduates are already excluded.[10]

Having observed and proved the phenomenon the rest of the paper tried to understand how and why this observation occurred and how to create a mathematical formula, which they were able to do. The final statement of their conclusions reads:

... it is recommended that these findings be considered in connection with allocation and training plans for National Service personnel ...

An interesting document – even by today's standards!

(c) Exemptions/conscientious objectors

The document last mentioned in the previous section touched on legislation for conscientious objectors. There were issues relating to conscientious objectors as late as 1946 – at least those relocated to Jersey.

Employment of British workers in Jersey
during the potato season of 1940

For eight successive seasons – 1932–1939 – the Ministry of Labour supplied all extra labour required by members of the Jersey Farmers Union to lift all their potato crop and assist with other agricultural work including tomato crop. The number of workers supplied per season varied from 1,500 to about 2,500.

Due to war conditions, the Ministry advised the JFU early in 1940 that no British labour would be available to assist with that year's crop but later agreed to receive a deputation in London of Jersey farmers. I was then carrying out temporary duty for NS4 Montague House, and because I had acted as the

10   National Archives AIR 77/271.

Department's Representative in Jersey during several earlier seasons, I was asked to attend the meeting.

At the Conference held on 3rd May 1940 at Queen Anne's Chambers, the President of the JFU said they needed at least a thousand extra workers immediately for a period of 6 to 10 weeks. Because of the difficult manpower position in Great Britain the Union had accepted an offer from the Society of Friends and the Pacifists Union, via Mr Flinn, to supply about 500 men, most wholly conscientious objectors …

… the nearby French coastline fell into enemy hands and nearly 20,000 persons were evacuated from Jersey by 20th June. The potato workers were regarded as fare-paid passengers for GWR or SR boats and were refused admission on refugee boats. They were eventually cleared by Southern Railway boats and I left the Island on 23rd June after satisfying myself, as far as possible, that no worker brought over under the Ministry's scheme was stranded. To the best of my recollection the few 'Ministry of Labour' men who elected to remain had spent some years on the Island having been brought over during earlier seasons and could please themselves. I feel sure, therefore, that the 11 men referred to on page 2 of Mr Flinn's letter relate to such persons … [11]

The letter referred to above is reproduced here:

Home Office
Whitehall

5th September 1946
To: H Flinn
Le Houmet
St Brelade's Bay
Jersey

Sir,
I am directed by the Secretary of State to refer to the letter which you addressed on the 9th July to the Ministry of Labour and National Service regarding reimbursement of expenses incurred in caring for certain seasonal workers and conscientious objectors left in Jersey at the time of the German Occupation.

Your case has already been under consideration by the Minister of Labour and National Service who has decided that he is unable to make any reimbursement from public funds at his disposal, and has forwarded the correspondence to this Department.

The Secretary of State regrets that there are no funds at his disposal from which financial assistance might be given to you.
I am Sir,
Your Obedient Servant[12]

11   National Archives LAB 6/2.
12   Ibid.

It is unfortunate, with the benefit of hindsight, that Mr Flinn received no compensation for his actions. The rest of the paperwork in the folio discusses the issues relating to his actions which were that of a volunteer. The Government were forced into paying for the actions of some residents. The issues relate to the National Service Hostels Corporation, a member of which wrote the following letter.

To: R L Bicknell
    Ministry of Labour and National Service
    80/92 Pall Mall
    7th June 1951

Undesirable Residents

Dear Mr Bicknell,

I have had correspondence and discussions on the above subject with your Branch in the past, and feel I should let you have the following particulars of a case which has just been brought to my notice.

A man named Alexander Craw was sent by your Ministry to Cowdenbeath Miner's Hostel on 16th April as a mining trainee. Certain offences subsequently took place and on 31st May he was found guilty of:

a)   Breach of the peace (3 charges).
b)   Flourishing an open razor.
c)   Breaking open and stealing various articles from residents' lockers at the hostel.

The disturbing thing is that the man's record contains five previous convictions for housebreaking which shows, I suggest, complete unsuitability for community life in a hostel.

The man is now in jail and he has been black-listed by our regional officers so as to prevent re-admission to any of our hostels in Scotland. The Coal Board, divisionally, have endorsed our action in barring the man from hostel accommodation.

Yours sincerely,[13]

Other letters in the same folio document cases of persistent gambling, fighting and other issues. The table below shows the incidents recorded by the National Service Hostels Corporation in a letter to the Ministry of Labour and National Service dated 5 March 1949. The comment immediately preceding the data shown in the table is included to place the data in context.

... in my earlier letter to Rossetti on this subject, I gave figures relating to certain hostels where most of the trouble was being experienced in June 1948. For the purposes of comparison similar information was obtained in respect of December 1948. The comparative figures are as follows:

13   National Archives LAB 26/273.

	June 1948	December 1948
Number of residents taken into police custody	93	101
Number of residents evicted	226	216
Number of residents who disappeared without booking out	270	248

Figure 3.12. Undesirable hostel residents.

These figures must have caused some concern at the time.

4   Education

Arguably, the most widely known education act of the 20th century was the 1944 Education Act, often known as the Butler Education Act. R A B Butler was the Minister of Education at the time and had overall responsibility for bringing in the Act, the infrastructure needed to bring the fledgling Bill to the Statute books and enable the Act to affect those in education. Undoubtedly the Act had a far reaching effect on education at many levels.

Whilst reproducing the Act here may add little value, Circular 5, published by the Ministry of Education and dated 15 September 1944, may help to understand some of the more important aspects:

Local Administration of Education
Schemes of Divisional Administration

1. Section 6 and part III of the First Schedule of the Education Act, 1944, provide for the setting up of a new machinery for the local administration of the public system of education in county areas. The object of these provisions is to secure that while, within the framework of national policy, the education service in county areas shall be administered under the general control and supervision of the Local Education Authority, it shall not lose the inspiration to be driven from more immediate local interest and local initiative.

2. The functions of the Local Education Authority which may be delegated to divisional executives by schemes of divisional administration are those relating to primary and secondary education. The extension of schemes of divisional administration to cover functions relating to further education is permissible at the discretion of the Minister on the application of the Local Education Authority or of the council of an excepted district ...

4. As was made clear in the course of debate during the passage of the Bill, it would be neither desirable nor practicable to attempt to lay down any hard and fast model scheme to which Authorities should be expected to conform. Such uniformity would be irreconcilable with the wide differences in the circumstances and requirements of different areas.[1]

1   National Archives ED 147/393.

(a) Administration/Education Act 1944

Such was the impact of this act that the National Archives store many reference documents written at the time. It would add no value to document all of those folios here, however, by way of an example and as a pointer to further research, the following table documents just some of the series folios in the National Archives.

Folio Description	National Archives Reference
16-19 Cost Effectiveness Study Steering Group and Committee (Russell Committee)	ED 208
Annual reports of the National Council for Domestic Studies and National Council for Home Economic Education	ED 276
Central Advisory Council for Education (England)	ED 146
Central Advisory Council for Education (Wales)	ED 263
Committee of Inquiry into Fircroft College	ED 177
Committee of Inquiry into Reading and the Use of English (Bullock Committee)	ED 256
Committee of Inquiry into Special Education (Warnock Committee)	ED 285
Committee of Inquiry into the Teaching of Mathematics in Schools (Cockcroft Committee)	ED 284
Committee on Adult Education (Russell Committee)	ED 175
Committee on Social Studies (Heyworth Committee)	ED 144
Committee on Technician Courses and Examinations (Haslegrave Committee)	ED 163
Committee on the Development of Day Release (Henniker-Heaton Committee)	ED 204
Committee on the Need for a National Film School and National Film School Planning Committee	ED 243
Computer Assisted Learning Programme Committee	ED 264
Disabled Rehabilitation and Resettlement Committee. (The Ince Committee): Tomlinson report recommendations; establishment of neuropsychiatric source	LAB 20
Industrial Policy Official Committee, Subcommittee on Management Education	ED 201
Joint Committees for Vocational Education	ED 182
Minutes and papers on the review of the University Grants Committee	ED 280
National Advisory Body for Public Sector Higher Education	ED 259 and ED 260
National Advisory Council on Art Education	ED 206
National Advisory Council on Education for Industry and Commerce	ED 205
National Committee for the Award of the Certificate in Office Studies	ED 200

Folio Description	National Archives Reference
National Committee of Enquiry into Higher Education (Dearing Committee)	ED 266
National Council for Domestic Studies and National Council for Home Economics Education	ED 237
National Libraries Committee (Dainton Committee)	ED 178
Records (mainly minutes, agenda and papers) of various councils, committees, working parties and other bodies concerned with education	ED Division 29
Reviewing Committee on the Export of Works of Art	ED 180
United Kingdom Advisory Council on Education for Management	ED 231
Working Group on Research into Comprehensive Education and Consultative Committee on Research into Comprehensive Education	ED 209
Working Party on Public Lending Right	ED 254

Figure 4.1. Some National Archives folio references.

Of course some of these Committees met many years after the war ended. They are included here to demonstrate the far-reaching effects of post-war education reform. Perhaps for our purposes it will be instructive to concentrate on just a few of the relevant committees active just after the War ended.

Working to enact the Education Act, The Central Advisory Committee for England met on many occasions, one of which was on Friday 11 January 1946. Sir Fred Clarke was the Chairman at the time with Mr W O Lester Smith as Vice Chairman. There were many notable members of this Committee including Sir Charles Darwin FRS, who made significant contributions to the development of technology during the war.[2]

This particular meeting addressed some points arising from the Ince Report previously mentioned (in figure 4.1). A member of the Central Advisory Committee quoted part of the Ince report. Part of paragraph 42 reads:

> The pivot of the life of almost every boy and girl who has left work is the job. It may not be their work that holds their main attention or interest, but the job is a job and is of paramount importance.[3]

The committee member who raised this issue in the meeting is on record for holding these thoughts:

> I should like to know at what stage you think the schools should begin to think about that and what influence, if any, the fact that when a boy enters into the job it is pivotal in his life should have upon the school in the handling of the boy. It is an omission in it, in that it seems to say very little about what used to be

2   National Archives ED 146/2.
3   Ibid.

known as secondary school leavers, boys and girls who leave school at 16 or over. The Report, I think you will agree, concentrated very much upon children leaving school at the minimum age, i.e., when they are 14 or 15 as it will be after 1st April 1947, and I think it is possible for that reason that there is so much emphasis upon the job as being the most important consideration in the child's mind ... [4]

Within two years of the above argument for producing children able to join the job market, a paper was presented to the Central Advisory Council titled *The Crisis in the Primary School*. Written by J L Longland, the paper suggests:

The result is the impression that the Junior School is drifting rudderless; that many teachers in them are badly puzzled about their job, above all the relation between the various parts of it. A similar sense of uncertainty, of the absence of any particular mark to aim at can be felt in many secondary modern schools. Is citizenship as useful as arithmetic, or English composition as profitable as local surveys, and if not why not? It seems likely that there has been a consequent drop in the standards of achievement in the kinds of knowledge that are readily measurable, and a complete lack of certainty among teachers about the proper balance between formal drills and informal activities – if indeed they admit that there is any difference between them!

There is a growing volume of complaint from teachers in secondary schools, especially in the grammar schools, that the children come up to them from the primary school ignorant of the simplest ways of handling language and number, that a secondary school course cannot be undertaken without competence in these basic skills and that they have to waste a lot time in teaching things that ought to have been learnt in the Junior Schools. Some parents at least make the same complaints. It is obvious that all this evidence must be looked at suspiciously, since investigation might show it was the methods of secondary school teachers and the things they expected of children entering their schools for the first time that were wrong, and not the methods of primary school. But the growing dissatisfaction of the secondary school teachers is a fact, and since the primary school exists partly to prepare its pupils for the secondary schools, it is a fact that seems to call for investigation ... [5]

As with any far reaching Act, there were authorities which were adversely affected. A case in point was the Borough of Morley.

Education Act 1944
Claim on the West Riding County Council for an annual payment to the Morley Corporation by way of Financial Adjustment under Section 93(3) to compensate for the continuing charge arising out of the Superannuation of Officers and Servants transferred to the County Council under the above Act

4   Ibid.
5   National Archives ED 146/21.

1. Until the 31st March 1945, the Morley Corporation were a Part III Education Authority but as from the 1st April 1945, their duties relating to Elementary Education were by the Education Act, 1944, transferred to the West Riding County Council.

2. The Morley Corporation under the Local Government Officers' Superannuation Act 1922, established a Superannuation Scheme as from the 1st April 1934, and the balance of the fund, together with outstanding liabilities, was transferred to the new compulsory Superannuation Scheme and Fund established under the local Government Superannuation Act 1937. The provisions of the Superannuation Acts applied to employees of the Education Committee equally with those of all other employees of the Corporation

3. On the 1st April 1945, the whole of the staff engaged on Elementary Education were transferred to the County Council under the provision of Section 6(4) of the Education Act 1944, although for the sake of administrative convenience certain Officers and Servants in connection with School Nurseries and Medical Inspection were not transferred until a later date ...

9 ... it will be clear therefore that unless some financial adjustment is made between the two authorities, the Morley Corporation will be paying an equal annual charge in respect of all the Officers and Servants previously employed by the Corporation's Education Committee and also through the County Rate a proportion of the Equal Annual Charge for all Officers and Servants employed by the County Council's Education Committee prior to the 31st March 1945. If a financial adjustment is not made between the two Authorities under Section 96(3) of the Education Act 1944, the Morley Corporation will therefore be involved in a double charge.[6]

This situation with the Morley Corporation was not unique. The Borough of Wembley also had issues to resolve when the County of Middlesex took over the responsibilities for education in that part of London.[7]

Some of the responsibilities delegated by the Ministry of Education to the local authorities was further devolved to the school's Governing Body, in previous years known as the School Board. In line with other legislation in the 1944 Education Act, there was a Government publication, in this case called the *Principles of Government in Maintained Secondary Schools*. The introduction for this publication starts:

Under clause 16 of the Education Bill every county and auxiliary secondary school is to have an instrument of government provided for the constitution of a body of governors, and is to be conducted under articles of government, which shall in particular determine the functions to be exercised in relation to the school by the local education authority, the body of governors and the head teacher respectively.

6   National Archives ED 147/420.
7   National Archives ED 151/90.

Hitherto in the sphere of education of pupils over eleven years of age there has been a clear distinction between Secondary Schools falling within the field of Higher education and Senior or Central Schools falling within the field of Elementary education. So far as schools of Higher education are concerned there is no statutory provision in the Education Acts relating to the constitution and powers of governing bodies and head teachers. In a certain number of schools, however, the governance of the school is regulated by a Scheme made under the Endowed Schools or Charitable Trusts Acts, and all Secondary Schools are required as a condition of grant to 'be governed and conducted under adequate and suitable rules'. So far as Elementary Schools are concerned the constitution and powers of the body of managers are regulated by Sections 30-36 of the Education Act 1921, and by rules made by the local education authority.[8]

I find this fascinating. I am in my 16th year as a primary school governor. We have an instrument of governance setting out how we work. From time to time we have updated it. In some cases central or local government has triggered the change. In one case it was for a name change as we were previously a First and Middle School and are now a Primary School. Other schools have changed their instrument of governance upon an amalgamation of two smaller schools. Additionally the school might have taken another class (or more) per year group and needed more governors within the governing body. Looking through the above document the sentiment and ethos of these changes will resonate with all current governors, be they in the Primary or Secondary Sector.

As part of their remit, school governors have oversight of curriculum delivery. The immediate post-war period offered many challenges, not least of which was adequate resources to ensure content delivery. Perhaps the issue of school books will serve as an exemplar.

The school books and library service covered many areas of reference literature for which there were oversight panels. They included: Art, Broadcasting, Drama, English, Handicraft, History, Industry and Commerce, Infants, Mathematics, Music, Needlecraft, Physical Education, Principles of Education, Religious Instruction, Rural Education, School Meals, Science, Secondary, Special Educational Treatment, Technical and Visual Methods. These panels were staffed by experts whose remit included book content, sourcing from a variety of publishers.[9] Obtaining paper and ink to print these books was a challenge all of its own!

Once the content and supply had been determined, there was then the matter of ensuring distribution. On its own, this would have been a challenge; coupled with post-war conditions and the changing needs of the curriculum, it must have seemed daunting at times!

The 1944 Education Act also impacted on physical education. Legislation in force prior to 1944 was enshrined in the Physical Training and Recreation Act of 1937. This was modified in 1944 in the following way:

8   National Archives ED 147/85.
9   National Archives ED 147/73.

Introduction

1. The amendment of the Physical Training and Recreation Act 1939, effected by Section 53(4) of the Education Act 1944, amplifies the administration of grants for the purposes covered by the Act and leave the Minister of Education direct responsibility for the consideration of applications for, and the assessment and payment of, these grants. Provision for this service has been made in the Ministry estimates for the financial year 1945/46.

In accordance with the undertaking given during the passage of the Education Bill through Parliament (Official Report, House of Lords 27th June 1944, column 475), a small non-statutory Committee is being set up to advise the Minister generally on the application of grants under the Physical Training and Recreation Act. The Chairman of the Committee will be the Head of the Branch responsible for the administration of the grants …

3. Schemes for the provision of facilities for physical training and recreation, which are intended mainly for the benefit of adults but will include some provision for juveniles, will also be considered for grant under Section 3 of the P, T and R Act.[10]

Clearly, in some cases land was also needed in order to enhance or establish existing playing fields. There was a form, a procedure and a Memorandum from the Ministry of Education which covered premises to be acquired with the aid of a grant by the Minister under Section 3 of the Physical Training and Recreation Act 1937.

The first two paragraphs of this Memorandum set the scene:

1. Before a capital grant can be obtained by a Voluntary Organisation in respect of the acquisition of land or buildings for Physical Training and Recreation, it will usually be necessary for the premises to be settled on suitable trusts. The Ministry is not issuing a specimen form of Trust Deed, but the following notes will be of assistance in drawing up the Deed.

2. The Ministry considers that it is desirable that the trusts should be declared in the Conveyance of the property rather than for a Conveyance on trust for sale to be executed, followed by a Declaration of Trust; this latter course is open to technical objection.

In drawing up the conveyance therefore the following considerations, among others, should be borne in mind … [11]

As with every other initiative in Government there was the inevitable procedure.[12]

(b) Communications and training

Victory in Europe brought with it the prospect of travel, albeit on a limited basis. Accordingly a Conference of Allied Ministers of Education took place on Thursday 12

10   National Archives ED 169/11.
11   Ibid.
12   Ibid.

July 1945 in London. Mr Richard Law, then Minister of Education, was in the chair. Fourteen governments sent their representatives, some travelling from Canada, China and the USSR. In addition to general discussion various Commissions reported their work, including:

- Books and Periodical Commission.
- Commission on the Protection and Restitution of Cultural Material.
- Commission of Enquiry on Special Educational Problems.
- Commission on Films, Broadcasting and Similar Aids.

In his opening remarks, the Chair made the following statement:

> The Chairman expressed his pleasure in the opportunity to participate in the work of the Conference, although it was a matter of regret that Mr Butler had had to abandon the chair just as the conference was reaching some finality in its deliberations.
>
> It was encouraging to know that Article 57 of the Charter of the United Nations made provision for international co-operation in the field of education and culture, and the task of the Conference of Allied Ministers of Education now would be to consider how to make this article effective.
>
> At the last meeting it had been unanimously agreed that His Majesty's Government should be invited to issue invitations for a United Nations Conference in London to adopt a Constitution for a United Nations Organisation for Educational and Cultural Co-operation. The Cabinet had been consulted and was willing to issue invitations for such a Conference to take place as soon as possible, probably in November. The invitations would be issued shortly and provisional arrangements for accommodation were already in train. Draft proposals for an Educational and Cultural Organisation had been drawn up by the Conference for submission to the United Nations Conference. The Chairman hoped that it was quite clear that this was only a draft, and that suggested amendments would be considered at the United Nations Conference.[13]

During the War, perhaps like no other time in recent history, the educational and cultural heritage of every European nation was at the forefront of attention, at least by some. Indeed there was a Commission for Protection and Restitution of Cultural Material which met regularly through the latter years of the War. A report from 25 April to 31 August 1944 set the scene.

1. Formation

This Commission was constituted at the 10th meeting of the Conference on the 19th April 1944, when Professor Paul Vaucher was appointed Chairman and Mr C P Harvey of the British Council was appointed Secretary. Its formation

13   National Archives ED 42/2.

was largely due to the initiative of Mr Archibald MacLeish of the American Commission for the Protection and Salvage of Artistic and Historic Monuments in War Areas (commonly called the Roberts Commission) who was present at the Conference as a member of the US delegation headed by Congressman J W Fulbright. The general purpose of its formation was to take in hand the task of co-ordinating the work on restitution and preservation of cultural material which had been and was being done by various other bodies. No definite terms of reference were laid down for the Commission, but at its first meeting on 25th April it propounded the following definition of its function:

To collect from all available sources (including the Allied Governments concerned) the fullest possible information of art and cultural material of all sorts in the occupied countries; to act as a pool for all such information; and to offer its services in any other useful capacity to such military or civilian authorities as may now or hereafter be concerned with the public administration of any liberated territory or of any enemy territory which may be occupied by the Allied forces.[14]

Shortly after VJ Day efforts were stepped up in an effort to contain the dispersal of material. In a note dated 10 September 1945, the Commission was concerned with the location and restoration of cultural artefacts.

... that 70-90% of all the artistic material officially taken from Europe was now located in the Western Zone although so far not much material from the Eastern Zone has come to light in the United States or British Zones. The Americans are facing very great difficulties. There are some 40 officers in all engaged in the work but there are at least 500 depositories scattered all over Germany. So far not more than a dozen are being investigated. The work of examining material and removing it from the depositories is enormously difficult. At Heilbron, for example, there are 40,000 cases down a mine. Only six of these cases can be brought up the shaft at one time. If all the material were taken from their present depositories, there would not be sufficient buildings in the whole of Germany to receive them.

The United States' policy is immediate restitution of looted property as quickly as possible against a guarantee that accredited representatives will receive it. The United States in other words have decided to go ahead on their own.[15]

Of course works of art are tangible and often well known. Perhaps of equal significance might be the restoration of the educational materials looted for other purposes or simply destroyed. Fortunately, the United Nations Relief and Rehabilitation Administration (UNRRA) was able to help. The UNRRA was founded in 1943:

The United Nations Relief and Rehabilitation Administration (UNRRA) was created at a 44-nation conference at the White House on November 9, 1943.

14   National Archives ED 42/12.
15   Ibid.

Its mission was to provide economic assistance to European nations after World War Two and to repatriate and assist the refugees who would come under Allied control. The US government funded close to half of UNRRA's budget.

The organization was subject to the authority of the Supreme Headquarters of the Allied Expeditionary Forces (SHAEF) in Europe and was directed by three Americans during the four years of its existence. Its first director-general was Herbert Lehman, former governor of New York. He was succeeded in March 1946 by Fiorello La Guardia, former mayor of New York City, who was in turn followed by Major General Lowell Ward in early 1947.[16]

National Archives documents take up the story of restoring educational materials and buildings:

As part of UNRRA's work in providing relief and rehabilitation to those liberated countries in Europe which have asked for the Administration's assistance, it is understood that provision can be made for the supply of materials to give aid in the restoration on an emergency basis of essential buildings for educational purposes. As part of the policy of 'helping countries to help themselves', it is understood that UNRRA is prepared to assist generally with necessary supplies and in the provision of scientific, technical and engineering equipment which is necessary to help the authorities of each country to train their own people to produce essential goods and services and thereby reduce their dependence on outside assistance in relief and rehabilitation. Under special conditions and as part of this policy, UNRRA is prepared to give aid in training or otherwise securing essential technical personnel. UNRRA will not provide textbooks.[17]

UNRRA was also in receipt of a Memorandum on *Post-War Relief of European Jewry* – a more intractable problem to solve as it involved far more intangible issues.

Whilst the international stage was restoring artefacts and educational institutions, the Government relaxed the arrangements for National Service so that those involved could complete their education where appropriate.

Arrangements for the Academic Year 1949-50
Universities and University Colleges, Agricultural, Medical, Dental and Veterinary Colleges
It has been decided that there shall be certain relaxations of the rules governing the deferment of the national service of students at universities. The universities will now be dealing with the entry of students on a peacetime basis, and it is desired henceforth to interfere as little as possible with normal academic education.

16 United States Holocaust Memorial Museum, Learn about the holocaust <http://www.ushmm.org/wlc/en/article.php?ModuleId=10005685>. (Accessed July 2014).
17 National Archives ED 42/18.

Admission of ex-servicemen

The system of fixed percentages and 'priority classes', set out in the Memoranda of Guidance issued in previous years, will no longer operate. Instead, the Minister of Labour and National Service will rely upon the undertaking given by Vice-Chancellors that preference in filling places will continue to be given to ex-servicemen

Men eligible for deferment

It has hitherto been the position that deferment to enter a university was granted only to men of a certain age group. This rule will no longer be applied, and men will be able to obtain deferment to go up to university at a later age provided:

a)   They go straight from school to university (except where it is part of the recognised training for a profession to spend some time in practical work) and

b)   They will not pass out of liability for national service. The age at which a man passes out of liability for national service is the 26th birthday (30th birthday in the case of medical and dental registered practitioners), and no one will be given deferment to start a course which clearly cannot be completed before that date. In all cases which appear doubtful, taking into account possible extensions for failure, the applicant will be required to sign a statement that he fully understands that, whatever the position of his studies, he will be called up before he can pass out of liability.[18]

(c) Wellbeing programmes

Even though the schools' rebuilding programme, more of which in Chapter 9, allowed for the creation of playing fields, the Marylebone Cricket Club (MCC) Chairman wrote to universities, training colleges and public schools expressing concern that insufficient attention was being paid to teaching the young the virtues of cricket.

15th April 1950

Dear Sir,

The MCC Cricket Enquiry Committee have for some time past been engaged in their study of the need for greater facilities for the playing and teaching of cricket to the youth of the country.

It is now clear to them that the primary difficulty lies in the inadequacy, both in number and quality, of the grounds and pitches available for those who wish to use them.

As part of an approach which is now being made to all those who may be able to assist in this problem, whether Cricket Clubs with grounds of their own, Education Authorities who control existing or projected school grounds, or Public Bodies administering parks and recreation grounds, the Enquiry Committee would appeal for their co-operation to university colleges, teachers' training colleges and the public schools.

18   National Archives ED 147/371.

They ask them to consider the possibility of placing their grounds or some portion of them at the disposal of a school or youth organisation in their neighbourhood. It may be that this would only be possible during their own vacations, but perhaps also on one or two evenings a week in term time.

They recognise that such facilities could only be granted to boys under the full supervision of a teacher or youth leader. They appreciate too the additional wear and tear to the ground and the extra burden on the ground staff that any such concession would involve; but they would emphasise the urgent need for increasing by every possible means the opportunity to play cricket for the thousands of boys who have at present so little chance of doing so.

They would suggest that where those to whom this appeal is addressed feel that they can help, every encouragement should be given to such organised bodies as apply or whom they may be good enough to approach either direct or through a Local Education Authority.

Yours faithfully

H S Altham

Chairman[19]

The findings of the MCC Enquiry Committee can be found in the National Archives.[20] This issue initiated correspondence within various government departments. On the one hand there was a desire to regain the tradition for sports enjoyed in pre-war times. There was also the need to ensure that the youth at the time were as fit and able as possible as it was from schools and universities that the armed forces received their future intake of national service men and women!

Whilst the fitness of our young adults exercised the minds of those in Whitehall, there was arguably a pressing need to train amateur athletes for the Olympic Games which were held in London in 1948. The Amateur Gymnastic Association (AGA) requested funds from Central Government to train athletes for the Games; however, the official response was that money was only available to train the trainers and not the athletes directly. The reply from the AGA to the Minister of Education is instructive of the level of frustration as the Games drew ever closer.

3rd February 1948

Dear Sir,

I am in receipt of your letter dated 22nd December 1947 in answer to my letter to Colonel S J Parker.

My committee wish me to express their profound disappointment with your official reply.

In our experience the Governments of many countries, against whom we shall be competing in the Games, are assisting the Governing Federations of

19   National Archives ED 147/366.
20   National Archives ED 169/66.

sports financially; and especially is this so in the case of Gymnastics, for on the Continent our sport is held in very high regard by all members of the community.

It is possible that, in view of our slender resources and your decision to withhold financial support as suggested in our letter, we may find it necessary to withdraw our teams from participation in the Games, an action which would cause much comment amongst our foreign competitors to the detriment of this country.

We trust you would place this letter before the Minister and ask him to reconsider his previous decision.

Yours faithfully

E A Simmonds

Hon. Secretary[21]

Now as then, not all education and training was accomplished in school classrooms. Vocational training fulfilled a large part of the training needs of certain industries. By way of examples the mining and catering industries, both employing large numbers of workers post-war, will be mentioned.

Coal Mines (Training) General Regulations, 1945

Monmouthshire and South Wales Mining Education and

Training Scheme

Object of the Scheme

The scheme is designed to put the mines in compliance with the above-named regulations.

The directorate will also take charge of all other training and educational activities of the association, and such other training as is at present undertaken or may be undertaken by the association or the associated undertakings.

In particular, the following grades of workers will be in the training scheme:

1. Juvenile entrants into the industry.
2. Adult entrants into the industry.
3. Workers prior to their first employment underground.
4. Craftsmen of the various types required in mining subject to the development of a craft apprenticeship training scheme.
5. All grades of officials below that of under-manager.
6. Supervision of the practical training of the various students of mining, such as the supervised practical training envisaged by the Institute of Mining Engineers and the practical work now undertaken by students under the present educational scheme of the association.
7. Groups or individuals of any of the above in respect of whom it is necessary or desirable that there should be continuation training … [22]

And in the same folio, a catering example, also from the Welsh records.

21   National Archives ED 169/35.
22   National Archives ED 220/9.

23rd May 1946
Welsh Department
Ministry of Education

Training for the catering industry

The catering industry is one of our major industries, employing some three-quarters of a million persons in its various sections. With the support of His Majesty's Government, leaders of the industry are anxious to raise its standard of efficiency, in order that the requirements both of the home public and of visitors from overseas may be more suitably and adequately met. If this aim is to be realised much greater attention must be paid to the training of the personnel of the industry. There are at present few training facilities, and a comprehensive system of vocational training is needed for workers of all types and grades, organised in progressive stages and leading to recognised qualifications. The Minister of Education hopes that Local Education Authorities will be prepared to play their part by providing suitable training facilities, a matter of particular interest to them in view of their own large responsibilities for school, hospital and other catering services.

This initiative was not just confined to Wales, many towns and cities throughout the United Kingdom were involved. For example Leeds College of Technology ran a

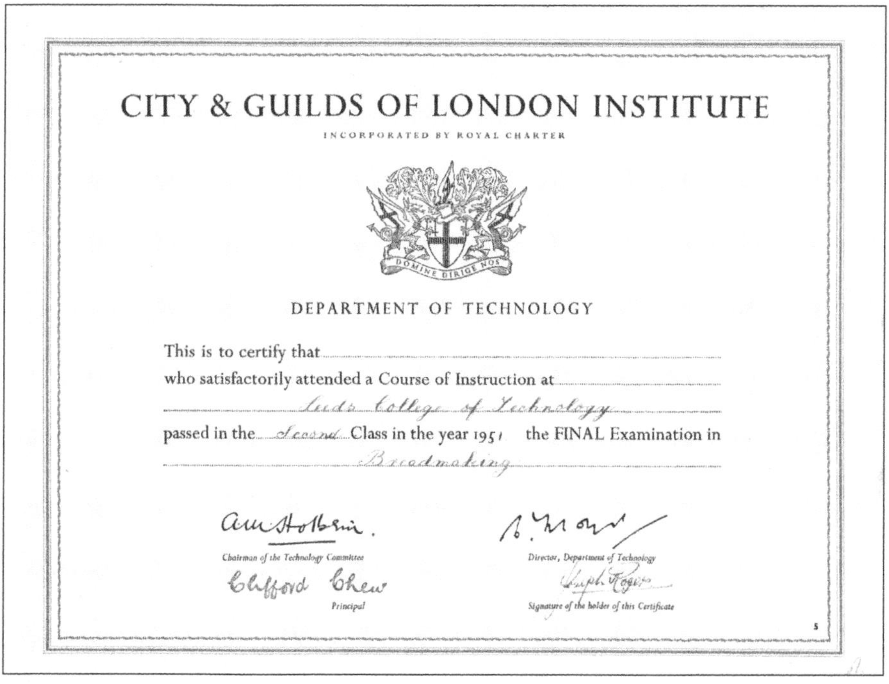

CITY & GUILDS OF LONDON INSTITUTE

INCORPORATED BY ROYAL CHARTER

DOMINE DIRIGE NOS

DEPARTMENT OF TECHNOLOGY

This is to certify that ....

who satisfactorily attended a Course of Instruction at ....

Leeds College of Technology

passed in the Second Class in the year 1951 the FINAL Examination in

Breadmaking

Chairman of the Technology Committee

Director, Department of Technology

Clifford Chew
Principal

Signature of the holder of this Certificate

5

Figure 4.2. A catering qualification from 1951. (Author's photograph)

whole series of catering courses including:

- Intermediate breadmaking.
- Intermediate flour confectionary.
- Final bread making.
- Final flour confectionary.

These courses all led to a City and Guilds' qualification which at the time was part of the London Institute. Figure 4.2 shows one such certificate for 1951.

5   Rationing

The Consumer Rationing Order 1941, dated 29 May 1941, made by the Board of Trade under Regulation 55 of the Defence (General) Regulations 1939 stated:

> The Board of Trade in pursuance of the powers conferred upon them by Regulation 55 of the Defence (General) Regulations 1939, hereby order as follows:
>
> 1. The provisions of this Article shall apply to the supply of rationed goods by a trader to a retail customer.
> 2. No trader shall supply any rationed goods otherwise than against the surrender of the appropriate number of coupons and in accordance with the provisions of this Order.
> 3. Except where the goods are ordered by post, a trader shall not supply rationed goods against the surrender of coupons of a kind comprised in a ration document unless the ration document shall have been produced to him and he shall have detached therefrom the appropriate number of coupons.
> 4. A trader shall not supply rationed goods ordered by post unless he shall have received from the retail customer to be supplied the appropriate number of coupons signed on the back by the customer.
> 5. The preceding provisions of this Article shall not apply to the supply of rationed goods:
>   a) Under the authority of a licence granted by the Board of Trade under this Article and in accordance with any condition attached thereto.
>   b) To, or for the execution of contracts of a Government Department.
>   c) By delivery outside or by exportation from the United Kingdom otherwise than in, or to, the Isle of Man.
>   d) To a local authority or
>   e) To the Women's Voluntary Services for Civil Defence.
> 6. The preceding provisions of this Article shall not apply before 14 June 1941, in pursuance of an order received before the commencement of this Order, of rationed goods a process in the manufacture or making up of which has been carried out especially for the purposes of that order ... [1]

---

1   National Archives BT 258/1231.

The following ten pages or so laid out all the regulations necessary at the time to enforce a period of rationing needed to sustain our infrastructure during, and indeed for some years following, the War. The headings used in this document show both the extent of the Order and also hint at the infrastructure needed to ensure it was enforced. They were:

i)   Basis of scheme.
ii)   What goods were rationed.
iii) Provision of the supply of certain rationed goods, coupon free.
iv)   Coupon printing.
v)   Coupons issued to the public.
vi)   Directed distribution to certain classes of users of essential goods in short supply (clothing or household textiles).
vii) Introduction of rationing.
viii) Coupon banking.
ix)   Arrangements for traders under rationing.
x)   Enforcement.
xi)   Rationing in Northern Island, the Channel Islands and the Isle of Man.
xii) Legal position.

The annexes provided further details of the necessary infrastructure and, in some cases, how the regulations applied to specific industries such as lace, household textiles and yarn.

Interestingly, civilian uniform wearers were not provided with extra rations, the argument being that whilst wearing the uniform there was less wear and tear on the owners' civilian clothes!

Whilst the introduction of rationing took place over a relatively small period of time, its withdrawal was gradual. The complicated process of rebuilding the many faceted social needs of Britain determined the phased withdrawal of rationing. Figure 5.1 shows some of the finish dates.

Commodity	Finish date
Clothes	14th March 1949
Milk	15th Jan 1952
Sweets	4th Feb 1953

Figure 5.1. End of rationing in Britain.[2]

Of course many commodities were rationed. Indeed sugar continued to be rationed until 1954. Although I have no recollection of the end of sugar rationing, I have personal experience of it in that I was issued a ration book in 1954, figure 5.2.

The process of rationing commodities required a complex procedure ensuring, as far as possible, transparency of process and execution. Such a complex process grew

2   Source – Rogers archive.

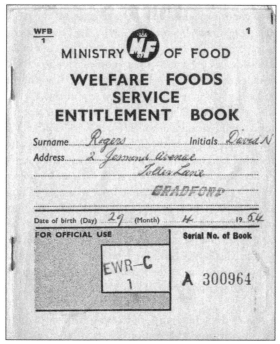

Figure 5.2. My ration book. (Author's photograph)

with time.

(a) Administration

Rationing arrangements in the Ministry of Agriculture, Fisheries and Food required policies covering such topics as:

a) Allocation and priority control of food.
b) Instructions to local food offices.
c) Storage.
d) Ship's stores.
e) Civil defence mobile columns.
f) Etc.[3]

Most of these arrangements were common across all commodities. Fortunately the Ministry of Food decided to compile a history of their involvement in rationing which is stored in the National Archives. The lead document is dated 19 April 1945 and titled 'Permanent record of the operation of all Executive Divisions', the first few paragraphs of which read:

---

3   National Archives folio series MAF 313.

1. Most of the control schemes and other activities of the Ministry of Food have been built up gradually since the war began. Much experience has been gained, many errors have been made and corrected, and many other errors have been avoided. A great part of the knowledge of how the scheme works is in the minds of those who are working them and many of these people are likely to leave the Ministry during the next year or two.

2. It has been decided that there should be a permanent record in reasonably small compass of the manner in which each Division of the Ministry carried on its work at what may be termed its zenith, that is to say, when full control had been introduced and the period of trial and adjustment was passed, but before decontrol or relaxation began. If such a record is to be prepared satisfactorily, it must be done while the accumulated knowledge and experience of those responsible for building up and working the schemes are still in the Ministry.

3. The records should in no sense be a history of the various Divisions. Each one should be a detailed guide-book for any person who might be called upon, when faced with some future emergency, to set up similar arrangements and have them in full working order in short time.[4]

Although this report does not purport to be a history of rationing within the Ministry of Food, it does form a record of events by those who designed and ran the system within the Ministry of Food and as such is of interest, and worth reading should time permit. Unfortunately, the document is too long to reproduce even as an Appendix.

That said, the initial paragraph in the 'Development of Control' serves as an example for the whole rationing process. It reads:

The policy of the Food Committee in August 1939 was to control bulk consumption rather than to regulate the use of rationed commodities in detail, and that restrictions upon the manufacture and display of particular foods and directions in regard to the service of particular dishes at meals would be unnecessary if bulk supply were regulated. It was proposed that no meals consisting of meat, bacon or ham should be served free of coupons.

Whatever took place behind the scenes, the 'customer interface' relied on the use of ration books. This was not a decision taken in haste as it was determined from the experiences of World War One.

The Ration Book

Any history of the ration book must begin by referring to plans which the Food (Defence Plans) Department made before the War, for controlling consumption of food in wartime, either by rationing or some looser form of control. The experience of World War One indicated a national rationing system based

4   National Archives MAF 313/3.

on a consumer/retailer tie, with a network of local food offices to administer the rationing scheme and to act as the focal point for contact with the public. Planning proceeded on this main assumption. Forecasts were made as to the food which might need to be rationed; decisions were taken on the question of printing different kinds of ration books for several special classes of consumers; the ration book, or rather books, were designed; and orders were placed for them to be printed and distributed to storage points throughout the country. The printing and distribution of ration books for nearly 50 million people takes several months, and the foresight of the planners, with almost no true picture of the conditions in which the ration books would be required, proved to be of great value to the Ministry of Food when it came into being in September 1939. Although rationing as such was not introduced until January 1940, when butter, bacon, ham and sugar were rationed, it would have been impossible for the newly formed department, even with the best endeavours, to have got ration books designed, printed and into the hands of the public within four months between September 1939 and January 1940.

With stocks of ration books available, the Ministry of Food was able to set about the task of issuing them as soon as the Government decided that some of the foods were to be rationed. National registration had provided a list of people and their addresses and the Local Food Offices prepared the books for distribution by post.[5]

Printing ration books was done under the authority of HM Stationary Office by whom the printers are paid.

In view of the urgency of most of the work and the volume thereof, this branch works direct with HMSO, and not through the Clerk of Stationery of the Ministry; to conform, however, with general Departmental practice all printing demands must be signed or countersigned by a senior officer of the Branch who has been nominated to HMSO.

Special arrangements have been made with HMSO whereby certain orders may be placed direct with printers without first passing through HMSO. These types of work are known as:

i)   Headquarters Printing (symbol HQP) – used for the urgent production of forms and circulars where quantities do not exceed 50,000. The printers, Messrs R E Jones and Bros Ltd of Conway are, however, paid by HMSO under contract terms. Orders are placed with them by means of a document provided by HMSO known as a 'Green' demand, which on completion of work the printer sends direct to HMSO.

ii) Divisional printing (Symbol DP) – used for the production of urgent circulars to readers authorised for issue by circulars of the DO, FO and FEO series. A printer has been allocated by HMSO in every Food Division

5   National Archives MAF 313/4.

to carry out this work on contract terms. Each Divisional Food Office is provided with a book of Green Demands and places an order direct with the printer for the quantity required, which may be as much as 100,000 in the largest Division for a circular with wide distribution down to 500 in the smallest Division for a circular with a restricted circulation.[6]

The numbers of forms and types of ration books were larger than one might first think. In addition to the types of ration books involved there was also the distribution, and indeed the surrender of unused outdated books. A document filed in the National Archives lists just a few of the administrative procedures involving:

a) Post-war changes to ration books.
b) Distribution of documents other than ration books.
c) Stocks of forms (reserve).
d) Stock records.
e) Security documents.
f) Ration books for civilians.
g) Royal Navy Personnel ration books.
h) Weekly seamen ration books.
i) Army and Royal Air Force Personnel ration cards.
j) HM Forces short ration cards.
k) Temporary ration cards – RB12.
l) Surrendered ration documents.
m) Old ration books etc. – disposal of.
n) Statistics of Service documents.[7]

Figure 5.3 is the instruction page from a general ration book. This section of the book contains sections concerning:

1. How to use this book.
2. How to register with your retailer.
3. Purchases and coupons.
4. Depositing whole pages of coupons with retailers.
5. Meals away from home.
6. Cooked meat.

There were other factors needing consideration for those less fortunate, especially the distribution of food. In concert with ration books was the initiative known as the Welfare (Foods) Schemes.

6   National Archives MAF 313/2.
7   National Archives MAF 313/5.

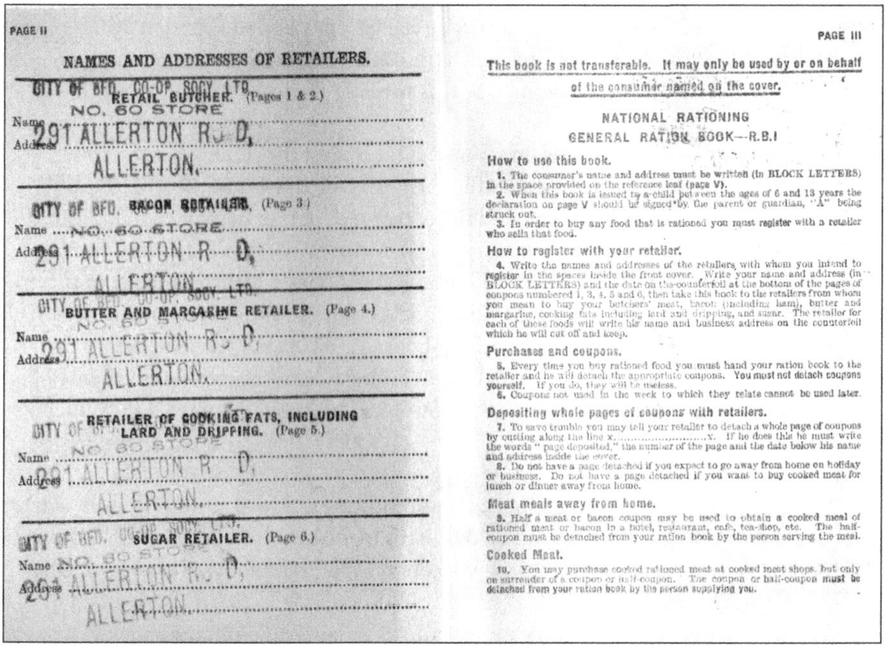
PAGE II

NAMES AND ADDRESSES OF RETAILERS.

RETAIL BUTCHER. (Pages 1 & 2.)

CITY OF BFD. CO-OP. SOCY. LTD.

Name NO. 60 STORE

Address 291 ALLERTON ROAD,

ALLERTON.

BACON RETAILER. (Page 3.)

CITY OF BFD.

Name NO. 60 STORE

Address 291 ALLERTON ROAD,

ALLERTON.

BUTTER AND MARGARINE RETAILER. (Page 4.)

CITY OF BFD. CO-OP. SOCY. LTD.

Name NO. 60 STORE

Address 291 ALLERTON ROAD,

ALLERTON.

RETAILER OF COOKING FATS, INCLUDING LARD AND DRIPPING. (Page 5.)

CITY OF

Name NO. 60 STORE

Address 291 ALLERTON ROAD,

ALLERTON.

SUGAR RETAILER. (Page 6.)

CITY OF BFD. CO-OP. SOCY. LTD.

Name NO. 60 STORE

Address 291 ALLERTON ROAD,

ALLERTON.

PAGE III

This book is not transferable. It may only be used by or on behalf of the consumer named on the cover.

NATIONAL RATIONING

GENERAL RATION BOOK—R.B.I

How to use this book.

1. The consumer's name and address must be written (in BLOCK LETTERS) in the space provided on the reference leaf (page V).
2. When this book is issued to a child between the ages of 6 and 18 years the declaration on page V should be signed by the parent or guardian, "A" being struck out.
3. In order to buy any food that is rationed you must register with a retailer who sells that food.

How to register with your retailer.

4. Write the names and addresses of the retailers with whom you intend to register in the spaces inside the front cover. Write your name and address (in BLOCK LETTERS) and the date on the counterfoil at the bottom of the pages of coupons numbered 1, 3, 4, 5 and 6, then take this book to the retailers from whom you mean to buy your butchers' meat, bacon (including ham), butter and margarine, cooking fats including lard and dripping, and sugar. The retailer for each of these foods will write his name and business address on the counterfoil which he will cut off and keep.

Purchases and coupons.

5. Every time you buy rationed food you must hand your ration book to the retailer and he will detach the appropriate coupons. You must not detach coupons yourself. If you do, they will be useless.
6. Coupons not used in the week to which they relate cannot be used later.

Depositing whole pages of coupons with retailers.

7. To save trouble you may tell your retailer to detach a whole page of coupons by cutting along the line x.........................x. If he does this he must write the words "page deposited," the number of the page and the date below his name and address inside the cover.
8. Do not have a page detached if you expect to go away from home on holiday or business. Do not have a page detached if you want to buy cooked meat for lunch or dinner away from home.

Meat meals away from home.

9. Half a meat or bacon coupon may be used to obtain a cooked meal of rationed meat or bacon in a hotel, restaurant, cafe, tea-shop, etc. The half-coupon must be detached from your ration book by the person serving the meal.

Cooked Meat.

10. You may purchase cooked rationed meat at cooked meat shops, but only on surrender of a coupon or half-coupon. The coupon or half-coupon must be detached from your ration book by the person supplying you.

Figure 5.3. Instructions for using a general ration book. (Author's photograph)

Purpose of the Welfare (Foods) Schemes

The purpose of the Welfare (Foods) Schemes is to ensure that adequate quantities of certain essential foods and vitamin supplements are available, on a priority basis, to the vulnerable groups, i.e. expectant mothers, infants, mothers of young children, invalids and adolescents.

The methods used are to control the production and distribution to ensure that supplies are available for the members of these groups; to subsidise certain foods and vitamin supplements, where necessary, so that they are available at low cost or, in certain cases, free of charge; and to undertake publicity to persuade numbers in these groups to take up their full entitlements.

The food and vitamin supplements referred to, and the qualifications for entitlement, are stated in Appendix I.

The principle schemes are:

1. The National Milk Scheme.
2. The Vitamin Scheme.
3. The Scheme for Invalids and Vegetarians.
4. The Scheme for National Milk Cocoa.
5. The National Juice Jolly, as a vehicle for vitamin C, for children taking school meals, for children resident in institutes and those in hospital.[8]

The end of the War in Europe and the imminent end to the War with Japan,

8 National Archives MAF 313/2.

brought with it the expectation of a more relaxed environment, anticipating greater availability. Accordingly, a more relaxed approach to rationing was announced – at least for children's clothing coupons – at this time.

> The Board of Trade announces that from the 1st August the children's extra clothes ration of 10 coupons may be used. The coupons which will now be valid for use are the eight numbered coupons and the two groups of four quarter coupons (but NOT the token marked 'D') on page 111A of the 1945-46 Child's and Junior clothing books (CB2/8 and CB4/8) – that is, the books which are already in the hands of the public, bound inside the food books. No other coupons in these books, and none in the General clothing books (CB1/8), may be used before the 1st September. The Order by which the children's extra coupons are validated is the Consumer Rationing (Amendment of 1944 Consolidation) (No3) Order S.R. and O 1945 No.[9]

This relaxation only applied to some commodities as bread rationing only started after the War ended. For example the Ministry of Food announced a supplement to the food rationing for the agricultural workers on 7 December 1947.

> Bread rationing. There was no case for a differential system of rationing so long as the two-main energy foods, bread and potatoes, remain unrationed. When bread rationing was introduced on July 21st 1946, however, it was necessary to adopt a scale of allowances which would meet the wide variations in need for bread which exist between different classes of the community. Manual workers in specified occupations receive a larger ration than the normal adult, figure 5.4.

Worker	Amount
Normal adult	9oz per day
Manual worker (woman)	11oz per day
Manual worker (man)	15oz per day

Figure 5.4. Bread rations.

Specified occupations include the following, which are concerned directly or indirectly with agriculture.
1. Agriculture; horticulture; forestry, land drainage; timber production; stock rearing and market gardening.
2. Handling and slaughtering of livestock for human and animal consumption.
3. Milling of cereals and of animal feeding stuffs.
4. Operation of wheel and track laying agricultural tractors.
5. Shifting, loading and unloading of heavy goods.

9   National Archives BT 64/1482.

Special Bread Allowance. Manual workers entitled to the special cheese ration because they cannot take advantage of canteen or restaurant facilities are also entitled to an extra bread allowance of 6oz per day.[10]

By the early 1950s there was a mixture of price control and rationing which had been introduced to ensure some measure of domestic stability. A question in the House of Commons on 13 June 1951 was asked by Mr Arthur Lewis of Mr Maurice Webb, the then Minister of Food. This question led to the publication, albeit to a limited circulation, of a lengthy document. It is not possible to reproduce that document here, however the introduction may be useful and the table of contents, providing for the interested reader an appreciation of the contents of the entire document.

Question by Mr Arthur Lewis: to ask the Minister of Food if he will give a list of the various price and ration controls operated by his department during the war, showing in each case the date of introduction and repeal of such Orders and those remaining in force at the current time.

Answer by Mr Maurice Webb: As the list will be a lengthy one, I will send it to my Hon. Friend as soon as it is compiled. Public Relations Division agreed to prepare the list, using the information contained in its own files and consulting the Divisions concerned as necessary.

The work was still in progress when Parliament was dissolved in October 1951. Although the General Election automatically cancelled Mr Lewis' question, it was decided to complete the reply, partly because a similar Question might be put down in the new Parliament and partly because the information would provide a useful addition to the Department's records. It was also decided to go beyond the original war period specified in the Parliamentary Question and to cover the post-war period also.

The report was published in two sections with the following format:

1. Section 1 – Food.
    a) Price control.
    b) Rationing and other restrictions on supply.
    c) Points rationing system.
2. Section 2 – Animal Feeding stuffs.
    a) Price control.
    b) Rationing.[11]

Of course there was also a need to restrict the import of goods which would demand dollar imports, particularly those involving semi-luxuries.[12] Later in this chapter (section c), the need to control food using dollar imported commodities will

10 National Archives MAF 156/262.
11 National Archives MAF 223/97.
12 National Archives CAB 134/215/20.

also be mentioned.

(b) **Clothing**

An article in the Board of Trade Journal, dated 21 August 1948 with the title *How the Clothes Rationing Scheme* is operated is instructive background reading. In setting the scene the article comments:

> To understand how clothes rationing was evolved and launched it is necessary to know something of the industries affected. They are, primarily, the textile industries – cotton, wool and rayon – which produce the yarn and cloth, and the secondary industries, including hosiery, which make the garments. Until recently, the manufacture of boots and shoes, which constitutes an industry rather separate from the rest, was also included, but this has now been freed from rationing control. The cotton, wool and rayon industries all use heavy and expensive machinery. They tend to consist mainly of fairly large productive units which are also to a great extent localised in a particular area. This made them more easy to regulate. Because of their vital importance not only for civilian clothing, but also for production for the Services, cotton and wool were fairly closely controlled from the outbreak of war. The same was true to a lesser extent of hosiery and footwear.
>
> By contrast, the clothing industry uses only light and inexpensive machinery. It is more easy to enter and so consists of a very large number of firms – up to 25,000 – of every type and size scattered throughout the county and employing about as many in total as clothes production. Control of this industry raised considerable practical difficulties and it was decided that to start with, control should be applied at the origin of supply the yarn and cloth.[13]

Accordingly, standard consumer clothing coupons and supplementary coupons, see later and figure 5.5, were issued from 1941 onwards.

Various releases of different coupons took place from the initial introduction until 1949, figure 5.6.

Rationing period	Description of coupons
1/6/41-17/8/41	26 'Margarine' coupons
18/8/41-31/12/41	20 Plain coupons on a buff and green clothing cards
1/1/42-31/5/42	20 'X' coupons on a buff and green clothing cards
1/6/42-10/10/42	20 Green coupons in 1942/43 clothing book
11/10/42-14/3/43	20 Brown coupons in 1942/43 clothing book
15/3/43-31/8/43	20 Red coupons in 1942/43 clothing book
1/9/43-31/1/44	20 Coupons in 1943/44 clothing book consisting of 18 yellow 'A' coupons and one each of 'W' and 'X' green tokens worth one coupon each

13   National Archives BT 258/1231.

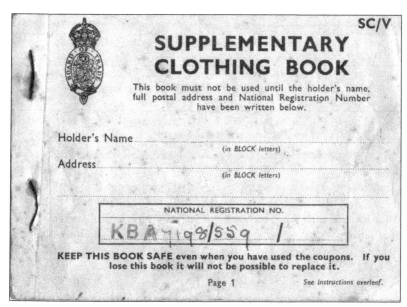

Figure 5.5. An example of a supplementary clothing coupon book. (Author's photograph)

Rationing period	Description of coupons
1/2/44-31/7/44	24 Coupons in 1943/44 clothing book consisting of 10 purple 'B', 8 black 'C' coupons and one each of 'Y' and 'Z' brown tokens worth 3 coupons each
1/8/44-31/1/45	24 Coupons in the 1944/45 clothing book consisting of 18 brown 'D' coupons and one each of 'A' and 'B' red tokens worth 3 coupons each
1/2/45-31/8/45	24 Coupons in the 1945/45 clothing book consisting of 18 green 'F' and 'H' coupons and one each of 'C' and 'E' red tokens worth 3 coupons each
1/9/45-7/4/46	24 Coupons in 1945/46 clothing book consisting of 20 blue coupons and 4 sets of blue quarter coupons
8/4/46-31/7/46	14 Coupons in the 1945/46 clothing book consisting of 20 green coupons worth ½ coupon each and one each of green 'R' and 'S' tokens worth 2 coupons each
1/8/46-28/2/47	30 Coupons in 1946/47 clothing book consisting of 20 red 'W' coupons, 2 red 'W' coupons, 2 red 'H' tokens worth 3 coupons each and 4 sets of red quarter coupons
1/3/47-30/9/47	32 Coupons in 1946/47 clothing book consisting of 20 brown 'X' coupons, 2 brown 'J' tokens and 2 lilac 'K' tokens, each worth 3 coupons
1/10/47-28/2/48	20 Coupons in 1947/48 clothing book consisting of 16 yellow 'E' coupons, 2 yellow 'F' tokens worth 1½ coupons each and 1 set of yellow ¼ coupons
1/3/48-31/8/48	24 Coupons in 1947/48 book consisting of 16 magenta 'R' coupons, 2 magenta 'L' tokens each worth 3½ coupons, 1 set of magenta ¼ coupons

Rationing period	Description of coupons
26/5/48	A special bonus issue of 12 coupons in the 1947/48 clothing book, consisting of 2 crimson 'O' tokens worth 6 coupons each
1/9/48-28/2/49	24 coupons in 1947/48 clothing book consisting of 16 olive 'T' coupons, 2 olive 'N' tokens worth 3½ coupons each and 1 set of olive ¼ coupons
1/3/49	17 Coupons in 1947/48 clothing book consisting of 16 crimson 'Z' coupons and 1 set of crimson ¼ coupons

Figure 5.6. Clothing coupons issued during and after the War.

An explanatory letter accompanying figure 5.6 commented:

All wearing apparel for men, women and children was rationed whether made of rationed material or not, except for a few items such as aprons not made of rationed goods, headgear, ballet shoes, asbestos garments, certain maternity and surgical belts and certain special industrial garments.[14]

Figure 5.5 above is a supplementary clothing book and not a standard adult issue. Clothing rationing was further refined to include extra clothing coupons for growing children and were issued in supplementary clothing ration books in the following way (reference as above):

When rationing was introduced in June 1941 it was accepted that in view of their rate of growth, and the additional wear and tear on their clothing some special arrangements must be made for children. In November of that year the first children's supplements were issued and consisted of 20 extra coupons for children aged 15 years 10 months to 16 years 5 months, 40 extra for those aged between 13 years and 8 months and 15 years 10 months and 40 for outsize children who were under 14 years 8 months. These supplements were varied in the following years but from September 1943, all children under 16 years received a supplement of 10 coupons in their ration books. By 1946 this arrangement had been extended to include all children under 18 years ... from 1941 infant clothing was rationed and a supplement of 50 coupons was given to expectant mothers. This was again increased by 10 to 80 coupons in August 1948 ... in addition to the other industrial supplements, arrangements were made whereby new entrants to certain industries received a supplementary grant of coupons to provide special or protective clothing for their new employment on the understanding they were continuing such employment. Briefly the arrangements were as follows, figure 5.7:

14   Ibid.

Occupation	Supplement
Agricultural and horticultural workers	15-18 coupons
Forestry workers	30 coupons
Home timber production workers	30 coupons
Land drainage workers	30 coupons
Miners	30 coupons
Students, research workers, teachers at agricultural colleges, institutes and advisory centres	30 coupons

Figure 5.7. Occupational coupon supplements.

As the economic and industrial output positions improved so too was the need to relax rationing. Accordingly the decision was taken to introduce a temporary bonus period during which the distribution of some clothing was less tightly controlled. In a letter dated 1 June 1948, Robert Hall makes the following comments to Sir Edwin Plowden:

> The wholesale stock figures, which just appeared in detail, allow us to compare stocks to turnover, and show that in the year stocks of women's garments have risen from about 5 to 7 weeks sales and in men's wear from about 3 to 5 weeks sales … The new decisions fall into four groups:
> a)   The removal from rationing altogether of children's shoes, gloves and some minor items.
> b)   The downpointing of a number of articles, and the arrangements for sales at half coupon rates for goods at reduced prices.
> c)   The unpointing of shirts.
> d)   The bonus issue of 12 coupons for four months.

Robert Hall was not a fan of the proposals and ended his letter with the following statement.

> It will be clear that I think that decisions which will lead to a marked change in the direction of consumer's expenditure ought not to be taken without discussions with those responsible for central planning. For they can easily make nonsense of the plans.[15]

Nevertheless the plan was introduced.

The majority of people living in their normal homes were able to form a relationship with the retail suppliers for all of their rationed commodities. Merchant seaman, however, were unusual but not unique in that they were constantly on the move when undertaking their normal employment and may have been away from their normal suppliers for a number of days or weeks. They carried their own identity cards, figure

15   National Archives T 230/152.

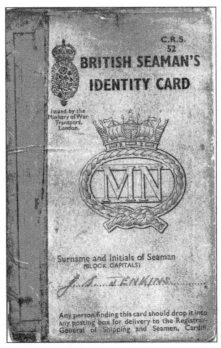

Figure 5.8. Seaman's Identity card. (Author's photograph)

5.8, and were issued with their different ration books, figure 5.9.

With the passage of time it is arguably difficult to appreciate some of the issues needing resolution during and after long sea voyages. Indian merchant seamen who travelled from the Indian subcontinent experienced many hardships.

> The Indian Seaman's Welfare Officer stated that he had noticed that Indian seamen were treated as visiting seamen for the issue of clothing coupons. He did not consider this was right. It was now very difficult for Indian seamen to obtain any coupons as a result of instructions recently issued by the Board of Trade and Ministry of Transport.
>
> He pointed out that Indian seamen were not able to obtain clothing in India for a very long voyage, and that they frequently arrived in this country with working clothes and shoes worn out. The seamen were pressing him very hard for a small issue of clothing coupons on arrival in this country. He would be grateful to know whether all the ship owners in Glasgow would issue a small number of clothing coupons.

The reply was interesting as it provides an insight into a much more complex problem.

> It is known that Indian seamen sell their clothing whenever opportunity offers, and in a recent case which came to notice the Master of a ship pressed a

Figure 5.9. Seaman's clothing coupons. (Author's photograph)

Superintendent very hard on behalf of his crew. On full investigation it was found that the reason the men were virtually in rags was that every man had sold all his clothing in Hamburg, where the ship had recently called. The Indian Seaman's Welfare Officer, London (Mr. Toto) did not contradict Colonel Montanaro, Board of Trade, when the latter said that Indian seamen did not want clothing or coupons, but money; and there are so many cases where these men DO sell their clothing, as owners well know, that they lose a great deal of sympathy which they might otherwise get.[16]

Any system is open to abuse, and for this one incident there will doubtless be many thousands where the system worked to the benefit of each individual.

(c) Food

Rationing food provided the most challenges to those administering the system compared with other rationed commodities. There was need to ensure a balanced diet and provide for the very young and vulnerable, those working in manual labour jobs etc. The Wartime Government was keen to ensure a healthy population during and after the War, and indeed stated as much in the draft of the White Paper on Nutrition. Consultation on the White Paper was extensive, including comments from Sir Edward Mellanby FRS who was at the time a member of the Medical Research Council and on the staff of the London School of Hygiene. The revised draft of the White Paper, dated 1 August 1944 provides some background to the then current thinking:

16   National Archives MT 9/4849.

The Government are determined to take all possible steps to ensure a healthy nation after the war. To this end they have already published their proposals for a National Health Service and for the prevention of poverty (in the White Paper on Social Insurance and Allied Services). But the nation cannot be healthy unless people are properly fed. In the following pages, therefore, the Government set out their proposals for ensuring satisfactory standards of nutrition after the war.

The United Nations Conference on Food and Agriculture (Cmd. 6451) held at Hot Springs in 1943, whose recommendations have been accepted by the Government, recognised, in the first of the Resolutions contained in the Final Act of the Conference, that 'the primary responsibility lies with each nation for seeing that its own people have the food needed for life and health; steps to this are for national determination. But each nation can fully achieve its goal only if all work together'. The Government accept this responsibility for ensuring that people of this country are at all times able to obtain the food they need and they will continue to do their utmost to collaborate with other countries in efforts to achieve the goal of 'freedom from want of food, suitable and adequate for the health and strength of all peoples'.

The Government believe that progressive improvement in the diet of the people must be sought by action with the following ends in view:

i)   To enable all individuals and households to obtain an income sufficient for a reasonable standard of living.

ii)   To secure that the foods required to provide an adequate, healthy and varied diet are available and within the reach of all, and

iii) To promote, through research and education, greater knowledge of nutrition and the better use of foods.

The means of achieving these ends are outlined in chapters V, VI and VII of this Paper.[17]

Both before and after the publication of this draft White Paper, various government departments were obtaining information on the dietary needs of various groups of workers. Some of these reports are available in the same National Archives folio[18] from which the following report titles have been taken.

a)   The nutrition of women workers in a Royal Ordnance Factory.

b)   The nutrition of coal miners.

c)   The state of nutrition of Sheffield steel workers.

d)   Report on an investigation into the nutritional condition of miners employed at a South Yorkshire colliery.

The theme of nutrition and balanced diets had been ongoing throughout the war. Indeed the aforementioned Sir Edward Mellanby FRS wrote the following on 14 May 1940.

17 National Archives FD 1/5438.
18 National Archives FD 1/5422.

Dear Colonel Manifold,

I have had an interim report on the inclusion of vitamin C in chocolate. According to Zilva, who has been doing this work, this method of ensuring vitamin C to the troops would be very effective. You will see that he has made an experimental batch of 24lb of chocolate and got good retention of C in the final product, so that an ounce of chocolate, which I believe is your army ration, would contain a complete daily supply of this vitamin.

It seems to me that you might find this suggestion useful for certain places. You will see that Zilva has only made an experimental batch of 24lbs of chocolate by this method and he would very much like the army or another service to make a large scale batch, and he would be glad to test it. I expect you would only be prepared to do this if you felt that the method was sufficiently promising to ensure the proper supply of this vitamin under all conditions. I understand that this is not to replace the jam about which I have already told you, as the results of the tests on the large scale preparation of 1000lbs of jam which have been made for the army are quite good. The chocolate method would apparently be an alternative to the jam for securing a supply of vitamin C.

Yours sincerely

Sir Edward Mellanby FRS[19]

Food supplements were just one of many issues taxing the minds of those civil servants running the food rationing system. Arguably more complex were the issues relating to varying supplies of home grown vegetables. Seasonal variations in yield from year to year brought with it issues needing resolution. It is worth including here a document written within the Rationing and Welfare Foods Division and dated 20 September 1954 as Appendix VI. This document looks back at the rationing system that had just ended, looking for ways in which the infrastructure of the rationing system could be modified should we ever need to implement the system in the future. It may also be instructive to glimpse into the world of supplying commodities to wholesalers.

Appendix VI mentioned the regions into and from which no movement of commodities should travel. The idea of providing locally sourced ingredients was underpinned with emergency powers some of which came into force during the War. For example:

Food and Food Transport (Carrots)
Order dated 7 December 1943 amending the carrots (1943 crop)
(Control and Prices) (No 2) Order 1943

On exercise of the powers conferred upon him by Regulation 55 of the Defence (General) Regulations 1939, and of all other powers him enabling, the Minister of Food hereby makes the following order:

1.   No person shall consign or cause to be consigned for transport wholly or partly by rail or transport or consign for transport or cause to be transported or consigned for transport otherwise than by rail any carrots:

19   National Archives FD 1/5460.

a) From or to any place in Great Britain to or from any place in Northern Ireland, or

b) From any place in the area comprising Scotland, Northumberland, Durham, Yorkshire, Cumberland, Westmoreland and Lancashire to any place in Great Britain outside that area, or

c) On and after the 1 March 1944 from any place in England and Wales to any place in Scotland.

2. It shall be an offence for any person charged with an infringement of this Article to prove that any carrots transported by him in contravention of the provisions of this Article were transported in the course of his business as a carrier and that he had no reason to believe that the provisions of this Article were being infringed.[20]

Keeping livestock for consumption was also subject to rationing. For example domestic poultry keepers needed a ration card in order to obtain supplies of feed. The instructions to poultry keepers within the ration book were interesting:

1. Register within 15 days of the date of issue of this card with the supplier whose name you insert at (§) overleaf. If no date has been inserted in the space provided at (**B**) the card is deemed to have been issued on 1st April 1944.

2. Sign your name in the space provided at ( ) in part 1 overleaf; enter the name and address of your supplier at (§); then take or send the card to him without delay.

3. This card must be produced each time you obtain Balancer Meal from your supplier, so that he may enter the quantities supplied in the table overleaf.

4. If you cease to keep poultry before 31st March 1945, you must inform your supplier and return this card, including the application form Parts 3 and 4 to the Food Office from which it was issued.

Note: You may be called upon to surrender this ration card if, during the period 15th September to 15th October 1944, any person who has surrendered a shell egg registration to enable you to obtain Poultry Balancer Meal applied to the local Food Office for its restoration. Your ration of Balancer Meal will then be adjusted to correspond with the remaining shell egg registrations surrendered on your behalf.[21]

Further in the same National Archives folio is a document titled *Special arrangements for Institutions for the rationing period commencing 1st March 1953* which indicated that this was one of the last commodities to be taken off rationing. Incidentally the amount of Balancer Meal issued was in line with the amount of land dedicated to poultry farming – at least that was the case on the 8th January 1945 (reference as above):

20 National Archives MAF 154/365.
21 National Archives MAF 79/63.

Now that the basic acreage deduction has been reduced to 1 bird per acre it is proposed that co-operative enterprises should be brought into line and a deduction of only 1 unit of Balancer Meal per acre be imposed as from 1st January, by the issue of a supplementary ration card allowing an additional Balancer Meal at the rate of 2½lb per month for each acre of agricultural land.

As in the case of hens mentioned above, the birds were kept for egg production and in some cases as food. Even in wartime there were cases where some animals were kept to maintain the bloodlines of rare breeds and to sell them for breeding. Perhaps the following general remarks about the pig industry might serve as a useful example. In this case relating to a proposed alteration to the existing rationing scheme in the late 1940s/early 1950s:

> In the case of Specialist Pedigree Breeders where very few pigs are sold to the Ministry of Food and it has been the practice to stick to all meal feeding thus keeping the number of stock at about the 1939 level or less the proposals would have the effect of retarding progress and may to that extent have a bad effect on the supply of breeding stock. In both cases quoted the quality of pigs is high and the effect would be a serious reduction in the supply of good breeding stock for breeding commercial purposes.
>
> In the cases where large numbers of pigs have been kept by using swill and a high proportion of pigs sold for bacon as distinct from being sold as young stores for breeding, the proposals would give a distinct advantage, so much so in fact that it is doubtful if the full allowance would be purchased. This applied also to feeders with 1939 registrations or extended scheme rations which have been taken up from the start except in one case where perhaps the true picture has not been extracted.
>
> In the case of people who have just started on the extended scheme the advantage is less marked.[22]

As one might imagine there were winners and losers to the proposed introduction of this modified scheme as the acreage used to rear the pigs was a factor in the calculation. Farmers who reared in a more intensive way and rearing on fewer acres would have been penalised. This issue took several months to resolve.

The average person knew nothing of the infrastructure mentioned above and was only concerned with converting their ration coupons into commodities of use to them on a daily basis. Figure 5.10 is of a part used page of coupons for cooking fats, lard and dripping.

Consolidating food stuff types into one ration book helped to simplify a complex system. This concept was applied to bread, flour (wheat and rye, but not malt flour, oatmeal or semolina), ryemeal, matzos meal and flour confectionary when they were rationed in one scheme from 21 July 1946. The above foodstuffs were defined in the Flour Confectionary (Control and Maximum Prices) Order 1946 'excepting any such

22 National Archives MAF 79/78.

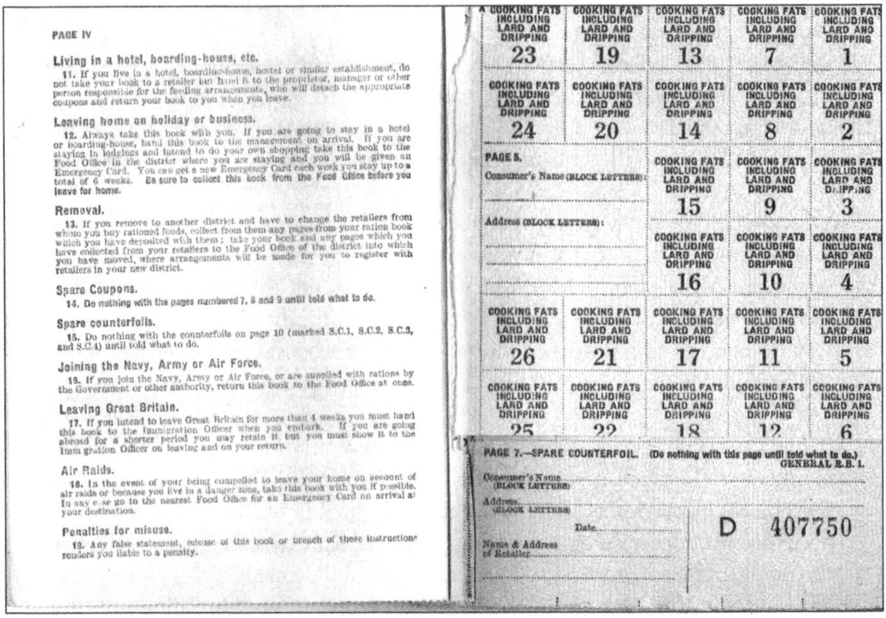

PAGE IV

Living in a hotel, boarding-house, etc.

11. If you live in a hotel, boarding-house, hostel or similar establishment, do not take your book to a retailer but hand it to the proprietor, manager or other person responsible for the feeding arrangements, who will detach the appropriate coupons and return your book to you when you leave.

Leaving home on holiday or business.

12. Always take this book with you. If you are going to stay in a hotel or boarding-house, hand this book to the management on arrival. If you are staying in lodgings and intend to do your own shopping take this book to the Food Office in the district where you are staying and you will be given an Emergency Card. You can get a new Emergency Card each week you stay up to a total of 6 weeks. **Be sure to collect this book from the Food Office before you leave for home.**

Removal.

13. If you remove to another district and have to change the retailers from whom you buy rationed foods, collect from them any pages from your ration book which you have deposited with them; take your book and any pages which you have collected from your retailers to the Food Office of the district into which you have moved, where arrangements will be made for you to register with retailers in your new district.

Spare Coupons.

14. **Do nothing with the pages numbered 7, 8 and 9 until told what to do.**

Spare counterfoils.

15. Do nothing with the counterfoils on page 10 (marked S.C.1, S.C.2, S.C.3, and S.C.4) until told what to do.

Joining the Navy, Army or Air Force.

16. If you join the Navy, Army or Air Force, or are supplied with rations by the Government or other authority, return this book to the Food Office at once.

Leaving Great Britain.

17. If you intend to leave Great Britain for more than 4 weeks you must hand this book to the Immigration Officer when you embark. If you are going abroad for a shorter period you may retain it but you must show it to the Immigration Officer on leaving and on your return.

Air Raids.

18. In the event of your being compelled to leave your home on account of air raids or because you live in a danger zone, take this book with you if possible. In any case go to the nearest Food Office for an Emergency Card on arrival at your destination.

Penalties for misuse.

19. Any false statement, misuse of this book or breach of these instructions renders you liable to a penalty.

COOKING FATS INCLUDING LARD AND DRIPPING 23	COOKING FATS INCLUDING LARD AND DRIPPING 19	COOKING FATS INCLUDING LARD AND DRIPPING 13	COOKING FATS INCLUDING LARD AND DRIPPING 7	COOKING FATS INCLUDING LARD AND DRIPPING 1
COOKING FATS INCLUDING LARD AND DRIPPING 24	COOKING FATS INCLUDING LARD AND DRIPPING 20	COOKING FATS INCLUDING LARD AND DRIPPING 14	COOKING FATS INCLUDING LARD AND DRIPPING 8	COOKING FATS INCLUDING LARD AND DRIPPING 2
PAGE 5. Consumer's Name (BLOCK LETTERS):		COOKING FATS INCLUDING LARD AND DRIPPING 15	COOKING FATS INCLUDING LARD AND DRIPPING 9	COOKING FATS INCLUDING LARD AND DRIPPING 3
Address (BLOCK LETTERS):		COOKING FATS INCLUDING LARD AND DRIPPING 16	COOKING FATS INCLUDING LARD AND DRIPPING 10	COOKING FATS INCLUDING LARD AND DRIPPING 4
COOKING FATS INCLUDING LARD AND DRIPPING 26	COOKING FATS INCLUDING LARD AND DRIPPING 21	COOKING FATS INCLUDING LARD AND DRIPPING 17	COOKING FATS INCLUDING LARD AND DRIPPING 11	COOKING FATS INCLUDING LARD AND DRIPPING 5
COOKING FATS INCLUDING LARD AND DRIPPING 25	COOKING FATS INCLUDING LARD AND DRIPPING 22	COOKING FATS INCLUDING LARD AND DRIPPING 18	COOKING FATS INCLUDING LARD AND DRIPPING 12	COOKING FATS INCLUDING LARD AND DRIPPING 6

PAGE 7.—SPARE COUNTERFOIL. (Do nothing with this page until told what to do.) GENERAL R.B. 1.

Consumer's Name (BLOCK LETTERS)

Address (BLOCK LETTERS)

Date

Name & Address of Retailer

D 407750

Figure 5.10. A part page of food coupons. (Author's photograph)

articles of which the flour, rye meal or matzos meal content does not exceed 15% of the weight of the finished product'.[23]

With the benefit of hindsight, rationing such a staple food as bread did lead to an interesting if not amusing issue. A circular dated 8 December 1947 highlighted an issue of counting bread coupons. Actually so many coupons came back to the Ministry of Food that they resorted to weighing the coupons!

Weighing of Bread Unit Coupons

I have now examined all the reports submitted by our Food Executive Officers in respect of the procedure for the assessment of bread units by weight, and give our observations in seriatim:

a) The consensus of opinion is that the weighing of coupons has its value in larger offices but in the smaller ones it is found to be much more accurate to count. A number of our Food Offices report difficulty in obtaining the loan of a balance, and in some instances the balance so obtained does not possess enough scientific accuracy to give a true weight of anything under say 30,000.

b) Some reports reveal that a number of test checks were made and it was found that in the case of period ½ there was a big percentage of error between the number of coupons according to weight and the actual number when counted. The cause of this was that strips of four coupons contained a side margin and also a portion of the margin at the top and foot of the strip. The

23 National Archives MAF 84/204.

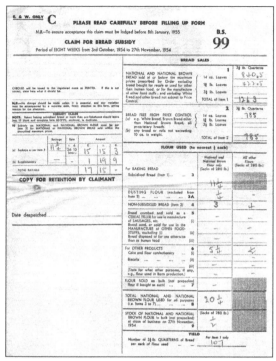

Figure 5.11. Form BS99 – claim form for bread subsidy. (Author's photograph)

results of tests discloses that a quarter of an ounce, which according to the scale, should represent 350 coupons was found only to contain between 290 and 300 coupons. On the other hand, in the case of coupons for period ¾ which, of course did not contain a side margin, there were very few coupons difference between that returned by weight and the number shown on an actual count.

c) The proportion of traders who sort coupons is very small, probably not more than 5%. In one instance it was found on the check that approximately 40% of the traders sort coupons into their respective categories. In some cases although requests have been made to all retailers to do so, blank refusals have been received. In the largest of our Food Offices approximately 50% of the traders sort coupons deposited.

d) etc.[24]

Whilst this is somewhat amusing now it must have presented many issues of tracking the number of coupons issued against the number returned and the amount of goods exchanged. Incidentally, flour continued to be of administrative concern well into the 1950s. Figure 5.11 is a form needed to claim for a bread subsidy. Many at the time who tried national brown bread might have been surprised at the level of control

24 National Archives MAF 99/1124.

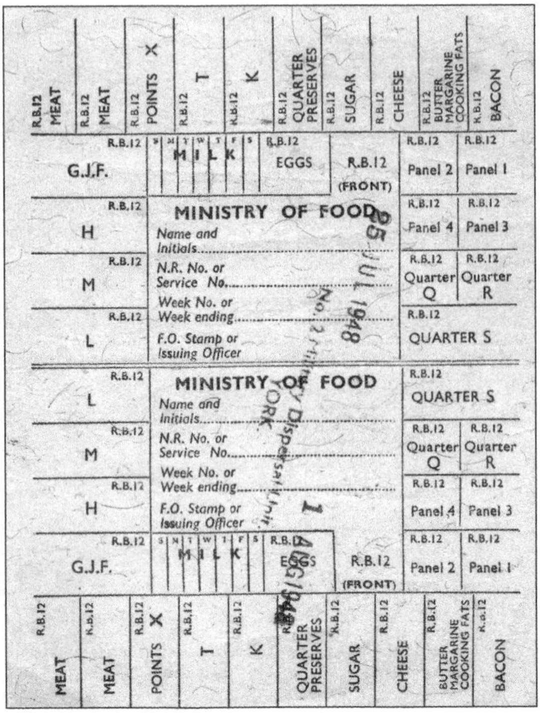
R.B.12 MEAT
R.B.12 MEAT
R.B.12 POINTS X
R.B.12 T
R.B.12 K
R.B.12 QUARTER PRESERVES
R.B.12 SUGAR
R.B.12 CHEESE
R.B.12 BUTTER MARGARINE COOKING FATS
R.B.12 BACON
R.B.12 G.J.F.
S M T W T F S MILK
R.B.12 EGGS
R.B.12 (FRONT)
R.B.12 Panel 2
R.B.12 Panel 1
R.B.12 H
MINISTRY OF FOOD
Name and Initials.......
R.B.12 Panel 4
R.B.12 Panel 3
R.B.12 M
N.R. No. or Service No.......
Week No. or Week ending.......
R.B.12 Quarter Q
R.B.12 Quarter R
R.B.12 L
F.O. Stamp or Issuing Officer
R.B.12 QUARTER S
25 JUL 1948
R.B.12 L
MINISTRY OF FOOD
Name and Initials.......
R.B.12 QUARTER S
R.B.12 M
N.R. No. or Service No.......
Week No. or Week ending.......
R.B.12 Quarter Q
R.B.12 Quarter R
R.B.12 H
F.O. Stamp or Issuing Officer
R.B.12 Panel 4
R.B.12 Panel 3
YORK
R.B.12 G.J.F.
S M T W T F S MILK
R.B.12 EGGS
R.B.12 (FRONT)
R.B.12 Panel 2
R.B.12 Panel 1
R.B.12 MEAT
R.B.12 MEAT
R.B.12 POINTS X
R.B.12 T
R.B.12 K
R.B.12 QUARTER PRESERVES
R.B.12 SUGAR
R.B.12 CHEESE
R.B.12 BUTTER MARGARINE COOKING FATS
R.B.12 BACON

Figure 5.12. The page of coupons issued to demobilised soldier. (Author's photograph)

still in existence in 1955!

Of course a member of the Armed Forces demobilised during the rationing would need some temporary form of ration coupons so that they would not be a burden on their families. Figure 5.12 is the single sheet page of coupons which was issued to at least one of the demobilised soldiers in 1947. It can only be assumed that this was a national scheme.

The reverse of this form reads:

> If found return to any food office
>
> 1. A member of the Army or Air Force whose leave is extended should receive a further form from his unit. If in difficulty he should apply to the food office and produce his pass.
> 2. Naval personnel whose leave is extended should take the authority for extension to a food office together with this form.
>
> <u>To the Retailer</u>
>
> Valid coupons are shown on the other side (front). Take no notice of printing on this side.

The Admiralty issued a Fleet Order on the 26 September 1947 the sub-title for which was 'Food Rationing – General Instructions'. The opening few paragraphs set the scene:

> The following details concerning the present application of food rationing to personnel of the Royal Navy, etc. are promulgated for information and guidance. These instructions revise and cancel existing Orders on this subject and incorporate certain new matter.
>
> It is desired to impress upon all personnel, and particularly upon those responsible for drawing up menus and the preparation and issue of meals, the great importance of the exercise of strict economy in the expenditure of all foodstuffs and the avoidance of waste.
>
> In no circumstances are letters on questions arising from these instructions to be addressed to the Ministry of Food. Any such problems are to be submitted to the Admiralty through the usual Service channels and direct correspondence with local officials of the Ministry of Food is to be confined to the specific occasions provided in these instructions and to such other minor matters about the supplies of foodstuffs from civilian sources as lend themselves readily to local settlement.[25]

The Order goes on to discuss:

a) The surrender of civilian ration documents by new entries.
b) Sources of supply of nationally rationed foodstuffs. Allowances for casual meals in officers' messes in Fleet establishments.
c) Contract messed establishments.
d) Ration books and cards – general.
e) Leave or duty ration cards RB12, RB12S and RB8A.
f) Personnel living ashore.
g) Arrangements for diabetic and vegetarian ration book or card holders.
h) etc.

Two years after Victory in Japan, and through a period of demobilisation and national service, numbers in the armed forces were slowly declining. Nevertheless there was concern within the Treasury on the cost of continuing the Services – even at this reduced level. Accordingly various military personnel met on the 23 December 1947 to discuss the hard currency expenditure on foods for the Services. Some extracts from this meeting appear below. In passing it is worth mentioning that Dr Magnus Pyke was at that time a scientific advisor at the Ministry of Food. Dr Pyke rose to prominence in the 1970s as perhaps one of the first scientifically trained television broadcasters to appear regularly on television and indeed he sometimes worked on programmes as the named individual in the programme title. Dr David Bellamy continued the trend in later years, appearing alongside Dr Pyke on a programme series called 'Don't Just Sit There'.

The purpose of the meeting in December 1947 was:

25   National Archives T 213/11.

To discuss the Treasury's opinion that the present Home Services ration scale is too generous in ration foods which involve dollar expenditure, and the overriding need to save dollars makes it urgently necessary to readjust the scale with a view to considerable saving.[26]

A letter dated 6 January 1948 (reference as above) provided the potential financial savings of the suggestions thus:

Dear Padmore,
You will have seen the minutes of the meeting of the Services Ration Scales Committee on 2 January.
It may be of assistance to you to know that we have computed the approximate savings based on the new proposals as follows:

Gross saving (meat, bread and cheese)   £3,425,000
Deductions (bread, sugar and fats)   £401,000
Net   £3,024,000

If the alternative calories equivalent of 2oz bread and flour per day is provided the additional cost would be of the order of £170,000, reducing the net saving to £2,854,000. This is an annual rate applicable as at today. Reductions in the size of the Forces will of course reduce the saving.

There are other references from the National Archives which may be of interest. Documents in the following folios were compiled or written at the end of rationing for the various commodities as part of the desire to write the history of each commodity for future generations of civil servants should there ever be the need for rationing in the future. They are:

a) Bread rationing: points rationing of cereal products. Used in connection with the preparation of *The History of the Ministry of Food during the Second World War*.[27]

b) History of meat rationing machinery 01 December 1952 – 31 May 1953.[28]

c) Admission of food shortages by Imre Nagy, the Minister of Food, in July 1951. 01 January 1951 – 31 December 1951.[29]

d) Flexibility of rations as a means of avoiding cold storage difficulties 01 January 1949 – 31 December 1950.[30]

(d) Petrol/Domestic fuel
Writing to Mr R Kelf-Cohen on 18 October 1950, A Franklyn Williams commented:

The work on the write-up of the Petrol Rationing Scheme 1939-50 has now been brought to completion and the story is told in the memorandum opposite.

26   National Archives T 213/9.
27   National Archives MAF 84/202.
28   National Archives MAF 99/1246.
29   National Archives FO 371/95216.
30   National Archives T 223/79.

The document is comprehensive and is supported i) by a series of appendices and ii) by a short memorandum on the working of the petrol rationing scheme in Northern Ireland ... .[31]

The memorandum was written by staff of the Petrol Ration Branch prior to it being disbanded. There were two sections one of 87 pages and discusses the rationing of motor spirit by that department, the second of 15 pages the rationing of goods and public service vehicles by the Ministry of Transport acting as agent for the above Department. Paragraph 3 of the overview documents various passages which were thought at the time to be of outstanding interest. This section reads:

a) Paragraph 45 page 10: by 1943 the numbers of private cars and motor cars in use had fallen to 34% of the pre-war figure and their annual consumption of petrol to 13% of the pre-war figure. Rationing can hardly go further.

b) Paragraph 90, page 31: from December 1947 to May 1950 the special section, which dealt with MP's letters, dealt with no less than 20,000. This shows that in peacetime petrol rationing cannot be kept out of politics.

c) Paragraphs 104 and 105, page 24: the Ministry at the end of the war, decided to grant private hire car allowances, irrespective of public need, for re-settling disbanded ex-servicemen and civilian workers. Unfortunately this concession was largely abused and had to be withdrawn.

d) Sections 191 and 192 page 42: the application of petrol to Ministers of the Crown and Members of Parliament.

e) Sections 225-227, page 49: the checking of coupons by the Ministry after the Petroleum Board had ceased to function was carried out conscientiously and meant a tightening up of control.

f) Paragraph 300, page 67: gives particulars of the staff employed in Regional Petroleum Offices at various dates. When the scheme was wound up in May 1950, the staff was as small as it had been at any date previously but was dealing with a much greater number of applications.

g) Paragraph 331, page 73: the power of Inspectors and Enforcement officers. In view of the recent interest in Parliament the number of Inspectors authorised by Departments to enter private premises, it is interesting that our Inspectors never had the right but could only go into undertakings which were concerned with the production or storage of fuel.

h) Sections 333-341, page 73: deal with the main difficulties of enforcement.

i) Paragraphs 345-354, pages 77-79: the workings of the Motor Spirit (Regulation) Act 1948 which introduced red petrol. The conclusion, as you will observe from paragraph 354, is that while the Act was effective, it was always being threatened and considerable effort and ingenuity were displayed in attempts to get round the Act. Defending Council were always looking for new methods to make it difficult to enforce the Act, and sometimes were successful. This report does not refer to the judgement given in the High

31 This report is stored separately to the main report and is located in National Archives POWE 33/1437.

Court in the St Albans case a few days before petrol was de-rationed, which would probably have made the continued enforcement of the red petrol act a matter of great difficulty. The lesson of course is, that however careful and thorough the provisions of an Act, its enforcement becomes difficult when public feeling turns against it.

The introduction of the Motor Spirit (Regulation) Act 1948 and the introduction of red petrol is interesting. The easiest method of ensuring 'commercial' and 'domestic' petrol were not sold and used by the 'wrong' sector was to dye petrol allocated to the commercial market. Red was the chosen colour and diphenylamine the chemical of choice. It was a simple matter for the analysts to check for the presence of this chemical in domestic supplies. As the memorandum pointed out there were very few instances where red petrol was found in domestic motor vehicles due to the heavy penalties for those caught selling commercial petrol for the domestic market. There were some prosecutions, however.

One hundred and sixty seven prosecutions involving the use of commercial (red) petrol in private vehicles were brought during the first three months of 1949. Of these 157 were successful. There were 66 cases in January, 44 in February and 57 in March.

Where the owner of the car is convicted of a red petrol offence both the driving licence and the road fund licence of the car are suspended for twelve months. In addition to these heavy penalties, which are automatic on conviction of an owner, fines totalled over £3,400. In four cases terms of imprisonment varying from one month to nine months were imposed. In seven instances the fine amounted to £100 or over. In seven cases, where the vehicle had been transferred to another owner, half the cost of the vehicle was forfeited, in addition to the other penalties.[32]

Wherever the course of supply, there was still the need to buy petrol from regulated sources using petrol ration coupons, see for example figures 5.13 and 5.14.

Figures 5.13 and 5.14 are for differently sized engines. Unlike modern times, most domestic users during and immediately after the war would only have owned one car – if they owned a car at all! Those that were motor car owners may only have known or seen petrol coupons for their engine size. Both common engine size bands are shown here for completeness.

Figure 5.13 is a book of N2 (two units) coupons. The notice to motor spirit dealers (September 1947) states the following:

'N' and 'L' basic ration coupons issued for September 1947, may be accepted by dealers during October 1947, and their value will continue on the basis of one unit equals one and a half gallons and half a unit equals one gallon ….dealers are

32 National Archives MT 55/237.

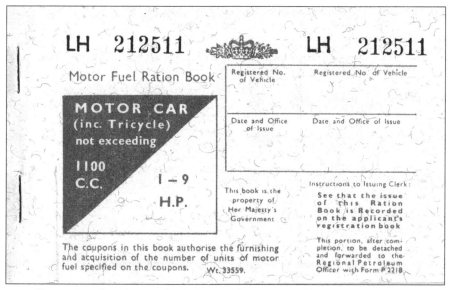

Figure 5.13. Petrol ration book for a small engine car. (Author's photograph)

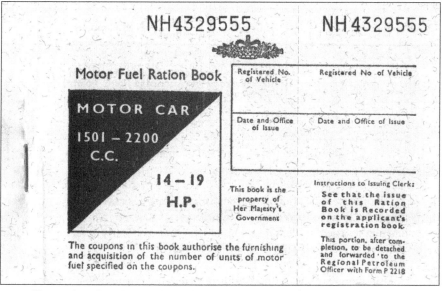

Figure 5.14. Petrol ration book for a large engine car. (Author's photograph)

asked to co-operate in preventing miss-use of motor spirit. Particular attention is invited to the following points:

1. No motor spirit may be supplied unless valid coupons are surrendered at the time of supply.
2. Before supply is made coupons should be examined to ensure:
    a) That coupons are valid by date.
    b) In the case of 'E' and 'S' coupons, that the registration of the vehicle is entered in ink on the coupon, and that such number corresponds with the registration number of the vehicle into the tank of which the supply is to be made, and
    c) In the case of coupons requiring endorsement with the name of the person, firm or company, that each coupon is signed by or on behalf of such person, firm or company.
3. Under NO circumstances may coupons be banked or deposited against future supply.
4. After 31st October 1947 the only types of coupons available for private cars and motor cycles will be 'E' and 'S'. Motor spirit must not be supplied into private cars or motor cycles against any other types of coupons.

Figure 5.15 shows the correlation of coupon units and gallons for three of the coupon types mentioned above. Incidentally for those used to measuring in litres a gallon is equivalent to 4.55 litres.[33]

'N' Coupons	Value in gallons	'L' Coupons	Value in gallons	'S' Coupons	Value in gallons
½	1	½	1	½	1
1	1½	1	1½	1	1½
2	3	2	3	2	3
3	4½			3	4½
4	6			5	7½

Figure 5.15. Petrol coupons and their gallon amount.[34]

The Enforcement Branch of the Ministry of Fuel and Power were active throughout the war and for some time afterwards. The work of this Department is documented in the National Archives in folio series POWE 3.

As one might expect there were some vehicles that required a different procedure to the standard profile for road vehicles. They included:

i) Dual purpose vehicles. In 1949 there were estimated to be 34,835 motor cars and 2,539 motor cycles that fell into the dual purpose vehicle category.[35]

33 National Archives POWE 33/1429.
34 Ibid.
35 National Archives MT 55/237.

ii) `A' & `B' licensed vehicles. Essentially these vehicles are commercial and could relate to road haulage, transporting felled timber, abnormal indivisible loads etc.[36]

iii) Taxi cabs. Arguably London supported more taxi cabs than any other major city in the United Kingdom during this period, if only because of the larger population. The Ministry of Fuel and Power issued motor fuel ration books called M.T. or Metropolitan taxicab. The coupons were labelled 'T' and were available in a range of units.[37]

As one might expect, domestic fuel was also rationed, for example there was an equivalent rationing scheme for paraffin.[38]

36   National Archives MT 55/239.
37   National Archives MEPO 2/6429.
38   National Archives POWE 33/1370.

6   Nationalisation

Nationalising any industry is a complex task. Transferring ownership of tangible assets is the least of the issues, although that could be a challenge in some cases. Additionally there are financial implications, perhaps new equipment not yet fully depreciated, the tax position may also be complex. Many of the other issues relate to the workforce involved in the industry in question and include:

(a) Pay scales.
(b) Pensions.
(c) Salary and career development.
(d) Worker rights and union involvement.
(e) Etc.

These issues, if handled incorrectly can lead to conflicts which may take many months if not years to resolve. Yet there was a need to nationalise the power industry and some of the transport infrastructure, notably the railways and the railway network. These two examples will be covered in some depth as examples of a much wider situation.

(a) Administration

Timing is everything when conducting takeovers, mergers or indeed nationalisation. There is always a period between lodging an intent and creating the necessary infrastructure to take the new venture forward. A high technology company or one requiring large development costs could incur large expenditure in this interim period. In the case of the nationalisation of the Iron and Steel industry the government set aside a large sum of money for this eventuality, for example:

Iron and Steel Nationalisation
Compensation for new development
At a meeting held in Mr Blunt's room at the Treasury on Friday 3rd May 1946, Mr Archer (Ministry of Supply) explained that:
... the Ministry of Supply had been giving consideration to the arrangements to be made with the industry for the period between the setting up of the new Interim Board and the date of vesting the industry with the Control Board

as finally constituted. One of the most difficult issues to be decided was that of finding means to overcome and tendency of manufacturers to delay action on their development schemes. The Ministry had provisionally approved such schemes to the value of £45,000,000 but a number of firms had said that they wished to suspend action pending clarification of the position of the industry as a whole. It was thought that industry generally would be reluctant to go on unless they could be given assurances that they would at least not be worse off than they would have been if nationalisation had not taken place. He would be glad of the Treasury's views on this point.[1]

The following documents the compensation plan adopted later in the year.

7th August 1948

Iron and Steel Bill
Compensation for Development Expenditure
Mr Lindsell
As requested by Mr Shirreffs, the attached schedule has been prepared as a possible means of honouring the pledge given by the late Minister on 27.5.46 that 'Whatever the final method and basis adopted, proper allowance will be made in assessing compensation for the results of any expenditure incurred from now onwards on approved schemes for development or rehabilitation'.

In brief, the scheme provides that the maximum compensation shall be a percentage on the estimated development expenditure to 31.12.50 (assumed date of transfer). The compensation payable will be reduced if the development work carried out at the date of transfer is less than that which was estimated to be carried out to that date.[2]

A complex funding issue came to light in the early 1950s once there were several nationalised companies.

29th August 1951
Mr Trend,
The question of inter-borrowing amongst nationalised undertakings has come to the fore again. You will remember that the Hydro-Electric Board and the Iron and Steel Corporation previously raised this question and we discouraged them.

The question was recently revived by the British Electricity Authority when they came to see us about the increase of the temporary borrowing rate from 2% to 2½%. Mr Drake gave them our general views but asked them to write if they wanted a considered opinion. This they have now done and we owe them a reply. If we are to stick to our previous decision then the attached draft by Mr Armstrong is I think adequate.

1   National Archives BT 255/263.
2   Ibid.

You ought to know however that the Gas Council are also very interested in this topic. We have nothing in writing from them but Bailey their Chief Accountant came to see me yesterday. I was suitably discouraging but I don't think the Council will let the matter rest there and I should be surprised if we don't get an official application from them later.

The Ministry of Fuel and Power know about these approaches but they are sitting on the fence at the moment and have asked to be consulted before we reject the British Electricity Authority's request. The next step therefore seems to be to send them a copy of the draft letter to Rix for their comments. Mr Armstrong will do this if you agree that we should continue to maintain our previous line.

Before we approach the Ministry however I think you ought to know that both the British Electricity Authority and the Gas Council may seek to press us strongly on this question and that we must therefore be ready to defend our decision; and I am not sure that this will be too easy now that the banks have increased their lending rate.

At the moment the question is of course somewhat hypothetical since with the possible exception of the Gas Council none of the industries has any money to spare. But I think they are looking to the future.

For R J Armstrong[3]

The Transport Acts of 1947 and 1953 brought other issues particularly for the Road Haulage Association. This organisation made a plea for:

1. Retrospective legislation giving exemption from balancing charges arising on the nationalisation of road transport following the Transport Act of 1947.
2. A method arriving at open market value of lorries on which balancing charges have been based. (The Association contended that, because of the glut of lorries on the market at that time, compensation received by hauliers was not the true measure of open market value.)
3. Treatment of purchase price of a transport unit following denationalisation under the Transport Act of 1953. (The Revenue contended that the sale price should be apportioned between the value of the vehicle and an estimated value placed upon the special A licences, thereby restricting by the latter amount the sum qualifying for Capital Allowances.)[4]

The Transport Act 1953 required the British Transport Commission to:

a) Dispose of the property held by them for the purposes of the part of their undertaking which was carried on through the Road Haulage Executive.

3   National Archives T 233/1032.
4   National Archives IR 40/12420.

b) Amend the law relating to the carriage of goods by road and to provide a levy, for the benefit of the Commission and for other purposes, on motor vehicles used on roads.
c) Provide for the reorganisation of the railways operated by the Commission and to amend the law relating to the powers, duties and composition of the Commission.
d) Repeal certain provisions of the Transport Act 1947 and to amend other provisions thereof.
e) Amend other provisions thereof, and
f) Amend section six of the Cheap Trains Act 1883.[5]

At a time when there were still unemployment issues, national service and demobilisation this must have been an unsettling time as the Act resulted in:

a) Disposal of the Commissions existing road haulage undertaking.
b) Sales of transport units.
c) Transfer of transport units to companies under the control of the Commission.
d) Transfer of property.
e) Disposal of property.
f) Etc.[6]

Not all of the immediate post-war events involved a cost in unemployment or the transfer of ownership of property between the Government and nationalised industries. A scheme was announced on 28 September 1946 for rural electrification at a cost of £72m. The collaboration was between the Farmers' Union and the supply companies and was to take five years to complete. The press release commented:

This is the first practical step towards the accomplishment of a service of extreme national urgency and involves supply to 150,000 farms at an estimated cost of £72m. It is an onerous responsibility, accepted with serious determination to discharge it …

State financial aid will not be sought. The supply undertakings have estimated that a capital expenditure of £45m will be required to connect up to 15,000 farms in the first year, 37,000 in the second, 52,000 in the third 30,000 in the fourth and 15,000 in the fifth.

The remaining £27m will be found by the agricultural industry to cover estimated expenditure on wiring installations, internal fitments and apparatus required in farmhouses and farm buildings.

5   Ibid.
6   Ibid.

The liaison committee of agricultural and electrical experts, who have been studying the problems for two years, believe the scheme now formulated recognises the needs of the agricultural industry and is a practical programme.[7]

Of course many of the resources needed for this undertaking, especially in the immediate post-war years, were difficult to obtain. A further report commented:

The main difficulties to be overcome are:
a)   Shortage of the materials for new developments especially wooden poles and, in certain areas, of labour.
b)   Wiring materials, motors and other electrical apparatus required for the farms do not enjoy the same priority as those required for new housing schemes.
c)   Insistence by some Supply Authorities on engineering standards which involve expensive line construction.
d)   The comparatively high cost of supplying electricity to isolated farms.
e)   That at the moment some of the terms and tariffs offered do not appear sufficiently attractive to the farmer.

The report went on to propose potential solutions which were submitted by the Committee to overcome some of these difficulties.[8]

Although some seventy years since this initiative was undertaken, most if not all of the rural farms are still benefiting from this scheme.

(b) Fuel – Coal/Electricity
The Coal Industry Nationalisation Act received Royal Accent on 12 July 1946. The intention and effect of this Act was to:

Vest colliery undertakings in a statutory corporation, the National Coal Board, whose function according to Section 1, Sub Section of the Act was threefold.
a)   To work coal to the exclusion of any other person save as in the Act provided.
b)   To secure the efficient development of the coal industry.
c)   To make supplies of coal available, of such quantities and sizes, in such quantities and at such prices as may seem to the Board best calculated to further the public interest in all respects including the avoidance of any undue or unreasonable preferences or advantage.
     By Sub Section 2 the Board were empowered to treat render saleable supply and sell coal.
     By Sub Section 3 the Board were further empowered to do anything and to enter into any transaction which in their opinion was calculated to facilitate the

7   National Archives POWE 38/13.
8   Ibid.

proper discharge of their duties under Sub Section 1 or the carrying on by them of any such activities was aforesaid or was incidental or conductive thereto.[9]

In this particular case, (nationalisation of the coal industry) the transfer of assets to the government was a complex undertaking.

The principle property of the Coal Commission is the coal acquired under the Coal Act, 1938. Under the Act, the private royalty owners received cash compensation in exchange for their coal, and the Commission raised the cash by issue of 3% Coal Commission stock under Treasury guarantee. The total nominal amount of Coal Commission stock issued and outstanding is £70,474,358 19s and 6d. All this stock was taken up by the National Debt Commissioners (NDC) as an investment for the Savings Banks Funds. All the stock is still held by the NDC, and by arrangement with the NDC, they will not part with any (except to the Coal Commission Stock Redemption Fund), till the transaction authorised by this clause has been completed.

It would have been possible to maintain the Coal Commission stock in existence, transferring the liability for its service from the Coal Commission to the National Coal Board. This course was not adopted for two main reasons:

1. Coal Commission stock is secured on the property and revenues of the Commission, i.e. on the coal royalties, so that if the stock had continued, it would have been necessary to draw up the constitution of the NCB so that its royalty revenue was kept permanently segregated from the rest of its finances.
2. The continued existence of Coal Commission stock would not have been consistent with the general scheme of the Bill which is to eliminate all stock specifically secured on or identified with the industry.

The alternative provided for in the clause is that, by agreement between the Treasury and the National Debt Commissioners (NCD), the Coal Commission Stock shall be cancelled and Government stock of equal value issued to the NDC in the place of the Coal Commission Stock. As a consequence, the National Coal Board instead of being directly liable for the service of the Coal Commission stock, will be liable to recoup the Crown for the service of the Government Stock issued to take its place ... [10]

In a further document titled 'Future of Coal Commission Stock and redemption and reserve funds' the following makes a comment on the possibilities.

It would be feasible to keep the stock in existence and for the National Coal Board as successors to the Coal Commission to service it, i.e. maintain interest and the agreed annual Sinking Fund contribution of £560,000. This is not, however, recommended for the following reasons:

9   National Archives COAL 35/1.
10   National Archives T 233/49.

a) The life of the stock and the Sinking Fund were calculated on the basis of the Coal Commission's royalty income. Equally the security behind the Treasury guarantee is the charge of the stock on the property and the revenues of the Coal Commission. A decision to maintain the existence of the stock would not make sense unless the property of the Coal Commission, i.e. its royalties, remain in existence on the same footing as now, and were kept separate from the other operation of the NCB so as to provide the specific security for the stock. Such a decision would probably be unacceptable as a matter of future coal policy.

b) Ministers have decided that the National Coal Board should not issue its own stock (whether guaranteed or otherwise) to the present owners of the industry as compensation, because it is necessary to avoid any appearance of ownership of the industry by members of the public.[11]

Having decided on a path forward for the financial aspects of the coal industry nationalisation, thoughts then turned to relationships with the workers and members of the Coal Board.

Minister of Fuel and Power meets Mineworkers

The Minister of Fuel and Power, Mr Emanuel Shinwell, today met representatives of the Executive of the National Union of Mineworkers to continue discussion on the proposals embodied in the 'Miner's Charter' in particular in relation to holidays with pay, the five-day week and the future of the Essential Workers Order in the mining industry. Mr Shinwell stated that it was intended that the members-designate of the National Coal Board would proceed shortly to prepare their plan for the future of the industry, and he suggested that the members-designate in association with representatives of the Ministry of Fuel and Power and the National Union of Mineworkers should in the immediate future undertake a study of these questions with the object of reaching agreement on measures which could be implemented when the National Coal Board assumed control of the industry. The Minister emphasised that he attached the greatest importance to the speedy establishment of good relations between the National Coal Board (through the members-designate) and the National Union of Mineworkers in co-operating to meet the future problems of the coal industry.[12]

The above report mentioned the members-designate. The obvious question was how they were appointed, what was their remit and terms of references – at least it is to me! Fortunately there was a Statutory Rule and Order no 1094 written in 1946 concerning the mechanism of appointment of the members-designate.

The Minister of Fuel and Power in pursuance of section two of the Coal Industry Nationalisation Act 1946, hereby makes the following regulations:

11 Ibid.
12 National Archives POWE 28/67.

1. The appointment of a member of the National Coal Board shall, subject to the provisions of these regulations, be for such a term not exceeding five years as may be determined by the Minister before the appointment of such a member and upon such conditions as may be determined by the Minister, with the approval of the Treasury, either before the appointment of such a member or, with his consent, at any time thereafter.

2.1. If a member of the Board:

a)   Except in so far as a Minister may approve.

    i)   At any time engages in any trade or business.

    ii)   Becomes, or continues to be, a director or officer of any body corporate.

    iii) Becomes, or continues to be, an officer or servant of an organisation of workpeople.

b)   Is absent from meetings of the Board for more than six months consecutively except for some reason approved by the Minister.

c)   Becomes in the opinion of the Minister unfit to continue in office or incapable of performing his duties.

The Minister may declare the office of such a member to be vacant and shall notify the fact in such manner as the Minister thinks fit; and thereupon the office of such member shall become vacant.

2.2. Any member of the Board may resign his office by not less than three months notice under his hand given to the Minister.

3.3 Every member of the Board shall forthwith disclose to the Minister full particulars of any interest or securities which he may at any time hold in his own name, or in the name of a nominee, for his own benefit ... [13]

The formation of the Coal Board provided a forum for the Federation of Small Mines of Great Britain to meet and determine a path forward that would enable small mines (less than 30 below ground employees) to operate. A meeting on the 16 April between these two bodies had additional agenda items. These included:

    i)   Revised arrangements for the exclusion of contracts of Small Mine Licensees.

    ii)   A guaranteed wage.

    iii) Opportunities for trainees.[14]

These issues were not resolved at that meeting. The meeting did, however, provide a forum to continue these and other discussions for the next few years.

The formation of the National Coal Board also allowed for meeting between it and other interested parties. For example the National Association of Colliery Overmen Deputies and Shotfirers and the National Union of Mineworkers. These three groups formed an agreement on 25 August 1952 where they agreed to:

a)   The provisions of wages and conditions of service.

b)   The provisions as to sickness, accident and industrial disease benefit.[15]

The document also discussed the necessary training requirements in addition

13   National Archives POWE 26/1290.
14   National Archives COAL 35/1.
15   National Archives LAB 10/1219.

to terms and conditions of employment – an all too familiar document for most agreements between employer and employee even now.

Of course the formation of the National Coal Board had some knock-on effects in some unusual enterprises.

For example in the organisation of the fuel research. Sir Edward Appleton FRS of The Department of Scientific and Industrial Research (DSIR – a Government funded body active in research and technology development), received the following letter.

3rd September 1946

Dear Appleton,

We have now had the opportunity of consulting our Minister about the proposals you made for future responsibility for Fuel Research, in your letter of May 22nd to Barlow. You will remember that while you felt unable to give up any of the responsibility which was placed upon your department by the Order in Council in 1915, and therefore, considered it necessary that the Fuel Research Station should remain part of the DSIR, at least for the time being, you were prepared to hand over to us the task of co-ordinating research over the whole fuel field. While the Minister appreciated your offer of a transfer of the latter responsibility, and is in general agreement with the suggestion that a Scientific Advisory Committee should be set up here, I am afraid that I can only report that he is quite unwilling to accept the suggestion that the Fuel Research Station should remain as part of the DSIR ...

He point out that the National Coal Board will be creating organisations for research into those sections of the fuel field that particularly concern them, and as the Gas and Electricity Industries are nationalised in turn, they will no doubt do the same. It will remain his responsibility as Minister of Fuel and Power to ensure the proper co-ordination of these three nationalised industries, and he is convinced that it would be impossible for him to carry out this task if he is not able to have the benefit of direct access to research ...

I am afraid, therefore, that it is quite clear that agreement along the lines you suggested after our previous discussion is not likely ...

I think I should mention one other point which may weigh heavily with him, especially as it may cause you less difficulty than the Fuel Research Station issue. It is whether it will be appropriate for the Government's financial assistance to the research constituents, whose industrial income will in future come largely from nationalised corporations, to be paid through DSIR ...

Signed

Sir Guy Nott-Bower[16]

The outcome of these deliberations are not recorded in the same National Archive folio. However, the National Archives AY7 series documents the Department of Scientific and Industrial Research, Warren Spring Laboratory, 1958-1965 within which are the records of the Fuel Research Station, 1919-1958. This suggests that

16   National Archives POWE 25/147.

the Station remained within the DSIR for some time following the discussions in the letter above.[17]

Another knock-on effect of coal nationalisation was with respect to ancillary activities such as brickworks. For example:

> This Company was incorporated in September 1936, with the principle object of erecting a brickworks and mining the clay lying immediately above the major coal seam. This clay had been subjected to exhaustive tests and found to be eminently suitable for producing first class engineering and facing bricks of a type not previously produced in Scotland. By July 1939, complete plans had been drawn up for the erection of the brickworks, but owing to the war these had to be held in abeyance and the colliery side of the undertaking was continued under your instructions. In course of the war, coal in the major seam in the area covered by our leasehold was practically worked out, but the clay remains and the Company is now developing the lower seams. In view of this, when the colliery side of the Company's undertaking is taken over, under the Nationalisation scheme, the coal could be worked quite separately allowing this Company to continue mining clay only.
>
> During the last two years the Board, having obtained the most authoritative advice, has revised the plan for the brickworks, making it larger and more comprehensive, with an estimated output of 200,000 bricks per week. This plan, for which the necessary estimates from supplying firms have been obtained, is ready for immediate execution. The Ministry of Works has been approached and has given its sanction and strongest approval to the scheme.
>
> It will be appreciated that the erecting of the brickworks cannot be commenced until a definitive assurance is received from you that this would not come within the scope of nationalisation and that the Company would be in a position to mine the necessary clay. In order to allow this project to proceed we shall be glad to know if you are in a position to give this assurance. Secretaries[18]

The British Coking Industry was also affected by coal nationalisation. Their Association met with members of the Ministry for Fuel and Power on a number of occasions throughout the latter half of 1945. Amongst other issues were their concerns on the transfer of the assets of their members into the newly formed nationalised industry.[19] It would add no value here to provide a seemingly endless list of affected industries, it would be too long and would be incomplete for one reason or another.

There are other ways in which third parties were affected by the industry nationalisation, one of which was the effect on local land owners. Land adjacent to collieries were affected in many ways as some collieries expanded. Extra traffic and

17 National Archives, <http://discovery.nationalarchives.gov.uk/SearchUI/details?uri=C2721>. (Accessed May 2014).
18 National Archives POWE 28/11.
19 National Archives POWE 28/29.

worker footfall was the least of their worries. Arguably of greater concern as some of the collieries expanded.

One issue was the price paid for land under which coal seams were evident and the possibility of subsidence. In this case there was a statutory rule and order written in 1946 which addressed the issue of a claim against the Coal Board from local landowners.[20]

(c) **Railways/canals**

A Committee was established by the Rt. Hon. Lord Leathers MP on 22 February 1944. As Minister of War Transport, he appointed the said committee with the following terms of reference:

> To investigate and report upon the technical and operational aspects of those suggestions made in the County of London Plan of 1943 which relate to the main line and suburban railway system of London, both surface and underground, bearing in mind that these suggestions are intended to contribute towards and form part of a comprehensive scheme for the re-development of the area in question.
>
> The Committee should include in their examination of the problem any alternatives to or modifications of the suggestions made in the Plan which the Railway Companies or the London Passenger Transport Board may wish to submit and should have due regard to the requirements of traffic and to the convenience of the travelling public, and to any schemes of improvement which the Railway Companies and the London Passenger Transport Board may have in mind.[21]

The Committee chair was Professor Sir Charles Inglis FRS. The Royal Society Fellows database lists Sir Charles as a Fellow of King's College Cambridge and Professor of Mechanism and Applied Mechanics.[22] Other information in this database documents the war contribution of Sir Charles which was of significance in the field of metal bridges.

This Committee published its findings in a report titled *Railway (London Plan) Committee 1944. Report to the Minister of War Transport 21 January 1946.*

Of course London is only a small part of the overall network in terms of linear miles of rail track, yet in other ways the hub of the overall plan. Even though the above report is London centric, Chapter XII of this report documents the Summary of conclusions and recommendations and is reproduced as Appendix VII for completeness.

Of more importance here is the nationalisation of the whole railway sector and its effects on staff and users.

A memorandum to general managers was written on 4 December 1946 which helps to set the scene – at least from the employees perspective. The opening remarks

20   National Archives POWE 28/74.
21   National Archives MT 6/2787.
22   Royal Society, *Collections* <http://royalsociety.org/library/collections/>. (Accessed May 2014).

appear below and the full report as Appendix VIII.

Nationalisation – Transport Bill 1946

In accordance with the request of the General Managers the Railway Staff Conference have examined the provisions of the above bill in regard to conditions of employment, pensions and compensation to Officers and Servants, as set out in Part VII in so far as the railway aspect is concerned and their comments are set out below.

As the bill provides for the establishment of a Transport Commission with Executives to assist the Commission which are referred to in several places in Part VII the Conference have thought it well to set out briefly at the outset of their report the constitution and functions of these bodies.[23]

Arguably unlike any of the other industries nationalised during the immediate post-war period, the canals and railways, at least in one particular regard, were unusual. The particular aspect in mind here is the large numbers of horses this industry kept as working livestock. This was the age of steam and therefore the need to transport coal and heavy materials, which at first sight might be seem an unusual industry to own so many horses. Perhaps the scale of this venture might be appreciated with reference to the total number of horses mentioned in the Horse Stock Record Book.[24] The horses were of various types including shire horses and were recorded in the aforementioned stock book for a number of years. By way of an example the stock for some of the London Boroughs and another towns within the Midland Region for two dates might provide a feel for numbers of horses involved, figure 6.1.

Station	17 July 1949	24 January 1953
Bedford	17	11
Camden	13	6
Dunstable	3	2
Haydon Square	63	45
Hendon	4	2
Kensington High Street	2	2
Luton	12	10
Northampton	23	16
Watford	2	1
Total across the whole region	1080	176

Figure 6.1. Some horse numbers from the Horse Stock Record Book.

Only a fraction of the total number of horses are listed in figure 6.1, however the total is for all of the stations/depots within the Midland Region. The rate of

23   National Archives RAIL 1172/1305.
24   National Archives AN 35/20.

decline from July 1949 to January 1953 is across all of the depots signifying increased mechanisation for the most part. Annotations in the aforementioned book, suggest that the surplus horses, retired from active work in the railways, were put to stud or farms. However this process needed a procedure which could not interrupt the transition from private to national ownership, and was an issue needing resolution.

Livestock was just one of a number of issues. There were instances where land was requisitioned from the railway companies under the Requisitioned Land and War Work Act 1945. Some of this former railway land was either built on or was used as a means of access to another structure. This was a difficult issue to resolve as requisitioned land was the property of the government as it would be within the nationalised railway. Returning the land back to the privately run railways and then nationalising the companies added to the complexity. An agreement was eventually signed by the various parties.[25]

A further complication was easier to resolve. Prior to the war some railway carriages were owned by non-railway companies who then used their own stock on the railway network. At the time of nationalisation there were estimated to be 12,520 privately owned wagons. Some were old and were sold to a breakers yard and some kept for internal use (2070) leaving 12,520 which were bought from private hands into the new Railway organisation for £22 10s each. Although a relatively small sum of money compared with the millions of pounds involved in the whole nationalisation issue, the cost to the government was still £326,025. A large sum of money in those days.[26]

Developments in engines, the move from steam to electricity and diesel and the need for general standardisation in the whole rail industry, prompted the formation of the Locomotive Standards Committee, the first report from which is available in the National Archives. The terms of reference for this committee were:

> To deal with all matters affecting standardisation of locomotive types and details. Co-ordination is specially desired between common features of steam, diesel and electric locomotives, and of electric motor bogies, and because of the specialised nature of the electrical equipment in the latter, a standing sub-committee should be set up which will deal with all forms of motive power having electrical transmission. Other sub-committees may of course be appointed as required to deal with other individual matters. The following may require immediate investigation simultaneously by the Main Committee and the Electrical Traction Sub-Committee.

1. Design of consumable details.
    a) To prepare a list of renewable details which it is desirable to standardise from the point of view of purchase and manufacture.
    b) To consider existing designs of such details and recommend the best for adoption on future new construction.

25 National Archives MT 47/223.
26 Ibid.

c)   To make recommendations as to how far, if at all, it is practicable to apply such standards to existing motive power units.

d)   To report on first stage (a) within three months.

2.   Recommendations for 1950 construction.

a)   Steam and diesel – mechanical.

b)   The possibility is to be examined, of selecting only one of the existing standard types in each of the operating categories for construction in 1950 and onwards until such time as new standard types are developed.

c)   In order that the selection can be made on rational grounds, the Committee should assemble as much information as is available under the following headings in respect of each of the existing standard types:

   i)   Power capacity of engine and boiler.

   ii)   Mileage between consecutive classified repairs.

   iii) Casualty record.

   iv)   Record of tests already carried out.

   v)   Costs so far as they are obtainable on a uniform basis …

   vi)   Diesel-electric and electric locomotives and motor bogies for multiple unit stock.

d)   To report on the constructional programmes which are already proposed for 1950 in the different regions, and to recommend on similar lines to a) above, what should actually be undertaken in that year, having regard to contracts already placed.[27]

There were many other initiatives that were put in place. More details of the overall process of railway nationalisation can be obtained from the National Archives.

27   National Archives AN 7/139.

7   National Health Service

It is difficult to imagine now how health care was administered prior to the formation of the National Health Service (NHS). From my personal perspective I have not known any other system of health care. The formation of the National Health Service was a complex task as there were not just the physical aspects to administer but also the welfare of those health practitioners of all ages and qualifications needing their personal issues resolved. It seems appropriate to use examples of the creation of the NHS from the whole of the United Kingdom where they add value as the NHS affected everyone.

(a) **Admin**
Any organisational change of this magnitude requires a degree of basic infrastructure underpinning the changes that follow. The formation of committees able to co-ordinate further activity was the obvious first step in the process.

National Health Services Act 1946

The Secretary
Ministry of Health
Whitehall
London SW1
26th September 1947

Sir,
The Joint Committee is giving preliminary consideration to matters which will require attention in connection with the transfer of hospitals to the Minister in the appointed day for the above-mentioned Act.

The employees of eighteen hospital boards and six joint hospital committees which will be dissolved on the appointed day are included in the scheme administered by this Committee.

The Boards fall into two groups as follows:
1. South West Yorkshire Board for the Mentally Defective which will be dissolved in pursuance of Section 78(1)(a) of the Act.
2. The under-mentioned Joint Hospital Boards which will be dissolved by virtue of Section 78(1)(b) of the Act.

Calverley, Castleford and District, Colne and Holme, Doncaster and Mexborough, Goole, Guisborough and District, Harrogate, Knaresborough and Wetherby, Keighley, Bingley and Shipley, Liversedge and Mirfield, North Bierley, Penistone, Pontefract, Richmond and District, Selby, South Rotherham and Kiveton Park, Wath, Swinton and District and Wharfedale Union.

An order in pursuance of Section 78(2) of the Act providing for the transfer of liabilities in respect of superannuation will be required in respect of each Board.

A perusal of the Orders under which the Boards are established shows that in the great majority of cases the expenses are apportioned among the constituent bodies by reference to either the rateable value of each constituent district or estimated population ... [1]

Further administration was needed as the local authorities set up the West Riding (Local Authorities) Superannuation Joint Committee. A committee must also have been formed in each of the authorities affected. The above, of course, was just one example from one part of the United Kingdom. Later in the process there was a Statutory Rule and Order titled National Health Service – Dissolved Authorities. In dissolving these authorities not only were assets transferred or sold and the relevant people transferred to the new scheme, there were also the financial accounts to resolve.

In tandem with the short term requirements to resolve issues of the transfer of ownership, resolve staffing issues and complete necessary financial arrangements for running superannuation schemes and the NHS, there was also the need for longer term planning. A typical exemplar is that of the Welsh National School of Medicine and their need to find land for and build a new teaching hospital.

16th July 1948
Dear Sir Frederick Alban,
The University Council at its meeting on the 9th July, decided to appoint a Committee consisting of three representatives of The Welsh National School of Medicine, one representative of the University College of South Wales and Monmouthshire and two representatives of the University to discuss with representatives of the Board of Governors of the Teaching Hospital the question of a site for a new Teaching Hospital and Medical School. The University representatives appointed were the Vice Chancellor and Principal Sir Frederick Rees. As it may be necessary to have meetings with representatives of the Board of Governors before the Council of the Medical School meets I shall be glad if you will agree to act as a representative of the School in the meantime.
Yours sincerely,
R M F Picken
Provost[2]

1   National Archives MH 77/220.
2   National Archives BD 18/1492.

Professor Picken was later quoted in the Western Mail (8 July 1949) that the proposed new facility would accommodate 1,000 beds with a large out-patient department and medical school buildings.

The website for Cardiff University School of Medicine offers the following quote:

> Since its foundation in 1893, the School of Medicine has been committed to the pursuit of improved human health, through education, research and engagement with the wider world. We are a major Centre for teaching and research and make a positive difference to the way medicine is practiced in Wales, the UK and internationally.[3]

The plans formulated in 1948 continue to bear fruit some seventy years later! In conjunction with the need to consider the future of medical science, involving vast sums of money in developing sites for new or improved facilities, there was also the need to exercise financial restraint in running costs. At a joint meeting of representatives of the Welsh Regional Hospital Board and the Chairmen of Hospital Management Committees, which met in Cardiff on 11 January 1949, the Chairman stated:

> The Government's economic policy called for the maximum economy in expenditure on all Government services. This applied equally to the hospital services and Chairmen were urged to do their utmost to prevent unnecessary expenditure. The budgets would shortly be returned from the Ministry to the Regional Boards with a request for their re-examination with this consideration in mind. Each Board would be told the total sum available for its area and asked to advise the Ministry of the apportionment which should be made between its various Management Committees.[4]

Even with these local committees working on centrally generated directives, there was still too much to accomplish with the infrastructure already mentioned. The old adage of how to eat an elephant springs to mind. Of course the answer to that question is simple! One eats an elephant small piece by small piece. The same is true of any large problem. In this case the way forward was to appoint specialist committees dealing with manageable sections of the overarching goals. Amongst others this led to the formation of the following committees:

1. Standing Pharmaceutical Advisory Committee.
    The terms of reference of this committee was to ensure that pharmacist members were invited to comment on the technical aspects of providing pharmaceutical services at health services. This led the Pharmaceutical Society of Great Britain to examine:
    i)   The number of entrants to pharmacy necessary to maintain the register of pharmacists as near as possible to its present level over a period (20 years).

3   Cardiff University School of Medicine, *home page* < http://medicine.cf.ac.uk/>. (Accessed July 2014)
4   National Archives BD 18/32.

      ii)   The existing need for pharmacists.[5]

2.   Standing Cancer and Radiotherapy Advisory Committee.

The Members of this Committee were, with one or two exceptions, hand-picked by Sir Ernest Rock Carling. He was anxious:

   a)   To include people who were part-time advisors of the Ministry or who had been associated with the work of the Radium Commission.

   b)   To get all the Regional Centres represented.

   c)   To get a proper balance of specialities represented.

It was not therefore possible in this case to pay much attention to the nominations received from representative organisations. The regional principle also led them in one or two cases into getting people who were not absolutely in the front rank, conversely although there were nine London members, there were still some eminent London men not included.[6]

3.   Local Optical Committee.

The City of Birmingham local committee Chair was Mr R J Lucking. In total there were ten ophthalmic opticians and three dispensing opticians.

There were other committees including the Standard Dental Advisory Committee, the Standing Ophthalmic Advisory Committee, the Standing Nursing Advisory Committee, the Standing Tuberculosis Committee, the Standing Maternity and Midwifery Advisory Committee and the Standing Mental Health Advisory Committee.

In tandem with these committees the Government established a central purchasing system.

The Minister has had under consideration the need for extension of central purchasing and contracting by the Department, in the interest of economy and better efficiency, to other major equipment and common-user stores, both medical and domestic. He has decided that this shall be undertaken wherever it appears economically or otherwise advantageous or necessary. Boards of Governors and Hospital Management Committees will be notified in advance by Supplies Division of the types of equipment and stores to be purchased in this way and are invited to suggest particular classes of goods to be considered for early action.

Contracts for supply to meet the needs of hospitals are negotiated by or on behalf of the Department under normal Government purchasing procedure, including cost investigations where applicable, which may result in even lower prices than those accepted under tender. Central arrangements are made for inspection of goods in course of production and for testing their quality.[7]

There were many other facets to the administration for the new health service. An issue close the hearts and minds of those working for the new health organisations be

5   National Archives MH 133/369.
6   National Archives MH 133/449.
7   National Archives MH 133/369.

they local or national was that of remuneration.

Functions of the Councils

i)   To secure the greatest possible measure of co-operation between the authorities responsible for the Nation's health and the general body of persons engaged in the health services, with the view to increased efficiency in the public service, and the well-being of those engaged in the services.

ii)   To provide machinery for the regular consideration of remuneration and conditions of service of persons within the ambit of Section 66 of the National Health Service Act 1946, and Section 65 of the National Health Service (Scotland) Act 1947, excluding persons in the administrative and clerical classes employed by local health authorities in Scotland by Education Authorities.

iii) To provide machinery for the determination of the remuneration of persons with whom an Executive Council may make arrangements for the provision of general medical services, general dental services, pharmaceutical services or supplementary ophthalmic services.

iv)   To provide machinery also for the consideration of the remuneration and conditions of service of persons in the service of Local Authorities engaged in employment analogous to those specified in i) above.

v)   To provide machinery also for the consideration of the remuneration and conditions of employment of any persons whom the General Council may from time to time decide to admit within its scope.[8]

(b) Provision of new services

From time to time the Ministry of Health issued circulars on a wide range of subjects. For example there were circulars on the immunisation against diphtheria, actually numbers 8, 23, 84 and 100 which were issued in 1946. Brochures were issued by the Ministry of Information accompanying some of these circulars. In this particular case a brochure covered:

- Local campaigns (how Local Authorities can cooperate).
- Combined Ministry/Local Authority advertisements.
- Advertisements available for 'combined advertising'.
- Material available free of charge.
- Material available from the Central Council for Health Education.
- How to plan for a campaign.
- How to order advertising material.

The introduction to this brochure explains its intended use:

8   National Archives MH 174/23.

This brochure is intended to help Local Authorities to plan and carry out local campaigns for the protection of children against diphtheria. The main emphasis of the campaign is now on immunisation of children before the age of one year.

The number of children immunised each year ought to keep pace with the number of births; and in Circular 194/45 Welfare Authorities have been asked, working in close co-operation with other Local Authorities, to make and sustain special efforts to secure that each generation of infants receives protection at the earliest age.

Personal persuasion by health visitors, doctors, teachers and voluntary workers remains the most important factor: but this direct contact with parents must be supported during 1946 by both local and national publicity campaigns. The Ministry of Health will continue to afford every possible assistance.

Publicity material available for use by Local Authorities, including press advertisements, posters, cinema slides, and special leaflets for use in conjunction with personal persuasion, is outlined in this brochure ... [9]

Circulars were issued for many reasons, most of which involved the medical profession but may not have reached the wider public, unlike the diphtheria campaign mentioned above. There were some circulars intended to set fears at rest or explain changes which may have led to peace of mind and perhaps a better sense of well-being, such as the brochure 'Pensions (increase) Acts 1944 and 1947 Pensioner's Questions Answered'.[10]

By the early 1950s, the National Health Service was well established and thoughts turned to overlap in provision, amongst other things. This was set out in a letter to Sir William Douglas of the Department of Health for Scotland.

28th February 1949
Dear Sir William,
The Lord President has written to the Minister (and sent a copy to the Minister of Labour and the Secretary of State for Scotland) telling him that it has been decided to set up a departmental committee to decide on the proper demarcation of functions between the National Health Service and industrial undertakings.

Alec Johnson of the Cabinet Office telephoned this morning seeking your guidance on how best to bring the Scots into the enquiry. He was doubtful whether it would be desirable to have a separate committee for Scotland and thought perhaps the best thing would be to settle the principles for England and then to see what modifications are required to cover Scotland. This was, however, only a tentative suggestion and he is most anxious to have the benefit of your advice on the point.

I thought that as you were in Scotland you might like to take the opportunity of mentioning the matter informally to the Department of Health.

9   National Archives MH 10/156.
10 National Archives MH 10/160.

Yours sincerely[11]

A committee of enquiry was duly commissioned. Sometimes known as the Dale Committee, the subject of which was industrial health services, with the brief to:

> Examine the relationship (including any possibility of overlapping) between the preventative and curative health services provided for the population at large and the industrial health services which make a call on medical manpower (doctors, nurses and auxiliary medical personnel); to consider what measures should be taken by the Government and the other parties concerned to ensure that such medical manpower is used to the best advantage; and to make recommendations.[12]

The chairman, and after whom the committee was known, was His Honour Judge Edgar T Dale. Other members of the committee included health care professionals as well as senior managers and medical personnel from industry. Some of the steps to be taken by the Government and other parties concerned were documented on page 19 of the report. It would add very little to quote all of these, however the first two may be of interest:

> We have come to the conclusion that the existing industrial health services are most important to industry and that they are in many ways complementary to the National Health Service. We advise that they should be maintained and encouraged to expand with due regard to the demands of all other health services for medical manpower. For the most beneficial development of the National Health Service, Public Health Services and industrial health services, the three must be co-ordinated.
>
> In our view it is desirable that there should eventually be some comprehensive provision for occupational health covering not only industrial establishments of all kinds, both large and small, but also the non-industrial occupations referred to in the Report of the Committee of Enquiry into Health, Welfare and Safety in Non-Industrial Employment (Gower's Committee). This, however, is a long term view which cannot be made effective without much more experience to be gathered from future surveys and experiments ... [13]

Independent surveys of this kind were useful but very time consuming and somewhat costly. Of course the argument for using this type of forum is that of independence and also potential payback. There were other surveys which were conducted from within the Ministry of Health, for example the Local Health Service Special Survey of 1952. Topics for this survey included:

11   National Archives MH 79/623.
12   National Archives BK 2/126.
13   National Archives BK 2/126 page 19.

a)   Co-ordination and co-operation with other parts of the National Health Service.
b)   Joint use of staff.
c)   Voluntary organisation.
d)   Care of mothers with young children.
    i)   Ante-natal and post-natal.
    ii)   Welfare centres.
    iii) Other provision.
e)   Domiciliary midwifery.
f)   Health visiting.
g)   Home nursing.
h)   Vaccination and immunisation.
    i)   Diphtheria immunisation.
    ii)   Immunisation against whooping cough.
    iii) Smallpox vaccination.
i)   Ambulance service.
j)   Prevention of illness, care and after-care.
    i)   Tuberculosis.
    ii)   Other illness.
    iii) Domiciliary care of old people.
    iv)   Prevention of illness.
    v)   Health education.
k)   Domestic help service.
l)   Mental health.[14]

Even though the formation of the National Health Service took many hours and countless millions of pounds to set up the threat of War still weighed heavily on the minds of those in Government. With National Service there was the ability to call on trained soldiers, the same was also needed for health workers, i.e. a reserve of able bodied trained personnel able to treat casualties in the event of further conflict. Accordingly in July 1950 a revised document was published outlining the National Hospital Service Reserve. Part 1 of this document concerns the organisation and training of this organisation:

Composition of the National Hospital Service Reserve
The National Hospital Service Reserve, which was established by the Minister of Health under powers conferred by Section 1 of the Civil Defence Act 1948, to provide a trained and organised body of men and women available to meet the needs of an expanded hospital service in the event of War, at present consists of two parts:
a)   Trained nurses and midwives, enrolled assistant nurses and nursing assistants class I (the last named for mental hospitals and MD organisations only).

14   National Archives MH 52/491.

These are recruited and organised by Regional Hospital Boards and Board of Governors.

b)   Nursing Auxiliaries. These are recruited, organised and given initial training by the St John Ambulance Brigade and the British Red Cross Society.

It is proposed in due course to extend the Reserve to include certain categories of medical auxiliaries and technicians – radiographers, medical laboratory technicians, bio-chemists, physicists, physiotherapists and remedial gymnasts.

Organisation

a)   National Hospital Service Reserve Advisory Committee.

After which recruitment commenced on 15 November 1949, the Working party which was responsible for recommending the organisation and training of the Reserve was reconstituted as the National Hospital Service Reserve Advisory Committee. It consists of representatives of the Regional Hospital Boards, Boards of Governors, the St John Ambulance Brigade, the British Red Cross Society, the Association of Hospital Matrons, the Royal College of Nursing, the Royal College of Midwives, the Trade Union Congress National Advisory Council for the Nursing Profession, the Minister of Labour and National Service and the Ministry of Health; with observers from the Department of Health for Scotland. The Committee meets from time to time to consider inter alia, suggestions for improvements in the organisation of the Reserve.

b)   Regional Hospital Boards and Boards of Governors.

c)   Regional Hospital Boards and Boards of Governors have responsibility for:

i)   The enrolment of trained nurses, midwives, enrolled assistant nurses and nursing assistants, class I.

ii)   The keeping of records of such members.

iii) The medical examination of both trained and auxiliary members.

iv) Providing hospital instruction for nursing auxiliaries and refresher courses for both trained and auxiliary members of the Reserve.

Executive responsibility for these matters (detailed in an appendix) is delegated by Regional Hospital Boards to Hospital Management Committees.[15]

(c) The Paralympic Games

Rehabilitation exercised the minds of many people both during and after the War. Harold Balme was the Medical Officer in charge of rehabilitation at the Ministry of Health and was also the Director of Welfare Services to the British Red Cross Society. He issued regular bulletins. One was titled *The Present State of Hospital Rehabilitation*. His summary in of the situation from 1943 to 1946 appears as figure 7.1.

---

15   National Archives BD 2/1.

	1943	1944	1946
Hospitals possessing all facilities for active rehabilitation and using them for all suitable patients	13	58	83
Hospitals with all such facilities but only using them for selected disabilities (e.g. traumatic)	35	73	121
Total hospitals with all facilities	48	131	204
Hospitals possessing partial facilities (e.g. remedial exercises but no occupational therapy)	102	136	129
Total hospitals employing active rehabilitation	150	267	333

Figure 7.1. Progression in hospitals providing rehabilitation.[16]

The report comments on the above information thus:

> One of the interesting points in the above table is the large increase in the number of hospitals possessing and using all facilities for active rehabilitation, from 48 in 1943 to 204 today. Once a hospital has made a start at developing an active rehabilitation department (that is one with a full programme with remedial exercises and occupational therapy and not merely massage and passive physiotherapy), it tends to go on. The 102 hospitals, which three years ago possessed only partial facilities, and now amongst the 204 offering full facilities, and the same development will probably occur in the 129 hospitals still only partially equipped. There are a further 75 hospitals planning to develop a modern rehabilitation department as soon as conditions will allow ... [17]

The report mentions a range of component factors which included:
a)   A rehabilitation officer.
b)   Physiotherapy departments.
c)   Gymnastic exercises and recreational therapy.
d)   Occupational therapy.
e)   Educational and cultural facilities.
f)   Out-patient and canteen facilities.

Good as these services were at the time and were to become as the National Health Service was developed, there were opportunities to improve this service. My brother contracted a serious illness in the mid-1960s resulting in a stay at a hospital in Leeds. This hospital was also a centre for brain trauma (usually caused by blunt force) and prosthetic limbs. Some 20 years AFTER the end of the War there were still in-patients who had entered the hospital during the War and were unlikely to ever leave it!

In some cases this would have been inevitable as there were then and indeed still are medical issues for which there is no current cure. It must have seen this way for some of the patients at Stoke Mandeville Hospital in Buckinghamshire in the post-war years. Fortunately for them there was an innovative doctor willing to try a totally new

16   National Archives MH 101/34.
17   Ibid.

Figure 7.2. Sir Ludwig Guttmann FRS. (Author's photograph)

form of rehabilitation. His name was Sir Ludwig Guttmann FRS, figure 7.2.

Sir Ludwig was born on 3 July 1899 in Tost in Upper Silesia which was then part of Poland. The first official British paperwork for Sir Ludwig and his family appears in the records concerning the British Nationality and Status of Aliens Act 1914:

Certificate of Naturalization

Whereas Ludwig Guttmann has applied to one of His Majesty's Principal Secretaries of State for a Certificate of Naturalization, alleging with respect to himself the particulars set out below, and has satisfied him that the conditions laid down in the above mentioned act for the grant of a Certificate of Naturalization are fulfilled in his case.

And whereas the said Ludwig Guttmann has also applied for the inclusion in accordance with sub-section (1) of section five of the said act of the names of his children born before the date of his certificate and having been minors, and the Secretary of State is satisfied that the names of his children, as hereinafter set out, may properly be included:

Now therefore, in pursuance of the powers conferred on him by the said Act, the Secretary of State grants to the said Ludwig Guttmann this Certificate of Naturalization, and declares that upon taking the Oath of Allegiance within the time and in the manner required by the regulations made in that behalf he shall subject to the provisions of the said Act, be entitled to all political and other rights and privileges, and be subject to all obligations and duties and liabilities, to which a natural-born British subject is entitled or subject, and have to all intents and purposes the status of a natural-born British subject ... [18]

There must have been relief in the Guttmann household when these papers were received. Some twenty years later the following appeared.

Honours and Awards

Home Office
Whitehall,
London S.W.I.
18th February 1966.

Her Majesty QUEEN ELIZABETH THE QUEEN MOTHER, acting on behalf of Her Majesty by authority of Letters Patent under the Great Seal dated 31st January 1966, conferred the honour of Knighthood upon the undermentioned gentlemen at Buckingham Palace on Tuesday, 15th February 1966:
    Sir Ludwig GUTTMANN, C.B.E., M.D., F.R.C.S.

(Her Majesty's approval of these Knighthoods was signified on 1st January 1966.)[19]

So what did Sir Ludwig do that in such a relatively short space of time from becoming a British citizen achieved such a reputation that he was awarded a knighthood?

Sir Ludwig's ideas revolutionised certain forms of rehabilitation involving spinal injuries. His Royal Society Biographical Memoir comments:

Guttmann gave orders that patients were to be turned prone to supine and back or from one side to the other every two hours, night and day, waking or sleeping. His first orderlies had been released from the RAMC and had learned little there. One man, asked what he had done in the RAMC, said 'shovelling coal, Sir'. Guttmann had to be in the wards for every hour of the night until his orders were carried out, and the benefits began to appear. Guttmann traced the outline of healing bedsores on transparent film and measured their area at regular intervals, and established that all antiseptics reduced the rate of healing by damaging epithelial cells ...

... with the major clinical problems overcome and the necessary investigations done, Guttmann was in a position to turn his energies to the social rehabilitation of his patients. Toy making as occupational therapy soon paled and pre-vocational workshops were set up in hospital in which patients could do woodwork, instrument making and clock and watch repairing ...

... after lunch one day in 1945 Guttmann came across a group of patients in their heavy leather padded wheelchairs sunning themselves on the concrete

18 National Archives HO 334/229.
19 *London Gazette* 18 February 1966, issue 43904, p. 1891.

Figure 7.3. The Paralympic Symbol displayed on Tower Bridge. (Author's photograph)

apron outside the wards, and hitting a puck with reversed walking sticks. His eye brightened as he said something to the effect 'games, sport, that is what we must have'. He had been trying exercise machines in bed and had the impression that a spell of muscular exercise decreased spasticity in paralysed parts. He and the chief physiotherapist took wheelchairs and tried out wheelchair polo in the gymnasium and made it a recognized game, using a ball and the walking sticks. As long as one could avoid bumping and boring with the chairs, this was a great success. On one occasion the carnage was such that the game had to be given up, and Guttmann started wheelchair basketball instead. This was an immediate success and led to the first Stoke Mandeville Games for the paraplegic in 1948 when 16 ex-service patients competed. The Dutch brought a team to Stoke Mandeville in 1952 and the first Olympic Games for the Paralysed were held in Rome in 1960. The list of track and field events grew rapidly. Archery was a favourite …

… after his retirement from the Directorship of the National Spinal Injuries Centre, Sir Ludwig devoted the greater part of his time to the organisation of games, national every year, Olympic every fourth year, with the Commonwealth and later regional games about every two years …

… since 1946, those interested in the treatment of paraplegics had been coming to Stoke Mandeville, sometimes visiting, sometimes working there for a year or so before going home to set up equivalent facilities … [20]

Little did anyone at the time realise the world importance this form of rehabilitation

20   *Biographical Memoirs of Fellows of the Royal Society* Vol 29 1983, pp. 227-244.

has achieved for countless thousands of men, women and children. Indeed just recently, London hosted the 2012 Paralympic Games and proudly displayed the logo on some iconic landmarks including Tower Bridge, figure 7.3.

Incidentally, there is a permanent Paralympic Symbol displayed just outside of Stoke Mandeville hospital. A plaque nearby states that:

> The Paralympic Symbol is made up of three Agitos (from the Latin meaning 'I move'). It represents the Paralympic Movement and Vision embodied by the International Paralympic Committee and its global organisation:
>
> To enable Paralympic athletes to achieve sporting excellence and inspire and excite the world.[21]

---

21 Plaque near the roundabout at the entrance to Stoke Mandeville Hospital.

8   Welfare State

Introduction

The Welfare State owes its origins to a report titled *Social Insurance and Allied Services*, written in 1942 – almost two years before D-Day. The above report was authored by Sir William Beveridge, a highly regarded expert on unemployment problems who was also an economist. The Beveridge Report, as it is known, became the blueprint for the modern British welfare state. Indeed, contemporary politicians still refer to this report as one of the landmark documents in its field.[1]

The National Archives website quotes some abstracts from this report.

> In proceeding from this first comprehensive survey of social insurance to the next task – of making recommendations – three guiding principles may be laid down at the outset.
>
> 7. The first principle is that any proposals for the future, while they should use the full experience gathered in the past, should not be restricted by consideration of sectional interests established in the obtaining of that experience. Now, when the war is abolishing landmarks of every kind, is the opportunity for using experience in a clear field. A revolutionary moment in the world's history is a time for revolutions, not for patching.
>
> 8. The second principle is that organisation of social insurance should be treated as one part only of a comprehensive policy of social progress. Social Insurance fully developed may provide income security; it is an attack upon Want. But Want is one only of five giants on the road of reconstruction and in some ways the easiest to attack. The others are Disease, Ignorance, Squalor and Idleness.
>
> 9. The third principle is that social security must be achieved by co-operation between the state and the individual. The state should offer security for service and contribution. The State in organising security should not stifle incentive, opportunity, responsibility, in establishing a national minimum it should leave room and encouragement for voluntary action by each individual to provide more than the minimum for himself and his family.
>
> ... The plan for Social Security set out in this report is built upon these principles. It uses experience but is not tied to experience. It is put forward as a

---

1   National Archives, <http://www.nationalarchives.gov.uk/pathways/citizenship/brave_new_world/welfare. htm>. (Accessed June 2014).

limited contribution to a wider social policy, although as something that could be achieved now without waiting for the whole of that policy. It is first and foremost, a plan of insurance – of giving in return for contributions, benefits up to subsistence level, as of right and without means test, so that individuals may build freely upon it … .

Briefly, the proposal is to introduce to all citizens adequate pensions without means test by stages over a transition period of twenty years, while providing immediate assistance for persons requiring them. In adopting a transition period for pensions as of right, while meeting immediate needs subject to consideration of means, the Plan for Social Security in Britain follows the precedent of New Zealand.[2]

One of the proposals of the The Beveridge Report, was the introduction of a family allowance. The National Archives website comments:

The Beveridge Report, proposed an allowance of eight shillings per week for all children (apart from for a family's first child if one parent was working), which graduated according to age. It was to be non-contributory and funded by general taxation. After some debate, the Family Allowances Bill was enacted in June 1945. The act provided for a flat rate payment funded directly from taxation. The recommended eight shillings a week was reduced to five shillings, and family allowance became a subsidy, rather than a subsistence payment as Beveridge had envisaged …

… during the late 1940s, although family allowance was substantially devalued by inflation, there was little support for increases within government. In 1952, the Conservative government reduced food subsidy, which had been in place since the war. From October 1952, family allowance was increased by three shillings per week in order to advance the potential effect on nutrition.[3]

There were four Acts of Parliament underpinning these reforms, figure 8.1. Of course other acts were also brought to the statute book at this time, however they were concerned with the formation of the National Health Service, education etc.

Act	Year	Summary
The Family Allowances Act	1945	Provided a regular sum for second and subsequent children to be paid to the mother
The National Health Service Act	1946	Provided a free and fully comprehensive health service

2   National Archives, <http://www.nationalarchives.gov.uk/education/topics/attlee-beveridge-report-aims-vision.htm>. (Accessed June 2014).
3   National Archives, <http://www.nationalarchives.gov.uk/cabinetpapers/themes/beveridge-report-child-benefit>. (Accessed June 2014).

Act	Year	Summary
The National Insurance Act	1948	Established the welfare state as recommended by the Beveridge report of 1942 with compulsory contributions to cover funeral grants, maternity, old age benefits, sickness, unemployment and widows
National Assistance Act	1948	An Act to terminate the existing poor law and to provide in lieu thereof for the assistance of persons in need by the National Assistance Board and by local authorities*

*   Government Legislation, <http://www.legislation.gov.uk/ukpga/Geo6/11-12/29/part/II/crossheading/the-national-assistance-board/enacted>. (Accessed June 2014)

Figure 8.1. Some of the immediate post-war Welfare State key Acts.

The National Assistance Board was created to assist those people whose funds were insufficient for a basic standard of living.

The Government website concerned with Acts of Parliament (www. http://www. legislation.gov.uk/) offers the following concerning the National Assistance Act:

1.   The Assistance Board shall be known as the National Assistance Board, and in addition to the functions for the time being exercisable under any other enactment shall exercise the functions conferred on them by the following provisions of this Act.
2.   The National Assistance Board (hereafter in this Act referred to as 'the Board') shall exercise their functions in such manner as shall best promote the welfare of persons affected by the exercise thereof.
3.   For the purpose of securing the prompt discharge of their functions under this Act, the Board shall by regulations provide for the local administration of their said functions, and in particular, but subject to any arrangements for the discharge thereof by officers of another Government department or of a local authority, for the discharge by local officers of the Board of the functions of the Board in relation to applications for assistance and the decision of all questions arising thereon.
4.   Annual reports on the activities of the Board shall be made by the Board to the Minister of National Insurance, and the said Minister shall lay each report of the Board under this subsection before Parliament.
5.   The constitution and proceedings of the Board shall continue to be governed by the provisions set out in the First Schedule to this Act. Being the provisions in that behalf of the Unemployment Assistance Act, 1934.

Advisory committees
a)   For the purpose of securing that full use is made of the advice and assistance, both on general questions and on difficult individual cases, of persons having local knowledge and experience in matters affecting the functions of the

Board, the Board shall arrange for the establishment of advisory committees throughout Great Britain to act for such areas as the Board think fit.

b)   The Board shall pay to members of advisory committees appointed by the Board such travelling and other allowances (including compensation for loss of remunerative time) as the Board, after consultation with the Minister of National Insurance and with the consent of the Treasury may determine.[4]

More details of the National Assistance Board and the help that committee provided appears in section a) below.

Unemployment

There were many ways of assessing the level of post-war unemployment. Arguably one of the most reliable is to follow the money, which is to say to look at the annual report of the Unemployment Insurance Statutory Committee. The annual report from this Committee was ordered by Parliament to be printed on 18 March 1947 for the previous year up to 31 December 1946. Some of the opening remarks of this Committee, which were signed by Hubert D Henderson (Chairman), H F Brand, J Kaye Charlesworth, Katherine J Stephenson and George W Thomson on 17 February 1947 are interesting. Addressed to the Right Hon. James Griffiths MP, the Minister of National Insurance, the opening remarks include:

> ... in our last annual report, we indicated the possibility that despite the prospect of a continuing shortage of goods and shortage of labour power, the process of demobilisation and of turnover to a peace economy might none the less be accompanied by an increase in unemployment benefit. For 1947, it is now clear that the increase that must be expected in the average of unemployment during the year as a consequence of a coal shortage may be substantial. In 1946, however, some increase in registered unemployment occurred during the first half of the year, this was never very considerable. The number of insured persons registered as unemployed rose from 285,000 in December 1945, to 372,000 in March 1946, and reached 376,000 in June. The substantial trend was slightly downwards, and in December 1946, the figure was 363,000 despite the normal seasonal increases of winter-time ... as compared with 1945, contributions from employers and insured persons showed an increase of £4,145,606. This represents an increase in the total labour force in insurable employment as a result of men and women being released from the Services, partly offset by an increase in the number of persons unemployed and by many married women and other persons retiring from industry as war-occupations came to an end or controls of labour were removed ...[5]

Now as then there is/was always the option of stimulating the economy by building

4   Government Legislation, <http://www.legislation.gov.uk/ukpga/Geo6/11-12/29/part/II/crossheading/the-national-assistance-board/enacted>. (Accessed June 2014).
5   National Archives PIN 19/80.

housing, developing the highway infrastructure etc. Development areas had already been identified, intending them to act as catalysts for changes within their respective regions. Whilst the Development Areas did indeed fulfil some of their goals, there were some initiatives within them which were less well received. For example a suggestion to build brickworks within the Development Areas did not meet with universal approval.[6]

There was, of course, the Cabinet Unemployment Committee whose remit was to explore work for the unemployed. A memorandum by the Minister of Health outlined government policy thus:

> The policy of the Government, as we know, is a long term policy to find work for the unemployed by restoring to activity the industries of the country. It is agreed that no temporary palliatives for unemployment should be allowed which would postpone the return to industrial prosperity.
> Relief Works
> That rules out further substantial outlay on relief works. Experience has taught us that they do less good in the direct provision of work than harm in the indirect increase of unemployment, by depleting the resources of the country which are needed for industrial restoration.
>
> This does not, of course, apply to works which, although they are unlikely to be put in hand by unaided private enterprise, would have the effect of directly increasing national income. But such works have been practically exhausted by the efforts of recent years. It is hard indeed now to put forward proposals for relief works that are economically sound.
> Effects of enforced idleness
> Nevertheless, the damages and evils of maintaining many hundreds of workers in idleness on unemployment benefit, transitional payments and public assistance, are obvious and gross.[7]

Monthly statistics of the unemployment position allowed for unemployment insurance (from 1947)[8], and credits for weeks of genuine unemployment.[9] Also, where possible there was a move to place contracts in development and unemployment areas.[10] Understandably, the cost of administration for unemployment insurance and unemployment assistance was closely monitored.[11]

Perhaps there is no coincidence that the National Insurance Act 1946 included provision for employment payments for those who have exhausted their entitlement – at least there was under certain circumstances. The introduction set out the scope of the new regulations.

6   National Archives T 161/1249.
7   National Archives T 161/1277.
8   National Archives FO 1051/323.
9   National Archives LAB 12/495 and LAB 12/497.
10 National Archives BT 177/1315.
11 National Archives LAB 9/178 and LAB 9/203.

1. The Minister of National Insurance has now made the 'National Insurance (Extension of Unemployment Benefit) Regulation 1946' dated 21st December 1946, under which benefit may be paid in certain circumstances to persons who have exhausted their title to standard benefit (including any additional days under the General Scheme) as outlined in ML Circ. 82/602. Copies of the Regulations have already been sent to LOs.

2. Under the Regulations the first payments will relate to pay weeks beginning immediately after 10th February 1947. This means that LO action will have to be completed in time to enable recommendations to be obtained from Tribunals and claims rated before computation is due to take place in respect of such pay weeks. Orders-to-pay unemployment assistance (including 'Nil' orders) will remain operative – unless reviewed for some reason – until the end of the pay week which includes 10th February 1947.

3. The introduction of the new scheme has been announced in the press and members of the public have been advised not to make application before 13th January. Supplies of posters for exhibition at LOs will be available shortly. Supplies of the leaflet for issue to persons identified by LOs as being within the scope of the scheme, as well as to enquirers, should reach LOs by about 5th January 1947.

4. The regulations apply to both general and agricultural benefit (direct and indirect) and these instructions should be read as covering both types of benefit except where otherwise stated.

5. LOs will be responsible for identifying persons on the Live Register (excluding non-claimants) or who come on to the Register and who appear to be within the scope of the Regulations. In such cases LOs will initiate action to bring the scheme to the notice of the persons concerned and arrange for the taking of applications. Persons who are not on the Live Register or persons registered as non-claimants will be required to make applications of their own accord if they wish to be considered for extension of benefit.[12]

There were also sectors of the working population who were unable to claim as they were resident abroad for the majority of their time. For example:

At a meeting held on Friday 12th March, between the National Maritime Board and representatives of the Ministry of National Insurance and the Ministry of Transport, Mr Bowden and Mrs Yates pointed out that seamen who serve in foreign-going ships spend a large part of each year outside Great Britain and have, therefore, less opportunity of receiving medical benefit under the existing scheme of health insurance or treatment under the new health service. They said that the present scheme of health insurance recognises this by making rebates to the Approved Societies in respect of seamen, and they urged that the new scheme also should recognise it and should return a part of the contributions paid by seamen, so that there would be funds available for welfare.

12   National Archives PIN 7/292.

The view of the Ministry of National Insurance is, that all contributions paid by employed persons must be at flat rates. There can be no reduction in the rate, and no return of contributions on the score that particular workers have no opportunity of qualifying for certain benefits of the scheme. This is one of the basic principles of the National Insurance Act 1946.[13]

This matter was raised at a meeting held at Carlton Gardens on 12 March 1948 which was attended by members of the Ministry of National Insurance and the Ministry of Transport as well as several unions. The first topic recorded in the minutes was titled 'Unemployment benefit outside the United Kingdom' with the following decision being documented:

> The Chairman said that after further consideration the Ministry now proposed to provide in the draft regulations that seamen should be able to qualify for employment benefit for periods when they were outside the United Kingdom, provided that they put themselves in the charge of the British Consul or Shipping Master within fourteen days of the time when they ceased to be employed in a British ship or, if they had been detained in custody immediately on their release. This entitlement to benefit would be subject to all the usual conditions, and in particular would be subject to a disqualification for anything up to six weeks where it was found that the seamen had lost his employment through misconduct or had left it without good cause. The benefit would be paid outside the United Kingdom. It would be paid to a deputy chosen by the seaman or alternatively it would be kept until he returned to this country.[14]

This is just one example where the legislation was altered in a minor way to accommodate a group of workers who would have been at a disadvantage. There were others but this should serve as an example of the process followed to rectify these types of issues.

Even at this early stage in the introduction of the welfare reforms and the NHS there were discussions concerning the classification of the sick and non-sick, which was another problem needing resolution.

> The question is bound to occur from time to time whether a particular person who cannot be looked after at home should be admitted, as sick to a hospital or part of a mixed institution administered by the Board or, as non-sick, to accommodation provided or administered by the local welfare authority. Boards may already have had some experience, in discussing the future of mixed institutions, of the factors to be taken into account; but the following broad classification may not be unhelpful in deciding on doubtful cases.
> i)   Sick and therefore proper to the Board – patients requiring continued medical treatment or supervision and nursing care. This would include

13   National Archives PIN 22/62.
14   Ibid.

very old people who, though not suffering from any particular diseases, are confined to bed on account of extreme weakness.

ii) Infirm – and therefore proper to the local authority – persons who are normally able to get up and who could attend meals either in the dining room or nearby day-room. This class would include those who need a certain amount of help from the staff in dressing, toilet or in moving from room to room and also those who, from time to time, e.g. in bad weather, may need to spend a few days in bed.[15]

This particular report goes on to discuss how best to help long term patients deal with their normal affairs, particularly those with small friendship groups or no relatives living nearby.

There were also other issues with the new systems needing attention:

i) The Cabinet Social Services Committee resolved issues relating to death benefits as part of the National (Insurance Injuries) Bill.[16]

ii) Further amendments to the Industrial Injuries Bill including:

    a) Abolition of hospital deduction.

    b) Extension of death benefit to post injury wives.

    c) Increase of widower's benefit.

    d) Extension of payment of constant attendance allowances to past cases.

    e) Payment of benefit for first three days. It is now proposed that this payment should be made only after 12 days of incapacity have been experienced in the injury benefit period whether or not these days are consecutive.[17]

iii) Recovery from Liable Relatives.[18]

As one group of civil servants were working through the finer points of the Act ensuring equitable arrangements were available to all, another group was looking at some of the other administrative changes needed to make the new system a reality, including:

a) Termination of arrangements with Associations under Section 68 of the Unemployment Insurance Act 1935.[19]

b) A survey of the progress made in the United States towards a welfare state.[20]

c) The need to establish provision for accommodation for persons not ordinarily living in the area or with no fixed abode. This liability fell to the local authorities.[21]

---

15   National Archives MH 154/341.
16   National Archives T 161/1248.
17   Ibid.
18   National Archives AST 7/1129.
19   National Archives PIN 7/311.
20   National Archives FO 371/81763.
21   National Archives AST 7/1148.

d)   The need to establish provision of clothing for those with no alternatives.[22]

(a) National Assistance

An online English dictionary offers the following definition of a welfare state:

> A system whereby the state undertakes to protect the health and well-being of its citizens, especially those in financial or social need, by means of grants, pensions, and other benefits. The foundations for the modern welfare state in the UK were laid by the Beveridge Report of 1942; proposals such as the establishment of a National Health Service and the National Insurance Scheme were implemented by the Labour administration in 1948.[23]

It is so very easy to get bogged down in the detail of the post-Second World War legislation that it becomes difficult to understand the intent of the various elements of the relevant acts. Fortunately, in the case of the National Assistance Bill, there was a press conference on the 30 October 1947, outlining the basic premise of the legislation. The opening paragraphs were:

> This bill will complete the Government's social security plan. In addition to the new National Health Service (to which the Minister of Health has referred) and the scheme of family allowances, there is already on the statute book legislation providing for the new and comprehensive system of national insurance to be administered by my Department. When national insurance is in full operation, every citizen who has paid the requisite contributions will be able to claim benefit in the event, among other things, of sickness, industrial injury, unemployment and retirement in old age.
>
> But however complete a national insurance system may be, it cannot cover all the requirements of everyone unless benefits were to be paid without regard to contributions and raised to an extravagant level; the rate of benefit must be governed by the contributions people can reasonably be expected to pay.
>
> Accordingly, behind the insurance scheme there must be some service which can fill in any gaps by meeting actual need, and Part II of the Bill will provide this – it will provide a new state service of assistance for those not entitled for the time being to pension or benefit or, because of a high rent or other special circumstances, requiring a supplement to their pension or benefit. It is the Government's desire that the new service shall be one to which those in need can look for financial help without diffidence or loss of their self-respect. National Assistance therefore will round off the Government's social security measures.
>
> The new service will be financed entirely by the Exchequer and not, as in the case of National Insurance, partly from insurance contributions. It will be administered by the Assistance Board, to be renamed the National Assistance

---

22   National Archives AST 7/1167.
23   Oxford Dictionary on line, *definition of welfare state* <http://www.oxforddictionaries.com/definition/english/welfare-state>. (Accessed June 2014)

Board. It will take the place of the unemployment allowances and supplementary pensions now administered by the Board, and of the blind domiciliary assistance, tuberculosis treatment allowances and poor relief now administered by the local authorities.

Thus the Bill marks the end of the ancient Poor Law, the end of a story more than three hundred years since some of its provisions originated in the Poor Relief Act of 1601 passed during the reign of Queen Elizabeth ... [24]

As mentioned above, an infrastructure was needed to ensure implementation of the above was properly conducted. Figure 8.2 documents the members of the Board and the date their term of office expired. The documentation accompanying this also details the make-up of the Board.

Name	Term of office expired
Lord Soulbury (Chairman)	21st July 1948
Mrs Adamson (Deputy Chairman)	21st July 1948
Mr Hallsworth	21st July 1948
Dr Mallon	21st July 1948
Mr Asbury	28th June 1948
Mr W Betty	Sadly died in office

Figure 8.2. Founding members of the Assistance Board.[25]

The National Assistance Bill provides for the Board to consist of Chairman, Deputy Chairman and not less than one, nor more than four, other members of whom one should be a woman. This continues existing arrangements. The salaries of the Board are charged on the Consolidated Fund and are determined by the Treasury at the time of appointment; but the aggregate amount of the salaries must not exceed £12,000. The terms of office are fixed by the warrant of appointment. Chairmen have been appointed for seven years, for a member the normal term is three years but some recent appointments have been made for shorter periods in view of the change to be brought about by the present Bill. No member of the Board can be elected to sit in the House of Commons.[26]

The National Assistance Board was not a new concept, its predecessor having been commissioned in the 1930's, however in this form it was a vital part of the introduction of the welfare reforms.

As one might imagine, granting national assistance required an assessment of need, and a formal appeals process should someone think the decision not to provide

24   National Archives AST 7/913.
25   National Archives PIN 73/1.
26   Ibid.

assistance was an error. There are documents in the National Archives detailing the work of the National Assistance Appeal Tribunals[27]. Also the Padmore Report, a committee on Government Local Offices, was submitted in June 1946, which was signed by Mr Padmore of the Treasury. Its remit was:

> ... to consider, without set terms of reference, how best provision might be made for the local work of the Ministry of National Insurance and the Assistance Board, both when the various schemes of National Insurance and National Assistance are fully in operation and in the intermediate period. In considering what form the local organisations of the two Departments should eventually take we have examined three different propositions, to all of which objections have been put forward from one side or another, and a fourth which we think would give a large measure of the various advantages which the members who advanced them saw in the three other propositions. The four propositions are set out and discussed below. Finally, we offer some comments on the problems which will have to be worked out in the intermediate period.[28]

The four propositions were:

1. Proposition 1. That there should be one local organisation for the work of both Departments at the Regional Office as well as the local office level.
2. Proposition 2. That the two Departments should have distinct local organisations apart from the visiting service, which would be a common service on behalf of the Board.
3. Proposition 3. That the two Departments should each have their own local organisation including their own visiting staff, though with arrangements for the staff of one Department to make visits for the other when and where this would mean an appreciable saving of time.
4. Proposition 4. That the two Departments should have their distinct local staffs, but as far as possible they should share premises and minor common services.[29]

The following accompanies the report in the National Archives:

> As one might have expected on the introduction of an extensive scheme of social security some unforeseen developments took place which affected the way in which the recommendations of the Committee could be carried out.
> 1. When the basic pension rate was increased from 10s to 26s in October 1946 it was found that a great deal of enquiry from individual pensioners was necessary to establish whether they were entitled to the increased rate. This in turn meant that many personal interviews with pensioners were necessary,

---

27 National Archives PIN 16/24.
28 National Archives PIN 23/144.
29 Ibid.

and as the Ministry's visiting service had not reached the stage when they could undertake this themselves the Board's visiting officers undertook this work. The volume of this work remained fairly heavy until about the middle of 1947 but gradually disappeared thereafter.

2. In the Spring of 1947, the Board took over from the Customs and Excise Department the administration of the Old Age Pensions Act 1936. There were roughly half a million pensions in payment; a considerable body of staff had to be transferred with the work, and absorbed into the Board's organisation.

3. The Polish Resettlement Act of 1947 laid an entirely new duty upon the Board which meant considerable calls upon their staff.

4. At a later stage it became clear that the load of supplementary pensions work, which had fallen in October 1946 with the increase in the basic pension rate, was rising steadily with the increase in the number of pensioners and that it would increase very substantially in July 1948 when other classes of persons would be eligible for national assistance and the Board's rates of assistance for all classes would be increased.

5. The Ministry of National Insurance on the other hand did not find it necessary to build up an outdoor visiting staff before July 1948; but after the National Insurance Scheme got going they found that in addition to visiting the sick, which they had foreseen, a large volume of visiting was needed in connection with the failure to stamp insurance cards properly and failure to link contribution records under the new scheme with the records under the old scheme. This altered the complexion of their visiting work and in due course they decided it was necessary to reorganise their outdoor staff and integrate their inspectorate with the visiting staff in local offices ... [30]

Having established an infrastructure, albeit one subject to changing demands and therefore somewhat fluid – at least in the early days – the issue became one of helping those in need. Some examples of benefits introduced by the scheme included:

i) Adjustment of arrears of sickness or injury benefit under section 13 of National Assistance Act 1948.[31]

ii) Consideration of a grant to meet funeral expenses.[32]

iii) Discretionary powers of the Assistance Board to grant assistance to firemen not specifically covered by the National Assistance Bill, 1947.[33]

iv) Maintenance of deserted wives who were claiming national assistance.[34]

v) National assistance: eligibility of dependants of HM Forces personnel.[35]

30 Ibid.
31 National Archives AST 7/1394.
32 National Archives AST 7/1165.
33 National Archives HO 187/1090.
34 National Archives HO 45/25320.
35 National Archives AST 7/1154.

vi)   Treatment of payments to the blind, and general assistance for tax purposes.[36]

Of course there also needed to be a robust process for recovery of overpayment. This could take the form of someone who claimed for national assistance and receiving national insurance and industrial injuries benefits,[37] or recovery from liable relatives.[38] These two examples are typical of the types of recovery and not an exhaustive list.

The Assistance Board provided a focal point for all those in need, including old age pensioners. Some pre-meeting correspondence between the Assistance Board and the National Federation of Old Age Pensions Associations is illuminating.

To: Stuart King
Assistance Board
Vicarage House
Soho Square
London
23rd February 1946

Dear Sir,
I have to thank you for your letter of the 20th February in which you are good enough to say your Board is willing to receive a deputation from this Federation on Friday 15th March, which I have the pleasure of confirming.

My Executive Committee have now met to consider the points the deputation wish to raise which are:
1.   The regulations governing a national minimum standard for those who have no resources other than the main old age pension.
2.   That in computing supplementary or non-contributory pensions, a flat rate of 20/- (20 shillings or £1) of income shall be disregarded.
3.   That all war savings, whether pre-war or post-war, be disregarded.
4.   The attitude of the Assistance Board on rent allowances.
5.   The position of supplementary pensioners who respond to the appeal to sublet as a national emergency.
6.   The question of dependants allowances and war pensions in regard to supplementary pensions.
7.   The future relations of the Assistance Board in respect of the aged people
    ...[39]

The meeting took place as advertised. Using the above list someone within the Assistance Board organised a pre-meeting briefing to the rest of the Board, which is interesting as background information, but not relevant here. The minutes of the meeting are also in the same file as is a memorandum written by the member of the

36   National Archives IR 40/13472.
37   National Archives PIN 18/67.
38   National Archives AST 7/1195.
39   National Archives AST 7/857.

Assistance Board dated 18 June 1946. This memorandum is useful as it provides some of the documentation collated after the meeting. The first paragraph explains:

> When the Chairman and members of the Board received a deputation from the National Federation of Old Age Pensioners' Association on 15th March 1946, it was agreed that the Federation should be allowed to submit as evidence in support of their contention that the existing scale rates of supplementary pensions were inadequate, household budgets collected from supplementary pensioners. The April issue of 'Old Age Pensioner' (the Federation's monthly paper) contained a front page report of the interview with the Board and invited pensioners to send in their weekly budgets. The Secretary of the Federation has now forwarded 33 of these budgets out of the 'many hundreds of such letters received'. He does not say why only 33 have been submitted, nor on what basis the selection was made ... [40]

There followed a meeting with the Minister and his team followed by an announcement of some changes, the summary of which was:

a) The Government promised to increase old age pensions before the winter of 1946-47. Action fulfilled.
b) The pension increased rate will be payable from the first week in October and applied to both contributory and non-contributory pensioners.
c) The exchange of pension order books was begun and on Thursday 26 September 1946 old age pensioners between ages 60 and 70 started to receive their new books.

Unfortunately with no formal plan in place linking pension increases to inflation, the whole process was repeated on 31 March 1949, documented under the title 'Demand for increased pensions – Minister sees deputation'. Perhaps that might explain why a further deputation met the National Assistance Board on 7 December 1950, in this case the Scottish Pensioners Federation and the Welsh Pensioners Federation were also included in the discussions.[41]

The plight of pensioners continued to cause concern with the Ministry of Pensions and National Insurance. In a letter to Sir Harold Fieldhouse, who was at the time a member of the National Assistance Board, from the Ministry of Pensions and National Insurance, the question of pride was raised.

> Dear Mr Fieldhouse,
> The Minister is anxious to have information if possible about the degree of reluctance of retirement pensioners to apply for National Assistance although qualified for it, and is asking two questions in particular as follows:
> The first is whether an indication could be given of the length of time successful applicants for assistance could have been having assistance if only they

40 Ibid.
41 National Archives AST 7/1213.

had applied earlier. You have no figures I believe about this, but would it be possible for you to make a small sample enquiry covering say new applications at some specimen offices over the next fortnight – or something of that kind?

His next particular question was how many unsuccessful claims there were by pensioners. You have I think the number of unsuccessful claims of all kinds but not of claims by retirement pensioners to claim assistance I am sure the Minister would be glad to have it ... [42]

Of course anyone in retirement in the early 1950s would have had to have been over 60 which meant that they had lived through both world wars. I know from talking to my own grandparents that particular generation had a different perspective on life, losing relatives in both wars and suffering hardships hard to imagine now. At least the Minister of Pensions and National Insurance was trying to ensure this particular group of people suffered no more than necessary.

Whilst some within the Ministry of Pensions and National Insurance were dealing with issues relating to reluctance to claim entitled funds, others within the Ministry were faced with addressing an emerging problem of an altogether different type.

24th November 1949
Dear Kearns
Voluntary Unemployment
Although we have not yet said much about it in our instructions, we are not unmindful of the need to exercise the punitive powers contained in sections 10 and 51 of the National Assistance Act in the more flagrant cases of 'workshyness'.

We contemplate that eventually we shall have a standing instruction as to the submission of the really bad cases but at this stage we are trying to get a measure of the extent of the problem by calling for information in the form of an experimental report from one or two Regions, such as your own, where it is known that some cases have already come to notice.

I am enclosing 30 copies of a draft A instruction on the subject and I should be glad if you would arrange for this to be issued to your Area Officers with any covering local instructions you may think necessary ... [43]

Almost a year later, September 1950, there was still a problem.

Extract from Items of Interest – September 1950
Long term unemployed
The need for a special form of report in a case of an apparently able-bodied applicant unemployed for very long periods has been evident to Headquarters for some time and the necessary instructions have now been issued to the local staff. The Executive Officer handling the case is now required to prepare this special report in every assistance case arising in the future where:

42 National Archives AST 7/1206.
43 National Archives AST 7/1007.

1. Unemployment benefit ceases to be payable and a Ministry of National Insurance Tribunal refuses payment of extended benefit (extended benefit is payable after an unemployed person has exhausted his title to standard benefit but may be refused if a Tribunal is not satisfied that his is co-operating with the Employment Exchange and that he is willing to accept work, if necessary outside his normal occupation or his normal district, or to undertake training, if appropriate).

2. Assistance has been in payment for a long time and the applicant does not take advantage of the jobs offered to him or is frequently reported by the Ministry of Labour to have refused or abandoned jobs without reasonable cause.

    The object is to ensure that the case receives proper consideration before the period of unemployment has continued too long for any efforts at rehabilitation to be effective, and, if possible, to discover at this stage what is the reason for continued unemployment and whether any action can be taken in the interests of the applicant, of his family and the community, to prevent his becoming a permanent charge on public funds … [44]

(b) National Insurance

As one might imagine, many hours of thought went into drafting the National Insurance Bill and bringing it to the statute books. Equally many hours were spent in working out how to introduce the concepts once the Bill became law. The first stage in setting out the proposed timetable of operations, was to document the present position so that all of the civil servants involved in the process could understand the far reaching implications. The then present position was that:

a) Unemployment benefit was paid by the local offices of the Ministry of Labour and National Service acting as agents. The records of previous contributions and benefits were held by the Claims and Record Office based at Acton.

b) Sickness and maternity benefits were paid by several thousand Approved Society units on the basis of records held by these units. These records were used as the basis for the present scheme for providing free medical treatment to insured persons.

c) Old age and widows' and orphans' pensions were awarded and paid centrally by the offices at Blackpool, Edinburgh and Cardiff, but with negligible exceptions these offices held no record from which title could be ascertained – the records of Approved Societies were used for that purpose.

d) Worker's compensation was administered entirely outside of the departmental machine with the ordinary courts used to adjudicate in disputed cases.

e) Family allowance, an entirely new service, was awarded and paid centrally by an office which was set up in Newcastle.[45]

---

44 Ibid.
45 Based on a National Archives document MH 77/149.

There were many complex issues to deal with during the cutover to the new Welfare State system. These involved:

a)   The preparation of the necessary regulations of which there were a great number.

b)   The creation of a comprehensive network of local and regional offices for the administration.

c)   The establishment of a central office or central offices outside London at which records of all insured people will be kept.

d)   The recruitment of staff to run these central and local offices.

e)   Training of new staff.

f)   Maintain a sound standard of administration of the present scheme.[46]

There was also the new pension scheme to introduce and manage.

The incorporation of the Approved Societies into the new scheme was one of the countless issues needing attention. The following is a letter written to Mr Hawton at the Ministry of Health:

1st November 1945

You may have seen our Paper on the future of Approved Societies (S.S.(45)16) which was considered and approved by the Social Services Committee a week ago. In it we indicate in broad outline the steps by which we should propose to convert the present Approved Society system of health insurance administration into a state service. One of the points emerging is that we shall, at a fairly early date, be faced with the problem of ourselves having to administer the present benefits of Approved Societies; a necessary consequence of this would be that we should have to do something about the present individual additional benefit schemes of Societies.

So far as the cash benefits are concerned the problem is comparatively simple: at some convenient date we shall simply increase the present standard rates of benefit to a level which will enable practically all the existing additional cash benefits to be absorbed into the increases. Most of the remaining additional benefits provided by Societies will, however, ultimately be replaced by provisions of the National Health Service. The question then arises whether our arrangements will be ready by the date when we shall have to make a start with winding up Approved Societies and if not, what arrangements can be made to bridge the gap.

There may also be some present additional benefits which will have no counterpart in the new arrangements and which therefore, ought to be allowed to die with the Approved Societies. I believe too, that a few Societies will be found to have assets such as convalescence homes, in which your Department will be interested.

---

46   National Archives MH 77/149.

CONTRIBUTION 1s. 10d. a week. Date of entry into Insurance if after 3rd July, 1939.	RECORD OF CONTRIBUTIONS.									
	CONTRIBUTION YEAR ending 5th July, 1942, governing BENEFIT YEAR 1943.		CONTRIBUTION YEAR ending 4th July, 1943, governing BENEFIT YEAR 1944.		CONTRIBUTION YEAR ending 2nd July, 1944, governing BENEFIT YEAR 1945.		CONTRIBUTION YEAR ending 1st July, 1945 governing BENEFIT YEAR 1946.		CONTRIBUTION YEAR ending 7th July, 1946, (53 weeks) governing BENEFIT YEAR 1947.	
5.8.42	Contributions Credited.	Initials of Society Official.	Contributions Credited.	Initials of Society Official.	Contributions Credited.	Initials of Society Official.	Contributions Credited.	Initials of Society Official.	Contributions Credited.	Initials of Society Official.
CONTRIBUTIONS { July to Dec. PAID { Jan. to June	41 42		42 43	22 (W)	43 44		44 45		45 46	
Contributions allowed { July to Dec. on account of proved { unemployment { Jan. to June	41 42		42 43	26	43 44		44 45	51	45 46	47
Contributions allowed for notified incapacity or weeks before insurance began			H	W						
TOTAL CREDITED ...			52		51		51			
ARREARS DUE										
ARREARS PAID										

EFFECT OF ARREARS ON HEALTH INSURANCE BENEFITS.

1. The Health Insurance benefits payable to you during a Benefit Year (which begins on the first Monday in January) depend upon the number of contributions credited to you for the Contribution Year ended in the previous July.
2. If any arrears for a Contribution Year are due from you, your Health Insurance benefits will be reduced or suspended during the next Benefit Year unless you make up the arrears within the period of grace (which runs from the end of the contribution year to the 30th November).
3. Particulars of the arrears due for any contribution year should be notified to you by your Society by means of an Arrears Notice, and the notice will set out the amount of the requisite arrears payment, the manner in which it should be made, and the effect upon your benefits if you pay only part of the arrears.
4. If, for any Contribution Year, arrears are due, but no Arrears Notice has reached you by the 1st October following, you should ask your Society for one.
5. The payment of arrears does not entitle you to receive any benefit after your insurance has ceased.

PENSIONS BENEFITS.
The conditions governing title to contributory pensions will be found in Leaflet W.P. 6 B. (Widows' and Orphans' Pensions) and Leaflet O.A.P. 107B (Old Age Pensions). Copies of these Leaflets may be obtained at any Post Office.
Application for old age pension may be made at any time within four months before the applicant's 65th birthday.

TERMINATION OF INSURANCE.

A person who has ceased to be compulsorily insurable is advised to apply to his Approved Society for Memorandum 247 X which gives information as to the period during which insurance as an employed contributor continues, and the conditions for maintaining insurance as a voluntary contributor.

Figure 8.3. A payment card for an Approved Society. (Author's photograph)

We have been pressed to have our Bill ready for introduction by Christmas and it is important that we should know exactly where we are on the question of additional benefits ... [47]

Payments into the scheme for an Approved Society were monitored using a form as shown in figure 8.3.

The arrangement of clauses of the National Insurance Bill adequately sets out the scope of the final Act. The Bill was broken down into two parts, one describing the contributions and the second the benefits. The clauses cover:

Part I – Insured persons and contributions
1. Description and classification of insured persons.
2. Source of funds.
3. Number and class of contribution for any week.
4. Special provisions as to contributions of employed persons and employers.
5. Payment of contributions by Minister of Pensions.
6. General provisions as to payment and collection of contributions etc.
7. Persons to be treated as employers.

Part II. Benefit

Preliminary.

47 Ibid.

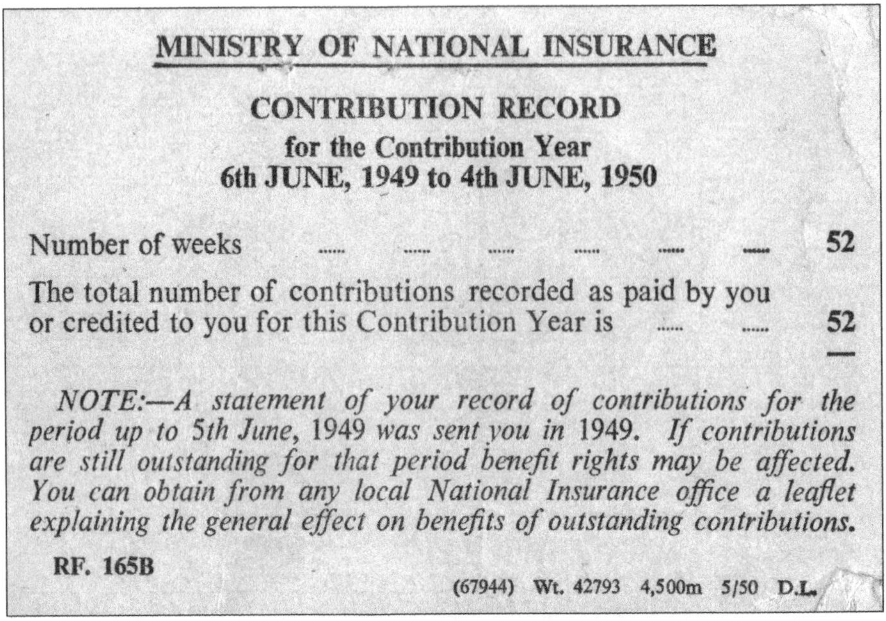

MINISTRY OF NATIONAL INSURANCE

CONTRIBUTION RECORD
for the Contribution Year
6th JUNE, 1949 to 4th JUNE, 1950

Number of weeks **52**

The total number of contributions recorded as paid by you
or credited to you for this Contribution Year is **52**

NOTE:—A statement of your record of contributions for the period up to 5th June, 1949 was sent you in 1949. If contributions are still outstanding for that period benefit rights may be affected. You can obtain from any local National Insurance office a leaflet explaining the general effect on benefits of outstanding contributions.

RF. 165B

(67944)   Wt. 42793   4,500m   5/50   D.L.

Figure 8.4. A contribution record card. (Author's photograph)

8.   Descriptions and rates of benefit and contribution conditions.

Unemployment and sickness benefit.
9.   Right to unemployment and sickness benefit.
10.   Duration of and requalification for benefit.
11.   Disqualifications and special conditions.

Maternity benefit.
12.   Maternity grant and attendance allowance.
13.   Maternity allowance.
14.   General provisions as to maternity benefit.

Widow's benefit.
15.   Widow's benefit.
16.   Widow's pensions in special circumstances.

Guardian's benefit.
17.   Guardian's allowance.

Retirement pensions.
18.   Retirement pensions.
19.   Retirement pensions for women.[48]

48 Ibid.

Payments into the new scheme were monitored using the form above, figure 8.4.

Underpinning the Act was the need for an efficient organisation able to provide the necessary service without requiring more staff than needed to fulfil the commitments. Mention was made earlier of the potential for the National Insurance organisation to work alongside of the National Assistance staff. Whilst the potential for combining both organisations where it was thought to be beneficial, there were some words of caution written by someone called EEB on 31 December 1946:

> Sir Godfrey Ince came to see me today. He said that he was seriously disturbed about Civil Service manpower and thought that unless something drastic was done quite soon there was a risk of another Geddes Axe.
>
> The Ministry of Labour has always been a decentralised department. Sir GI believed in decentralisation, but there was no doubt that a lot of local offices meant a big total staff. He had been disturbed to find that, notwithstanding the reductions in other branches, the growth of the Training Department meant that the total staff of the Ministry would not decrease by more than a thousand over the next twelve months.
>
> What disturbed him was to find that the Ministry of National Insurance were proposing to set up an organisation of local offices throughout the country which would parallel the Ministry of Labour organisation and would be two or three times as big; at least, in places in which the Ministry of Labour has a staff of 20, the Ministry of National Insurance were proposing a staff of 40 to 50.
>
> At the present time the Ministry of Labour were doing the unemployment insurance work for the Ministry of National Insurance on an agency basis. The proposal which had been agreed was to transfer the work from Labour to National Insurance, and Sir GI was disturbed to find that the Ministry of National Insurance were proposing to employ much larger staffs to do the job.
>
> Fundamentally he thought that the decision to have separate local offices for the two Ministries was wrong. It was impossible to separate the administration of unemployment insurance from the work of finding jobs ... [49]

The problem of how to organise staffing requirements for these two departments continued to cause some consternation and on the 8 January 1947 the following was written by J Wood.

> To: Mr J A C Robertson
> Staff Economy – Local Offices
> On the 1st January 1947 you were given a memorandum on the question of amalgamating local offices. The idea is prima facie attractive and in theory would lend itself to staff economies and reduce the vexatious trailing from office to office for the public. One can envisage a Central Government Office standing pari-passu with the Civic Centre.

49   National Archives T 216/15.

A closer examination of the proposal immediately brings one against a major difficulty, the absence of suitable buildings in which combined offices could be housed. On this point alone the policy must, therefore, be a long term policy, but I feel that the suggestion should not be shelved on this point alone. As a short term policy something might be done to coordinate the work of local offices, as, at the lower levels, I am sure there could be interchangeability of staff and it is at the level of clerical and sub-clerical staff that the bulk of the Civil Service now is ... [50]

The Minister also had a view.

21st January 1947
    Extract from a letter from the Minister of National Insurance
I have now had a chance of looking into the important questions raised in your letter of 10th December about our staff and premises requirements to bring the new National Insurance Scheme into effect. I have read the Economic Survey for 1947 and I fully realise the gravity of the position. You may take it as common ground between us that I shall do my utmost to restrict demands both for new manpower and premises to a minimum. At the same time I must stress the point in which you will agree, that we must not launch the new scheme of insurance without adequate equipment. To do so would bring lasting discredit on the scheme and on the Government ... [51]

Whilst the majority of the problems needing resolution were easy to deal with as they fit a set formula, the large number of people whose applications needed processing was one of the main issues. Additionally, there were problems to deal with issues of great complexity, for example:

In our discussion of the financial conditions to be offered under the Care and Maintenance Scheme last week, we considered in general terms the position of the pensioner admitted to hospital with an Unemployability Supplement (Un. Supp.) in payment or who applied for his supplement while still a patient in hospital.
    We have decided to refuse the Un. Supp. to single men without dependents where they are likely to be maintained in the institution for life or for a lengthy period, e.g. pensioners in mental hospitals or pensioners admitted for permanent institutional care.
    The forgoing minute sets out another aspect of the problem – the anomalies which arise where a pensioner drawing Un. Supp. is admitted for short periods of treatment or lengthy periods of remedial treatment. Such pensioners, being no longer eligible for sickness benefit by reason of the award of Un. Supp. do not suffer any home savings deduction irrespective of the length of the period of

50   Ibid.
51   Ibid.

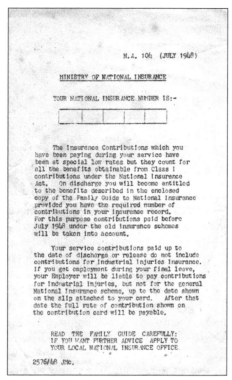

Figure 8.5. Service contributions to National Insurance. (Author's photograph)

treatment, until it can be determined or it is decided that the course of treatment is no longer remedial and the pensioner is classified 'permanently maintained'.

Now that the Un. Supp. has increased from 30s to 35s, with the possible addition 10s Comforts Allowance in suitable cases, it behoves us to reconsider our attitude to home savings and thus reduce the amount available for the use of pensioners during periods of in-patient treatment, having regard to the amount paid to other pensioners eligible for sickness benefit or additional treatment allowance, where after eight weeks hospital treatment a home savings deduction is made from the amount of sickness benefit paid by MNI (or additional treatment allowance paid by this Department).[52]

Those people serving their national service during the cut-over period were credited with the requisite contributions, even though their payments were at special lower rates than was normally the case, figure 8.5.

52   National Archives PIN 15/3703.

9   Rebuilding works

The ever increasing range of the German bombers, and the introduction of V1 and latterly V2 rockets, ensured that virtually every county of England and some in Wales, Scotland and Northern Ireland suffered bomb damage. In some cases the damage was extensive for example Belfast, Coventry and London, in other areas of the country the damage was less so. The War Damage Commission was set up to deal with some of the redevelopment of domestic and commercial buildings and roads, helping where it could those in dire need. In some cases, where there was a public building of national significance, such as the Houses of Parliament, offers of help arrived from many Commonwealth countries as well as the public purse.

Undoubtedly, the available, but meagre, public funds were never enough as all walks of life were affected. The Church of England suffered damage to cathedrals and churches, so much so that they made appeals in the United States for help as they realised they would never be able to cope on their own.[1] Perhaps the most iconic damage to a major church or cathedral which was so extensive it needed rebuilding, was that of Coventry Cathedral, more of which later. Buckingham Palace and the Houses of Parliament needed partially rebuilding and will also be discussed later.

A stroll round most of our larger towns will uncover plaques telling stories of post-war rebuilding. Three churches in London immediately spring to mind. One in the Strand which was later restored and is now perhaps the church in London most closely associated with the RAF. The second in East London near the Barbican has been left derelict as a permanent reminder, the third is in Piccadilly.

Designed by Sir Christopher Wren FRS, this church is now thriving with a notable attached coffee shop. One wonders how many of the coffee drinkers have noticed the plaque, figure 9.1, on the outside of the church.

This church was next door to major bomb damage in the commercial building the shop front for which is on both Piccadilly and St James'. Plans for the extensive work on this building are still available to view in the National Archives.

Of course the damage could have been worse – not that the people of London's East End may agree with me. The Civil Defence Camouflage Establishment at Leamington did what they could. For example the entry in the Biographical Memoir for William Edward Curtis FRS records the following:

1   National Archives FO 371/51753.

Figure 9.1. Restoration dedication plaque at St James's Church. (Author's photograph)

Professor of Physics at King's College Newcastle upon Tyne (1926-55). Appointed a Scientific Advisor to the Ministry of Home Security where he was put in charge of the Civil Defence Camouflage Establishment at Leamington with the title of Director of Camouflage and Decoy. This establishment was responsible for the camouflage of factories and civil airfields and was originally staffed by artists. Work was first concerned with daytime camouflage and later with night camouflage. One of the most successful pieces of work was creating a decoy of Sheffield which diverted numerous bombing raids from that city.[2]

More information concerning the work of the Civil Defence Camouflage Establishment is available in *Men Amidst the Madness*.[3] Good as this department was there was still damage to many properties.

(a) War Damage Commission/totally destroyed houses
Although the War Damage Act was passed into law in 1941, there were reservations in some quarters that there would still be problems at the end of the War. This letter, written almost two years before VJ Day expresses some of the concerns:

2   *Biographical Memoirs of Fellows of the Royal Society* Vol 16 1970, pp. 71-72, and *Who was Who 1961-1970*, (London: A. & C. Black Limited, 1967) p.270.
3   Rogers, David, *Men Amidst the Madness: British Technology Development in World War II*, (Solihull: Helion and Company, 2014).

8th November 1943

Dear Vincent,

In connection with our attempts to ensure that everything is ready which would be needed immediately hostilities ceased, one problem that has arisen is whether or not industrialists whose factories have been substantially damaged by enemy action will be in a position to repair or rebuild them immediately. This seems to raise three questions:

1. Whether the building labour and material will be available; this is part of the general problem of building capacity after the war which the Ministry of Works is co-ordinating.

2. Whether the approval of the local Planning Authority would be required and if so whether all Local Panning Authorities are or will shortly be in a position to give a decisive answer to applicants on this matter.

    You will appreciate that firms are already anxious to begin making their post-war plans and if they are held up while Local Authorities are considering the re-planning of their cities, the possibility of securing full employment in the immediate post-war may be seriously prejudiced.

3. Whether industrialists who have suffered from enemy action have yet been informed how much war damage compensation they will receive and when. I believe this matter concerns your Ministry, at any rate to some extent, since it links up with the question of whether or not town planning schemes will prevent the rebuilding or repairing of the damaged premises.

    I should be glad for any information which you can give me on points 2 and 3.

Yours sincerely[4]

There followed a flurry of letters between various government departments.

The issue of building materials and trained workers was not unique. Southampton was in urgent need. Their Chamber of Commerce wrote the following:

A Survey of adjustments of materials and personnel as a necessary preliminary to rehabilitation of Southampton.

General

a) The crux of the situation is in the building industry – the problem being to restore the fabric of the town to provide housing, schools, factories and shops in a balanced proportion.

b) As a preliminary an immediate survey of the town and docks areas should be undertaken and a long term programme of restoration planned in conjunction with the Town Planning and Reconstruction Committee.

c) It is assumed that in the early stages housing construction, both temporary and a permanent character, will be undertaken by the Local Authority. It is hoped however, that as quickly as possible the enormous potential of production by private enterprise will be called to action in this field.

4   National Archives HLG 71/1114.

d) It has been stated that twenty-two blitzed towns, of which two are on the south coast, one being Southampton, are to have priority in the first instance in order to achieve rehabilitation. In order therefore to implement this priority early release of materials and personnel to these twenty two areas should have a special priority of release over and above any other towns.

e) Before general building, even of a temporary nature can start, certain essential preliminary steps must be taken in order to provide the necessary ways and means or 'the tools' to make a start.

f) It is in this regard to this latter aspect of the problem that this Chamber submits the following observations.

g) Agreement is assumed on the necessity to provide employment and education, pari passu with the provision of increased housing accommodation.

Materials and goods
Priority of supply of all building materials together with the means of housing them by temporary hutments, should be granted to these towns, together with further hutments for the storage of food and clothing.

Planning
a) Little if any progress can be made in the very earliest stages of building without a definite declaration by the Local Authority as to their policy for acquisition of land etc. These can roughly be classified under three headings.
    i)   Properties through which new roads have been planned, as well as land, the depth of which is materially affected by road widening on one frontage and a new road at rear.
    ii) Properties facing Above Bar and High Street.
    iii) Road widening necessitating new building lines.

b) No building, even of temporary buildings, can be erected by existing means without knowledge of their tenure of the site.

c) It is further considered in the interests of the town and commerce that wherever possible some contribution to the ultimate lay-out of any building should be incorporated in the temporary building ... [5]

This lengthy document then addresses buildings other than for housing, schools or other institutions and personnel. Although this is one document from one town, the small number of other documents from other sources express common sentiments with those above, suggesting that there was common concern both at national and local level.

As with materials and labour, certainly at one time during the War, rubble from destroyed buildings was hard to obtain as its uses were many and varied.

5   National Archives CAB 124/841.

14th December 1943
To J H Burrell
Ministry of Home Security
Home Office

Dear Burrell,

Hardcore ex Portsmouth

Since the commencement of the Fire Risk Clearance Schemes the requests for hardcore, though numerous and sizeable, have up to now come in a steady flow, and have been satisfied without too much difficulty, but the reduction in labour which the War Debris and Disposal have suffered recently now coincide with increased demands, and the question of priority arises.

With the exception of one small demand for rubble for Fareham Labour Camp, we have not had demands which purported to be directly connected with the 'Phoenix' programme, but there is reason to believe that a number of recent requests are for works closely associated to Phoenix, as for instance, and Admiralty (RNAS) request, one for the Air Ministry No 14 Works Area for jobs in Hampshire, and certain War Department demands Via London Region ... [6]

The Air Ministry used vast quantities of rubble, mainly as hardcore for runways. Some of the rubble came from bombed buildings and some from pits. A meeting of the London Civil Defence Region discussed the issue of hardcore for the Air Ministry one agenda item of which was the distribution of tippers between Freckenham (a village just north of Newmarket) and No 10 Works Area:

> Mr Talbot said that 85 War Debris Survey lorries had now been sent to Freckenham, out of the 150 originally promised. Mr Miler stressed the urgency of this work, and agreed to lend 50 lorries to the War Debris Survey. It was agreed that the War Debris Survey should find additional drivers and work up to a total of 100 lorries as soon as conditions at the pit were suitable. The Air Ministry agreed to obtain the remaining 50 lorries from Sir Robert McAlpine and Sons ... [7]

In a further document in the same National Archives folio, some of the needed quantities of hardcore were documented:

> ... as a result of this review the Air Ministry have asked for the supply of approximately 300,000 cubic yards of hardcore for priority work on aerodromes in No 10 Works Area and a further 115,000 cubic yards for delivery to Eye and Ely, on a basis of a 10 week programme. It was proposed

6   National Archives HO 186/2483.
7   Ibid.

to arrange for monthly deliveries of approximately 120,000 cubic yards by rail and water and 13,000 cubic yards by road to the nearest sites …

With so much need for rubble, and therefore a ready market, perhaps it is not surprising that some of the removal was not sanctioned!

Dear Sir,
                    Removal of building materials from bombed sites
Enquiries are being made into the unauthorised removal of a large quantity of building materials and rubble from bombed sites in Southampton, and it will be necessary to produce to the Court, before which proceedings may be instituted in these matters, evidence of the ownership of the materials removed. There is some doubt in the minds of the former owners of the properties concerned as to the ownership of the materials at the time they were removed, that is, after a claim for total loss had been made to the War Damage Commission.

The position is further complicated by the fact that in some instances the powers of the local authority under Regulation 50 of the Defence (General) Regulations has been made for the Borough Engineer to enter upon the premises and remove materials for use in repair work on other damaged properties or similar grounds authorised under the Regulations.

From my Detective Sergeant Gibbon's telephonic communication with you, I gather that the building materials referred to remain the property of the original owners until such times as they are actually removed by the Corporation, and if they are stolen before an order made by the Council can be put into effect, the property is still vested in the owners of the premises.

Would you kindly let me have a statement in writing from yourself, or let the name and address of the person who can give this evidence …
Yours faithfully
F T Tarry
Chief Constable[8]

Some undated notes of a meeting of members from the Royal Institute of British Architects (RIBA), the Chartered Surveyors' Institution (CSI) and the War Damage Commission discussed the formation of an advisory committee the remit for which was to offer guidance on the rebuilding programme. The first order of business was to appoint officers.

The appointment of a Chairman was first discussed and there was a general opinion that before this happened the meeting should have an outline of what the duties of the Committee would be. Mr Murphy was invited to furnish a broad outline of the procedure for rebuilding flat houses (see below) and the direction in which it was felt the proposed Advisory Committee

8   Ibid.

could assist in resolving difficulties on the professional advisors side which would inevitably arise during the 'teething' stages of the scheme … [9]

Although the aforementioned meeting remained undated, a letter written on the 20th October 1945, outlined the formation of this advisory committee, inviting regional housing managers to submit concerns and questions. The topic of most concern was that of so called 'flat' houses, the generic name for a scheme to rebuild houses in groups using as far as possible one building contractor and one architect. The rationale for using one contractor and architect was one of economies of scale where professional fees were concerned and reduced building waste/increased buying power/ lower materials costs. Naturally where a whole street or neighbourhood was destroyed very few builders were of sufficient size to deal with the whole project. Additionally with so many house owners there was usually at least one owner who appointed his own architect. There was much to do.

As part of the cost reduction effort the War Damage Commission produced an explanatory pamphlet in agreement with the Federation of Building Trades Employers, detailing the procedure in arranging for the repair of war damaged buildings and the assessment of payments of costs and works. The first paragraph of this pamphlet outlines the scope of the document.

> Under the War Damage Act 1943, the War Damage Commission is required to make payments in respect of war damage sustained on land. When the land includes buildings the value payments will usually be made if the property is classified as a total loss under the general provisions of the Act, but payments of cost of works will usually be made in other cases. This pamphlet is concerned solely with payments of cost of works. [10]

There were many letters and applications for funding as one might imagine. Even streamlining the process as much as possible and endeavouring to work with one builder and architect, the costs were still high, as mentioned in a letter to the Director of Claims dated 17 September 1945.

> … it may be that we can satisfy the objection you are raising to early agreements of this kind by alteration in the phrasing of the letter. Suppose I amend it to read:
> 'The Commission will be prepared to consider a claim for the actual cost not exceeding £765, plus a fixed fee of £113.5.0 per house, on completion of the work specified. Regard will be had to important changes in conditions or circumstances which occur at the time of or during the rebuilding, provided there is immediate consultation and agreement with the Commission for such an adjustment …' [11]

Then as now builders need space. Small domestic jobs require somewhere to work

9   National Archives IR 34/1162.
10   National Archives IR 34/1141.
11   National Archives IR 34/1165.

away from the area under construction. Rebuilding houses, indeed whole streets in some cases, required land. Some for the site office and the stocks of building materials, yet more land for temporary accommodation for the workers. In some cases these temporary villages were there for a long time – especially if there were a number of houses in one street needing rebuilding. On occasions this caused problems.

28th September 1945
Dear Sir
I have been asked by the Clerk of Kent County Council to write to you regarding the possibility of releasing the site of 53, Sherwood Park Avenue.
   The present position is that this site is occupied by one of the camps used for housing SRS building labour and I am not in a position to give you any ideas as to when it will be possible to dismantle the camp and release the site.
Yours faithfully
Assistant Director
Mobile Labour Services[12]

The return letter further outlined the problems of land utilisation.

Ministry of Works
Dean Bradley House
Horseferry Road

18th October 1945
Sir,
                        Special Repair Service camp no 43, Sidcup
With reference to previous correspondence held with the Assistant Director of Mobile Labour Services of this Ministry regarding the site of 53, Sherwood Park Avenue, Sidcup, I am directed by the Minister of Works to state that owing to the shortage of accommodation for men employed on repairing bomb damaged houses, it has been decided that it is not possible to give up the Special Service Repair Services camps at present.
   It is regretted that your site cannot yet be released, but the camp will be removed as soon as is practicable.[13]

It will add no value to this discussion to list all of the service camp sites. This particular example was site number 43, it suggests that there were many of them! Other correspondence in the same folio is of a letter documenting that there were 24 men employed on this site, which suggests many houses needing repair and therefore a significant time needed to occupy the land.
   Of course the builders needed a formal process to obtain land for these camps. The land was requisitioned for the camps by the County Councils on behalf of the Minister

12   National Archives IR 34/1168.
13   Ibid.

of Home Security. Reversing this requisition notice was additional paperwork needed at the end of the job. Unfortunately in at least one case the paperwork for the land requisition did not take into account the land used for the camp was to have had a rebuilt house on it. An example of this is documented in the same folio as the above. Incidentally in London alone there were camps in Fulham, Hammersmith, Hampstead, Islington, Hackney, Poplar, Stepney, Greenwich, Woolwich, Lewisham, West Ham, East Ham, Camberwell, Acton, Barnet, Brentford and Chiswick, Ealing, Harrow, Enfield, Twickenham, Heston and Isleworth – to name a few![14]

With skilled labour in relative short supply, the idea of moving builders from one camp to the next took shape.

9th July 1946

Dear Murphy,

We have spoken in the past about a programme of work which our Mobile Labour Force, which has taken the place of the old SRS, might do in blitzed towns and other difficult areas where the Labour Force is too small for local needs.

We have recently discussed things further with the Ministry of Health, and the programme is beginning to take shape. The question has two aspects, first during the life of the Mobile Labour Force, and then after it has been taken over by a semi-independent National Building Corporation.

As you know local committees exist in most of the blitzed areas, including representatives of your Commission with those of other Departments and Local Authorities concerned. These Committees have been working out a programme according to the labour force which they have at their disposal, and I gather most of them have waiting lists of jobs which require imported labour. No doubt a proportion of these consist of totally destroyed houses, which are to a large extent your responsibility … [15]

With so many houses to rebuild and locations to supply it was not surprising that delays for wood were common.[16,17] Where materials could be re-used there was the inevitable issue of who paid for the pre-work needed in the salvage of the materials, for example:

5th June 1946

Dear Murphy,

Deptford have raised a question on LS3 contracts regarding salvaged bricks. They feel that as things stand it does not appear that a contractor would obtain the percentage normally applicable to salvage materials in respect of bricks cleaned and restacked on the site by himself and that accordingly there is no incentive for him to take the maximum of care when demolishing or stripping existing work.

14   Ibid.
15   National Archives IR 34/1173.
16   National Archives IR 34/1170.
17   National Archives IR 34/1174.

Moreover, Deptford point out that no provision has been made in the contract for the handling, cleaning and stacking of bricks.

I should like to know what you feel about this. I should have thought we ought to say that where the Supervising Officer considers that there is a substantial number of bricks becoming available in the course of the contractor's necessary work of demolition, then if the Supervising Officer considers that cleaning and stacking for re-use is advisable, charges at day rate might be allowed as an addition to the contract.

Yours sincerely.[18]

In an ideal world the rebuilding work would have been quick and involved the occupants prior to war damage, i.e. the property retained by the owner throughout the process. We don't live in an ideal world!

3rd November 1945
E Price

War Damage Commission

Dear Sir,

I have purchased the above site, together with war damage rights for rebuilding from Mr Wootton and the solicitors who have acted for me are Messrs Few and Kester.

Mr Few has written to tell me that you warned him privately that it was desirable to deal with the matter within two years. I would like to make my position clear; I have purchased this site with a view of building in about two or three years' time when I retire and as I am at present living in a railway company's official house, it is better for me to remain where I am until such time as I retire. If, on the other hand, the house is completed before my retirement, there might be some difficulty regarding its non-occupation for a period.

I should be extremely obliged if you would let me know whether, in these circumstances, you still consider that it is desirable that the house should be completed within two years.

I gathered in an interview which Mr Hammond was good enough to give me some time ago that it was immaterial whether I commenced building now or five years hence but my requirements would best be met if I could know that I could build in say three years.

Yours sincerely.[19]

Others held back their rebuild until more materials became available:

… it has been suggested that in some cases, owners have consulted architects who are already over-burdened, and that considerable delay in preparation of the necessary specifications, etc. is therefore occurring; it has also been

18 National Archives IR 34/1171.
19 National Archives IR 34/1177.

suggested that owners are holding back until all kinds of materials are more freely available, and until they can have their houses rebuilt more nearly like the original than is now possible. Clearly both these reasons are correct in a proportion of cases, but we are not sure that there may not be other reasons which have not so far emerged ... [20]

Clearly materials costs were part of the reason houses were built to a lower specification than those they replaced. At every stage the local authorities were asked to reduce costs or to keep costs fixed as far as possible.[21]

In some cases, alternative uses for the land were proposed (this example from 14 October 1946).

> ... you wrote some time ago regarding the proposal to build schools on the sites of a number of destroyed houses in East Ham. Much has happened since you wrote, and it now appears that some sites will be compulsorily acquired under the authority of the Board of Education, and others under the authority of the Ministry of Town and Country Planning.
> A number of sites, however, will remain available for reinstatement of the destroyed houses ... [22]

There are always dilemma when running a business. Balancing current needs against future capabilities, positioning assets against potential expansion. In many ways reconstructing housing was the easier task compared with business districts. Business leaders continually look to the future evaluating strategies for growth and in some cases creating opportunities. However, it is easier to plan for the future if your business is operating in premises capable of satisfying the needs of the day. The Hull Incorporated Chamber of Commerce and Shipping report of their sub-committee to their main Council provides an insight.

> The views of the Chamber of Commerce on the Abercrombie proposals for dockising the River Hull have already been conveyed to the Hull Corporation, to the City Engineer and to the experts appointed by the Corporation.
> Whilst the Chamber is strenuously opposed to any proposals for dockising or canalising the river, the Old Harbour remains an essential element in the Hull water carriage system and, as such, should be properly conserved as a tidal waterway.
> In order that Hull may be in a position to cater and compete for post-war trade, the port must be properly equipped. The immediate restoration of all facilities in the river Hull area which are necessary to meet trade requirements and which have been destroyed by enemy action is paramount – coupled with improvements on pre-war accommodation and lay-out.

20 National Archives IR 34/1176.
21 National Archives IR 34/1179, IR 34/1183, IR 34/1184.
22 National Archives IR 34/1188.

For the same reason, it is imperative that there should be no further demolition of sound assets. One of the strongest objections to the Abercrombie proposals is that, if adopted, they would probably result in greater demolition and the temporary loss of buildings and trading and manufacturing assets than resulted from air raids. It is recognised that long-term alternatives involve some demolition.

It is a matter of regret that the continued delay in arriving at decisions regarding applications from commercial interests for permission to rebuild is holding up enterprise. In view of the present military situation, it is to be deplored that many industrialists have not even been able to instruct their architects to draw plans. It is emphasised that many members of the forces will return to find their places of employment and their plant and tools destroyed and not replaced. This will have a serious effect on the restoration and development of trade, with repercussions on prosperity, employment levels and local rate income ...

... the sub-committee appointed by the Chamber submits the following suggestions for immediate improvements in the River Hull areas:

a)   The proper planning and widening of streets and roads in the area in order to enable existing businesses to develop in those cases where further immediate demolition is unnecessary. The bridges over the Victoria Dock entrance need strengthening to meet the needs of heavier motor traffic.

b)   Removal of air raid debris from the River Hull – after over four years, the consequential silting is abnormal and will require special attention.

c)   The general dredging of the river to secure safe navigation and berthing; the levelling of adjacent berths; and the repairing of the banks of the river.

d)   Reinstatement of destroyed mooring piles and the re-siting and/or repair of the remaining mooring piles together with the provision of new mooring piles to meet the requirements of river traffic.

e)   Adequate lighting of the roads, streets and staithes adjoining the river.

f)   Completion of the change-over from DC to AC power in the river area.

g)   The ladders for the use of vessel men on the banks of the river need overhauling. Some need extensive repairs. In other cases, the spikes or pegs should be replaced by new ladders.[23]

Of course most of the wish list above did not relate to bomb damage but a desire for the rebuilt area to be better than it was pre-war. There is nothing wrong with the plan, it is merely a case of resources and the balance of longer term potential against the shorter term need to create a workable infrastructure.

As one might imagine the problems faced in Hull were typical of many ports.

Privately owned port warehouses

The Board of Trade's investment programme includes an estimate of £750,000 for building licences in 1950 for port warehouses. This is nearly £500,000 less

23   National Archives HLG 79/263.

than had been hoped for but is necessary to meet the very substantial reduction required in the miscellaneous sector of investment.

1. Bristol. Approximately 540,000 sq. ft. was lost, of which 125,000 sq. ft. has been rebuilt and a further 176,000 sq. ft. provided on an existing estate at Avonmouth. The only scheme likely to come forward this year is for Bristol Industries, Brandon Wharf, at a cost of £12,000, with an area of 8,000 sq. ft.

2. Hull. Of the total estimateed loss of 500,000 sq. ft. (230,000 sq. ft. by civil fire), the reconstruction of 100,000 sq. ft. at a cost of £130,000 has been approved. No further schemes are expected within the next twelve months.

3. Southampton. Most of the damaged warehouses were Southern Railway property and any projects coming forward this year will be very small.

4. Liverpool. Estimated loss by enemy action was 3.2 million sq. ft. of which 750,000 sq. ft. was reinstated prior to 1948. 443,000 sq. ft. at a cost of £552,000 was licensed in 1948 and 1949. The proposed programme for 1950 is for warehouses covering 190,534 sq. ft. at a cost of £240,000 and a steel consumption of 852 tons. All the schemes are for the Liverpool Warehousing Company who own over 75% of the total private warehouses in the port.

5. Manchester. Although the loss of capacity in Manchester was smaller (590,000 sq. ft.) than in Liverpool, the individual premises are much larger and the programme cannot easily be spread over a long period. 170,000 sq. ft. at a cost of £236,000 was approved in 1948 and 1949.

The North Western Region have now submitted the following proposals for 1950, figure 9.2.

	Coat	Area	Steel tons
Port of Manchester Warehouse Ltd.	£93,977	35,200	698
Lloyds Packing Warehouses Ltd.	£275,000	171,250	1,060
Total	£368,977	206,450	1,758

Figure 9.2. North Western Region proposals for 1950.

6. London. Estimated loss by enemy action was 3¾ million sq. ft. of which about 1.3 million sq. ft. has been reinstated or is in process of reconstruction. Approval is required in 1950 for an area of 302,377 sq. ft. costing £432,000 with a steel consumption of 1,764 tons. The Regional Office advise, however, that licences for £150,000 worth of the work on these projects will not be required until 1951. The lower figure of £266,675 has, therefore, been included in the 1950 programme. To this must be added £35,800 for supplementary licences for schemes started in 1948 and 1949. Rising cost is the main reason for the supplementary licences. There are two major projects, figure 9.3.

	Area	Cost	Steel tons
PR Buchanan	116,530	£152,500	606
Butlers Wharf Ltd.	114,000	£185,810	900

Figure 9.3. London projects.[24]

The examples above are just that. A small sector within a much larger problem. In all cases there was competition for funding, labour and materials. However, this example does demonstrate the vast sums of money, the time taken to restore this financial sector and the extent of the damage.

Whilst there were many issues to resolve in the warehousing industry, arguably more complex problems were faced with war damage to buildings involving the health sector.

> St Thomas' Hospital
> London
> 30th September 1950
> Dear Godber,
> You will remember that I mentioned to you a short time ago the question of approaching the Ministry about temporarily taking over a property near the Hospital for accommodating departments which have to be turned out of their existing quarters, to enable the demolition of the buildings in which they are housed to take place as the first step in the reconstruction of the Hospital.
>
> The property concerned is a large warehouse at 8, Leake Street and the Governors own the leasehold in it as part of their endowment fund. It is very near the main building here and its use for decanting purposes would be a much more satisfactory and cheaper alternative to the erection of temporary buildings … [25]

There were many and varied issues needing resolution here so that patients could be treated in hygienic facilities in a timely manner.

Adding further examples to the above may not add value. Whilst each case had unique elements, all involved the basic requirements of money, time and resources.

(b) Transport infrastructure

A falling bomb wreaks havoc wherever it lands. Roads, bridges, railway lines etc. There are recorded instances of all types of bomb damage to these and other parts of the transport infrastructure. There was a wartime government establishment part of which assessed impact damage so they could determine the type of explosives used. This organisation, known as the Department of Scientific and Industrial Research or DSIR, was active in many fields during the War[26] including bomb damage to roads. As

24   National Archives BT 64/2976.
25   National Archives MH 89/158.
26   Rogers, David, *Men Amidst the Madness: British Technology Development in World War II*, (Solihull: Helion and Company, 2014).

early as January 1942 they proposed publishing information on a number of aspects of bomb damage to roads including:

i)   Earth movements – permanent and transitory – penetration depth of bombs – crater sizes – compression chambers.
ii) Visible signs of bomb damage and how to assess damage below ground – in towns, on embankments and in cuttings.
iii) Radius and extent of damage to services of various kinds.
iv) The filling of craters – importance of consolidation, with settlement to be expected.
v)   Temporary surfacings.
vi) Repair of damaged surfaces, order of repair, precautions to be taken during repair, temporary and permanent repairs.
vii) Temporary bridges over craters.
viii) New roads over bombed ground.
ix) Damage to building foundations by bombs in roadway.[27]

The point here is that there was an organisation whose expertise was available in dealing in all of the issues presented to them by many local and national government officers faced with the task of roadway repairs. The damage to services was extensive, figure 9.4. The following information covers the period 1 September 1940 to 31 December 1941. The total number of incidents affecting highways was approximately 9,860, though several minor cases of damage are not included in this figure.

	Incidents
Gas mains	10,519
GPO mains (defined as one containing over 50 pairs – the number of smaller cables damaged was considerably larger)	1,685
Water mains	6,845
Main sewers (LCC)	411
Main sewers, Groups 6-9	23
Thames floods defences	101
Bridges over roads or carrying roads over railways, rivers or canals	61
LPTB incidents affecting highways	23

Figure 9.4. Damages to services over a 16 month war period.[28]

This same report also documents bomb damage to sewers etc. in Coventry, as an example of a town badly affected by air raids. This table covers four pages and includes the street names and the types of pipes affected. There were so many projects affecting the transport network that I doubt any one person read information on all

27 National Archives DSIR 27/39.
28 Ibid.

of the programmes. There was an organisation called the Investment Programmes Committee which was able to take a holistic view of the rebuilding programmes at a high level.

Dated 24 March 1948 there was a document concerning the *Incidence of investment cuts in dock and road programmes on development areas and Merseyside*, part of which reads:

> ... as regards road works, it was agreed that the arguments put forward by the Ministry of Transport in IPC (WP) (48) 36 were sound, i.e. that it was impracticable to alter the balance of road work in favour of particular areas within the very limited resources now available, and that it was illogical to ask highway authorities in the areas under consideration to discharge road-men already in their employ, and, at the same time to reduce cuts in road improvement works in those areas as compared with the rest of the country. It was felt that there must be some relaxation in the restrictions which had been imposed on labour for road maintenance, if additional road work in the development areas and Merseyside was to be encouraged. It would not, however, be possible to make a separate allocation of materials for this particular purpose.
>
> The Committee were informed that the Ministry of Labour had prepared for the Distribution of Industry Committee a list of other areas which should be treated for this purpose in the same way as the development areas and Merseyside, and it was agreed that similar considerations with regard to road maintenance would apply in these areas.
>
> It was also understood that the Ministry of Transport were proposing to suggest that over the country as a whole there should be some machinery developed for relating the discharge of men from road maintenance to the demand for agricultural and other essential work. Some alarm was felt at this suggestion, which might have the effect of nullifying capital investment cuts ... [29]

The effect of closing bridges for repairs sometimes created more impact than closing roads, for the obvious reason that in most cases there were other roads available, whereas in some towns there may have been only one bridge over a particular river. At first glance one might think that the larger cities with more than one bridge might have been able to cope. This was not always the case as there were often more bombs dropped on larger cities.

> The following are the available particulars of damage to railway bridges over the Thames. I do not think that either of the Charing Cross cases can be called damage to the bridges.
>
> i)   Victoria, Grosvenor Road Bridge. 23:43 hrs. on 8th September. HE bomb dropped on Grosvenor Road Bridge stopping traffic on all lines.
>
> ii)   Charing Cross. 01:08 hrs. on 25th September signal box on fire, but as far as is known, no damage to the structure of the bridge.

29   National Archives MT 39/463.

iii) Charing Cross. 08:48 hrs. on 8th October, oil and HE bombs fell on station adjacent to bridge. Considerable damage to station but, as far as is known no damage to the bridge itself.[30]

Bridges over the tidal portion of the
River Thames damaged by enemy action

i) Tower Bridge (City Corporation). Hydraulic main transmitting the power for operating the bascules was severed and a portion of it carried on one of the high level foot bridges and destroyed; the bridge was in the 'closed to road' position when this happened, and until the main was repaired could not be moved. The bridge was out of action for a little less than six days.

ii) Waterloo Bridge (LCC).
a) 8/9th September. Oil incendiary on new bridge. Shuttering burned and some reinforcing bars damaged.
b) 28/29th September. Temporary bridge. Bomb on footway and bottom boom of main girder damaged. Repaired 30th September.
c) 7/8th October. New bridge. Four small incendiaries, damage to shuttering.
d) 14/15th October. New bridge. Small incendiary. No damage.
e) 15/16th October. New bridge. 2 HE bombs, small damage to concrete and plant.

iii) Westminster Bridge.
a) 7/8th September. Damage to parapet and pavement on Lambeth Approach. No damage to bridge.
b) 16/17th September. Bomb or shell on footway, slight damage to paving and parapet on bridge.

iv) Albert Bridge. 17/18th September. Incendiary bomb on Toll House. Slight damage to woodwork.

v) Battersea Bridge. 10/11th September. Two incendiary bombs on wood block paving. No damage.

vi) Kew Bridge. Slight damage to parapet on one occasion. No interruption to traffic.[31]

London bomb damage also affected the underground network. This report covered bomb related damage over a 24 hour period ending 7:00am 2 November 1940.

a) District Line. Suspected unexploded bomb. Line suspended between Southfields and Wimbledon.
b) Piccadilly Line. No trains from Kings Cross to Finsbury Park due to damaged tunnels.
c) Northern Line. No trains between Mornington Crescent and Warren Street due to damage between Mornington Crescent and Euston. No service

---

30   National Archives MT 6/2765.
31   Ibid.

between Tooting Broadway and Clapham Common due to damage at Balham Station.

d) Metropolitan Line. No service operating between Kings Cross and Farringdon due to the damaged tunnel between these two places. No services Hammersmith to Ladbroke Grove due to the unexploded bomb which still exists at Latimer Road.[32]

Of course post-war reconstruction plans started during the war for transport infrastructure as they did for everything else. The Railway (London Plan) Committee 1944 were no exception. The Final report to the Minister of Transport was dated 3 March 1948. Sometimes known as the Inglis report it has the following composition, figure 9.5, and terms of reference.

Member	Background Information
Professor Sir Charles Inglis FRS	Chairman
Mr Geoffrey Crowther	Editor of *The Economist*
Mr F A Harper	Principal Assistant to the Chief Mechanical and Electrical Engineer, British Railways (London Midland Region)
Sir Eustace Missenden	Chairman of the Railway Executive (Formerly General Manager of the Southern Railway)
Lieut.-Col. Sir Alan Mount	Chief Inspecting Officer of Railways, Ministry of Transport
Sir George L Pepler	Late Chief Technical Advisor, Ministry of Town and Country Planning
Mr J C L Train	Member of the Railway Executive (Formerly Chief Engineer, London and North Eastern Railway)
Mr A B B Valentine	Member of the London Transport Executive (Formerly Operating Manager (Railways), London Passenger Transport Board)

Figure 9.5. Membership of the Ingles Report.[33]

Terms of Reference

To investigate and report upon the technical and operational aspects of those suggestions made in the County of London Plan 1943, which relate to the main line and suburban railway system of London, both surface and underground, bearing in mind that these suggestions are intended to contribute towards and form part of a comprehensive scheme for the re-development of the area in question.

The Committee should include in their examination of the problem any alternatives to or modification of the suggestions made in the plan which the Railway Companies of the London Passenger Board may wish to submit, and

32 National Archives MT 6/2767.
33 National Archives MT 6/2791.

should have due regard to the requirements of traffic and to the convenience of the travelling public, and to any schemes of improvements which the Railway Passenger Transport Board have in mind.

The Committee were further requested to take into consideration the relevant recommendations of the City of London and Greater London Plans.[34]

Professor Sir Charles Inglis FRS was an interesting choice for Chairman, given the experience of the other Members. His Royal Society Biographical Memoir provides some insight.

The bridge stress work did not exhaust Inglis's interest in railway problems. In 1931 he accepted an invitation to become a member of the Advisory Committee on Scientific Research which had been set up by Sir Josiah Stamp under the chairmanship of Sir Harold Hartley. The object of the Committee was to guide and stimulate scientific work in the London Midland and Scottish Railway and to define problems that could best be studied extra-murally. Inglis was quick to see that many of the fundamental railway problems arose from the interaction of the wheel on the rail. He was first attracted particularly by the problem of overcoming the phenomenon of bogey hunting, the violent lateral oscillation that occurs under certain conditions and which can render passenger travel so uncomfortable.[35]

Sir Charles was a Fellow of King's College, Cambridge and Professor of Mechanism and Applied Mechanics in the University of Cambridge. He was knighted in 1945.[36] Interestingly, his sponsors for his election to Fellowship of the Royal Society included some impressive figures, active in both World Wars; J A Ewing, D Clerk, J E Petavel, H Darwin and R T Glazebrook.[37]

The summary of conclusions of this report were:

i)   *Inner goods ring.* The use of northern arc of the Inner Circle is not recommended, as the proposals in our previous report require its retention for passenger traffic.

ii) *Outer goods ring.* The main work required would be a connecting tunnel under the river at Greenwich, the project requires early investigation in relation to Route 7 of our previous report.

iii) *Land in central areas.* Some concentration of railway depots may be possible as the result of zonal schemes now being worked out. Street cartage could be reduced by the construction for goods traffic of automatic tube railways similar to that of the General Post Office, and this is worthy of investigation.

34 Ibid.
35 *Obituary Notices of Fellows of the Royal Society* Vol 8 1952-1953 p. 451.
36 Royal Society, *Collections* <http://royalsociety.org/library/collections/>. (Accessed June 2014).
37 Rogers, David, *Top Secret British Boffins in WW I*, (Solihull: Helion and Company, 2013) and Rogers, David, *Men Amidst the Madness: British Technology Development in World War II*, (Solihull: Helion and Company, 2014).

iv) *Coal.* A more concentrated system of handling coal would be of advantage, but some of the issues involved are outside our terms of reference.

v) *Main markets.* Co-ordination between any scheme for market decentralisation and railway services is essential. An early decision on the location of markets is desirable.

vi) *Electrification.* The view expressed in our previous report remains unchanged, and the proposals of the County of London and Greater London Plans are generally endorsed, but diesel or gas turbine traction should not be excluded. Electrification of freight traffic in London must be linked with the question of main line electrification, which is outside our terms of reference.

vii) *Watford-Chelmsford orbital link.* We consider that construction would necessarily be expensive, and more evidence than is now available of likely traffics would be required to justify such a project.[38]

Some of the recommendations were implemented soon after the war, others since. Of course this was just one aspect of the overall improvements in the national railway network, other plans were developed and some of the recommendations implemented.

The rail network was not the only issue under discussion. Plans were also being developed for a series of airports. Perhaps Heathrow might serve as an example as it is still one of the principle airports of the United Kingdom.

Inter-departmental Committee on Heathrow
Memorandum by the Ministry of Civil Aviation

1. In CAC (45)10, the Minister of Civil Aviation sought authority to present a hybrid Bill for the acquisition of 4,219 acres of land at Heathrow for the development of an international civil airport. It was pointed out in paragraph 10 of the paper that failure to acquire the whole area now would probably result in the loss of portions for all time on account of building development. It was also explained that when the final layout had been agreed it would be possible to dispose of some of this land. If the area were now to be reduced it would prejudice the planning of the airport. It cannot be too strongly emphasised that most transport aerodromes built in the past have proved quite inadequate owing to the rapid development in the size and landing requirements of modern aircraft.

2. Every possible site in the London neighbourhood has been considered and over 50 sites have been surveyed. Heathrow is undoubtedly the best and is, in fact, the only site within easy reach of London at which an airport of this size could be constructed. It has a meteorological record which compares very favourably with any other in the London area.

3. The major portion of overseas traffic to and from this country is destined for or departing from the metropolis and it is, therefore, essential that the main terminal airport should be as close to the centre of London as can be achieved. Access to Heathrow is better and quicker than to any other site of comparable area.

38   National Archives MT 6/2791.

4. The number of scheduled movements per day of British and foreign civil traffic in the London area over the next five years is estimated very roughly as follows ... [39]

The report continues to outline the many benefits from choosing Heathrow as the new London airport. Interestingly, in 2014 there is still a debate concerning the need for greater flights into and out of the airport. One can only speculate on the size of the airport today if all of the proposed land had been bought in the post-war period!

The expansion of transport links went hand in hand with dismantling the wartime defence infrastructure. Removal of the defence works in these cases naturally led to an improvement in resources and opportunities, or a reduction in the inconvenience to local residents or travellers to the area.

Relaxation of anti-invasion precautions
Removal of Defence works.

One of the conditions to removal of defence works was that removal should be in the public interest, and in such cases pillboxes, rail blocks, barbed wire and so forth the Chairman thought it would be generally accepted that removal would be in the public interest. He assumed that the Companies desired to get rid of practically the whole of such works as speedily as possible.

Mr Endicott agreed, but observed that the order of removal would depend on the labour situation. The companies would wish to concentrate upon those works which are a handicap to operation and/or maintenance and he suggested that the Ministry should accept the opinion of the Railway Companies on this point, as a criterion of public interest in removal ...

It was agreed that gun spurs and stabling sidings should come under general arrangements for removal of defence works, and a general modification had been received by the Ministry that these were no longer required. In these cases the Railway Companies' immediate problem was the removal of the unwanted connections from their running lines.

As regards bridges which have been decked, dismantled or otherwise interfered with for defence purposed, the Chairman referred to the list of such cases he had received from the REC, and it was agreed that removal of decking and the structural re-instatement of the bridge itself should come under the general defence works arrangements. An exception was Rochester Bridge, the decking of which for road traffic had been carried out as a MWT work ... [40]

Ports were also affected by wartime modifications to their normal operations.

39   National Archives MT 6/2800.
40   National Archives MT 6/2822.

28th May 1948
Dear Sir,

Folkestone Harbour – Special Reconstruction works.
Hard (NT) and Dolphins LST Berth and Ramp

With reference to your letter of 31st May 1947, the first stage of this work involving the reinstatement of the three bay sidings in the continental shed was completed towards the end of last year and consideration has now been given to the question of undertaking further restoration work.

It is felt that the time has now arrived when the proposals for reconstructing the sea wall across the Admiralty Hard should be proceeded with and I enclose plans 77/111 and 77/112 indicating the extent of the work involved.

The reinstatement of a wall across the Hard is a matter for immediate attention owing to the risk of a breach developing through the existing hard. During the past winter, erosion of the tow has become extensive in spite of temporary repairs executed last Autumn ... [41]

(c) Education Buildings

Buildings used for education purposes were bombed just like every other types of buildings. In some cases the resources within these buildings were unique, such as museums. In other cases they were used every day as schools. In all cases protection of scarce resources were key.

When a school has been damaged the first step should be an examination of the debris and, if it is safe, the removal of any books, furniture etc., which can be salvaged. As the war proceeds, furniture and other educational equipment will become more and more scarce and it is therefore of importance to avoid all unnecessary waste from exposure to the weather.

Where school premises within the Board's (of Education) jurisdiction are damaged and it is considered important to make more than urgent first-aid reports, the normal sequence of events will be:

a) Notification of damage to the War Damage Commission and to HM Inspector.

b) Carrying out of urgent first aid repairs (i.e. the minimum necessary to make the building for the time being waterproof, water-tight and safe).

c) Submission of proposals, for repairs over £100, to the Board (or to HM Inspector acting for the Board).

d) Approval of proposals by the Board or HM Inspectors.

e) Application, if necessary, to the Licensing Officer under Defence Regulation 56A.

f) Submission to the War Damage Commission of a claim for cost of works payment on completion of the repairs.

41 Ibid.

In cases in which is it decided not to repair the damage at present payment of compensation will be deferred until the repairs are done. If, however, the cost of repair would exceed the value of the building when repaired, no 'cost of works' payment will be made but a 'value' payment at some future date, probably after the war. It is hoped that 'value' payments may not be repaired either now or after the war, e.g. schools with very unsatisfactory premises have been seriously damaged.[42]

Figure 9.6 further explained the process.

Schools to be continued on present site	Proposed war damage
School repairable and should be repaired to former state	A cost of works payment
School repairable but Minister may wish school to be remodelled	A cost of works payment equivalent to the amount which would have been required had the school been restored to its original state
School demolished but must be rebuilt	Value payment
Schools which the Minister of Education says must be removed to a new site	**Proposed war damage**
School damaged and site sold	Cost of works payment which would be equal to the cost of repairs if building had been restored to original state. Money used for establishment of school in area where children attend
School demolished and site sold	Value payment

Figure 9.6. School war damage.[43]

Although written with Church of England schools in mind on the 23 May 1945, the following set the scene for determining the repair or rebuilding of a property used for education:

... it was explained on behalf of the commission that the question of whether a property was a 'total loss' within the meaning of the War Damage Act or not did not depend solely on the extent of the physical damage; the statutory test was an economic one – was it worth repairing? (i.e. taking total costs and values as at March 1939 would the cost of reinstating the property be greater or less than the excess of a) the value which the reinstated property would have had at that date, over b) the value of the property as a site with the damage not made good at that date). Thus a school which was entirely demolished might be 'not a total loss' if it was a modern up-to-date school, whereas an oldish school with a substantial degree of depreciation on account

42   National Archives ED 147/387.
43   Ibid.

of redundancy, obsolescence and structural defects might be a 'total loss', even though it was not a physical total loss.[44]

Some school buildings were also earmarked for other purposed should bomb damage or invasion deem it necessary.

6th February 1945
Mr G G Williams
Ministry of Education
Belgrave Square
Dear Mr Williams,
You will remember that in 1940 or thereabouts we had some discussions here as to the earmarking of certain public schools for use as 'shadow' or reserve hospitals in the event of an invasion of this country or other special emergency which might place an exceptional strain upon our hospital system.

I thought you would like to know that with the general relaxation of invasion of preparations we have finally abrogated this scheme of reserve hospitals. I enclose a copy of the instructions sent to our Regions (ROA 1161) from Part II of which you will see that we have asked that the owners of the reserved premises should be thanked for this co-operation in the arrangements.

If you have ceased to be concerned with this subject you will no doubt pass on this letter to whoever is now interested in it.
Yours sincerely,
Ministry of Health.[45]

Implementation of the 'Butler Education Act' of 1944, allowed for the Voluntary Schools to be created. This also led to issues of accommodation.

18th March 1946
To: The Secretary
Ministry of Education
14, Belgrave Square
London

Dear Sir,
I am writing to ask whether your Ministry is prepared to authorise Local Education Authorities to erect pre-fabricated huts to serve as temporary accommodation for Voluntary Schools, under powers granted by Section 109 of the Education Act 1944.

I have received a report that the Ministry is not prepared to give such authorisation, and I shall be obliged if you would please let me know whether this report is correct or not.

44 Ibid.
45 National Archives ED 147/384.

Yours faithfully,
Catholic Education Council[46]

In some cases a derelict school could not be rebuilt on the same land. In these circumstances land needed to be acquired, sometimes through compulsory purchase orders. For example there was a case in Cheshire.

The land is being acquired under the Education Acts 1944 and 1946. I understand that in the circumstances of this case the land is being acquired in accordance with the provisions of Part II of the Town and Country Planning Act 1944 subject to the special form of contract envisaged under Section 91 (4)(C) of the Town and Country Planning Act 1947 ...

... the land lies within the City of Chester and comprises the following, figure 9.7.[47]

Proposed use of land	Description or colour on plan	Apportioned area (acres)
County Modern Secondary School	Edged blue	18.362
County Modern Secondary School (Farm Cottage)	Indicated on plan but not coloured	0.047
College of Further Education	Edged yellow	40.733
City Grammar and City High Schools Playing Fields	Edged brown	15.376
Roman Catholic School	Edged green	0.292
Occupation road (for joint use)	Indicated on plan but not coloured	1.022

Figure 9.7. Some land bought by compulsory purchase for use in education.[48]

The land was formerly the property of the Duke of Westminster.

In some cases, it was not possible to obtain land through compulsory purchase and educational establishments needed to raise funds to buy the land on the open market. I have chosen this example as I attended the University of Salford (as the Royal Technical College became) in the 1970s, and walked passed these buildings on my way into Manchester.

July 1947
Specification and bill of quantities for an additional electrical engineering laboratory at the Royal Technical College.

27th September 1947

---

46 National Archives ED 147/55.
47 National Archives ED 160/154.
48 Ibid.

To the Council and the City of Salford

Your committee submit herewith a report of the Governors of the Royal Technical College with reference to a proposal to borrow the sum of £3,500 to cover the cost of the adaption of premises 28 and 29, Crescent, Salford, for use as a School of Chiropody.

Your Committee are advised by the City Treasurer that the loan charges upon the expenditure of £3,500 referred to above, which will have to be met by the Corporation ...

4th November 1947

I am directed by the Town Council of Salford to make application to the Ministry of Health, subject to the approval of the Lancashire County Council, for sanction to borrow the sum of £700 to cover the cost of the construction of a Fittings Workshop at the College.[49]

A further folio documents a large building programme for the same institute (Royal Technical College in Salford). The departments included: Bakery, Building and Civil Engineering, Chemistry and Applied Chemistry, Commerce, Domestic Studies, Electrical Engineering, General Educational Facilities, Mathematics, Mechanical Engineering, Physics, School of Art and Textiles. The total area involved in the upgrade programme across these Departments was 211,744 sq. ft. This represented a significant investment and increase in the College facilities.[50]

By the time I went to Salford University as it became in the early 1960s, the Chemistry Department was rumoured to have been one of the largest in Europe with over 600 students and 80 members of staff. This Department had strong links with major chemical companies based in and around Greater Manchester. Some of the other Departments were equally strong.

This significant increase in floor area was able to accommodate a large increase in student numbers. It would be hard to imagine this was unique to Salford and suggests that some of the demobilised Service personnel were taking advantage of returning to their studies as well as the College attracting its share of the youngsters who were of an age to attend.

(d) Bomb Damage to Public or Landmark Buildings

In one sense restoring public buildings might be more connected with symbolism than with the practical daily grind of living. Certainly those vast numbers of people made homeless during the many air raids all over the United Kingdom must have been more interested in having a roof over their heads than restoring a grade one listed building. Undoubtedly government departments could function in a contemporary building just as they did in a Georgian office block.

Three historic buildings at least, were to greater or lesser extents, intimately connected with the need for continuity, creating an atmosphere of business as usual,

49   National Archives ED 166/230.
50   National Archives ED 166/231.

defiance, or a connection with the suffering of millions. In no particular order they are: Buckingham Palace, the Palace of Westminster often known as the Houses of Parliament and Coventry Cathedral, more of which later.

Whilst these buildings in particular were to use tried and tested materials in their reconstruction, there were other techniques becoming available, even during the war.

> 28th July 1942
> The Director
> The Building Research Station
> Bucknalls Lane
> Watford
>
> Sir,
> A month or two ago, I attended a lecture by the Principal Scientific Research Officer of the Building Research Station, and Mr Fitzmaurice very kindly asked me to visit Watford, and said he would be glad to make an appointment to see me.
>
> I have been devoting all my spare time recently to the study of post-war problems in building, and in particular would be very glad to have the benefit of any advice on scientific and constructional subjects which it is possible to discuss at the present time. I am thinking of prefabrication, questions of heating, lighting and ventilation, which were the subject of the lecture I referred to, the possibilities of district heating (which formed part of the lecture I attended last week by Mr Marsh, the Secretary of the Smoke Abatement Society) and so forth.
>
> Although I believe my name is chiefly connected with churches, actually for a period of ten years after the last war, I was intimately concerned with housing …
> .and it was a great disappointment to me that progressive proposals for planning and housing in all its aspects did not receive much support, either from the public or the Government … [51]

Plans for the use of one of the new materials met with some concerns.

> 10th December 1943
> The Director
> Department of Scientific and Industrial Research
> Building Research Station
> Garston
> Watford
>
> Dear Sir,
>   Re North Radford Church Hall, Coventry
> Since calling at the Building Research Station on November 24th, when I discussed the Thermocrete slabs which are being used at the above Hall with

---

51 National Archives DSIR 4/642.

Mr Bagenal, I have heard from the builder informing me that the slab had been despatched by goods train on November 26th, as it could not be accepted on the passenger train, owing to its size.

I had instructed them to pack it carefully and hope that it has arrived without further breakage other than that which occurred during its transit from the Shockrete works at Rye House.

As it is impossible to hold up the progress of the job, the hall being urgently required, I am arranging for some extra reinforcement in the form of purlins under the slabs. But it would be a great help to me to have your opinion of the strength of this material ... [52]

Whilst some buildings were being rebuilt with newer materials attempts to restore others were fraught.

21st March 1951
The Secretary
War Damage Commission
Devonshire House
Mayfair
Piccadilly
London.

Dear Sir,

                    Corn Exchange Buildings Liverpool

These buildings were destroyed by enemy action at the beginning of May 1941, and after prolonged negotiations with the Commission in Manchester and with other parties concerned, the Directors of the Association were informed by the Chief Regional Manager, Manchester, that the Ad Val Forms would be cancelled and that 'in view of the change to a payment of cost-of-works, will you please request your appointed architects to contact Mr Rupert Medcalf at the War Damage Commission's Technical Centre, in Liverpool upon a permissible amount in respect of the war damage sustained' ...

... at the beginning of October 1948, Messrs Davies were advised by Mr Rupert Medcalf, Senior Assessor in Charge, Central Land Board and War Damage Commission, Technical Centre, Liverpool, of his recommendation to the Regional Manager of the sum of the permissible amount, which would be £259,222 excluding fees, and that the permissible amount should be this figure brought up to current prices at the date when the work is carried out.

Mr Metcalf asked for confirmation of this, so that a record can be kept in the file.

On the 19th October 1948, Messrs Davies advised Mr Medcalf of the Director's approval.

52 Ibid.

On 25th October 1948, Mr Medcalf noted Messrs Davies's clients accepted his recommendation to the Regional Manager in the above case.

Believing (and they had no reason to doubt it) that the basis of the permissible amount had been agreed between the Commission and the Association, – the Directors proceeded with the preparation of their plans for rebuilding the Corn Exchange, and they appointed Quantity Surveyors and prepared to seek a Licence for Clearing of the site as a preliminary to the commencement of building operations. They also instructed their surveyors to negotiate with the owners of certain adjacent property for the acquisition of their lands, as it appeared to be certain that the Planning Authorities would require the Association to purchase additional land for car parking or other purposes.

To the surprise of the Directors and their professional advisors, in October 1950 – and not until then – did the Assistant Regional Manager, Manchester, inform our surveyors that 'recommendation of £259,222 at March 1939 prices was a recommendation from the Senior Assessor in Charge at Liverpool, but 'this has not yet been submitted to, or confirmed by, my headquarters' ...

... I am instructed to inform you that the Directors hereby enter a most emphatic protest against this repudiation of an agreement made as long ago as October 1948. They submit that the War Damage Commission must accept responsibility for the prior actions and decisions of their officials, and they request that Mr Harrington be now instructed to withdraw this letter of 23rd February 1951, and that the Officers in Manchester and Liverpool be informed that the agreement of October 1948 is approved by the Commission itself and must be adhered to.[53]

An unsatisfactory state of affairs to say the least!

As mentioned above, Buckingham Palace was also bombed during the war. Indeed the then Queen Elizabeth commented after the war that it gave her a common bond with those who also suffered bomb damage. The King took a keen interest in the restoration, which started soon after the war ended.

At a meeting on 13th March 1946, the King decided to retain the concrete structure forming the exit from the shelter below the north terrace. This exit encroaches on to the normal carriageway through the arch of the colonnade and in order to avoid a sharp deviation of traffic the King agreed to the re-positioning of the archway about 12 ft. to the north and as indicated on the attached drawing (marked B), which the King eventually approved. I also attach a drawing (marked A) indicating the original façade of this colonnade.

The revision does not affect the length of the colonnade but introduces a plain panel against the Palace proper and the omission of the pavilion end to the north. It was explained to the King that the south and north colonnades were originally the same treatment and he agreed that any change in that to the north would not be seen in relation to that on the south.

53   National Archives IR 36/107.

A re-alignment of the grass verge as indicated in yellow in plan B becomes necessary.

The King questioned the stability of the remaining wall of the north colonnade, he having read in the Palace history of its doubtful construction. I have arranged for the wall to be examined. The re-positioning of the archway so affects the remainder of the colonnade that it may be necessary to rebuild the wall in question. Approval was also given of the plan indicating the line of hoardings for the enclosure for building areas for the colonnade, swimming pool and forecourt railings.

The King suggested that the motif on the shield of the central feature surmounted the archway of the colonnade be redesigned and he used the word 'modernise'. It is suggested the new design is prepared by the Royal College of Heralds and I have arranged for photographs showing the details of a similar shield over the south colonnade be prepared.

It is practically impossible to estimate the cost of the rebuilding of the colonnade including the proposed modifications. The extent of the re-use of materials and old foundations cannot be ascertained until operations are commenced. I would suggest the present estimate remains until a more accurate cost can be assessed following upon the receipt of tenders.

The revisions now proposed necessitate a certain amount of re-drawing etc., and every endeavour will be made to adhere to the original building programme.
E C Mee
18th March 1946[54]

Whilst Buckingham Palace suffered relatively minor damage, the Palace of Westminster suffered more extensively. The first course of action was to appoint a committee through which ideas for renovation could be routed. The Rt. Hon. William Whitely MP, wrote the following on Downing Street paper:

4th June 1947
To the Rt. Hon. Charles Key MP
Ministry of Works
Lambeth Bridge House
London

Dear Charles,
I can now send you the proposed names for your House Committee. They are as follows:

Labour:	Mr T J Brooks
	Mr T Braddock
	Mr M Phillips Price
	Mr S P Viant
Conservative:	Rt. Hon. H F Crookshank

54 National Archives WORK 19/1152.

Mr P Buchanan-Hepburn

Liberal: Mr W H W Roberts

You will of course be the Chairman and call the committee together whenever you see fit. I spoke both to Mr James Stuart and to Mr Byers about the project. I think it would be useful for you to have a note sent to each of the Members stating generally what you will expect of them and the kind of issue upon which you may want to consult them. If you decide upon this, will you please send me a copy of your letter because I think I should inform Mr Speaker and the authorities of the House of the existence of this body … [55]

The committee did indeed become a focal point for suggestions and incorporation of ideas into the eventual design. However, almost inevitably progress was slower than originally anticipated.

a)   The demolition contract was timed to start on the 1st April 1945, and to be completed on the 1st October 1945. The inclusion of additional work delayed starting until the 4th June, and the contract was finished on the 4th February 1946.

b)   The foundation contract was due to start on the 1st October 1945, but owing to delays in completing the demolition contract it did not start until the 4th February 1946. The estimated time for completion was six months, but in fact the work was not finished until the end of September. The superstructure contract was not ready to start at that date, and the foundation contract was, therefore, extended to cover work not originally planned.

c)   The total delay up to the beginning of the superstructure contract on the 15th March 1947 is therefore:

Demolition contract	2 months late in starting	
	2 months longer than expected	4 months
Foundation contract	7 months longer than expected	7 months
Total delay		11 months

d)   The superstructure contract was due to start on the 1st April 1946, but as already explained, it did not start until the 15th March 1947. The contract started with WBB priority, and it was not given WBA priority until August 1947. Completion date is April 1950, after which some time will be required for the installation of furniture, but in the first five months of the work approximately three months were lost because of the low priority and consequent labour difficulties.[56]

Some of the new features were useful additions:

55   National Archives WORK 11/449.
56   Ibid.

i)   Air-conditioning of new chamber.[57]
ii)   Fireplaces and central heating.[58]
iii) Inscriptions above doorways.[59]
iv)   House of Lords: rebuilding of west front staircase and provision of lift.[60]
v)   House of Commons Chamber: alterations to official boxes.[61]
vi)   Rebuilding of new Palace yard arcade.[62]

Uniquely, the restoration of the Palace of Westminster garnered offers of support from across the Colonial and Dominion Governments who were only too happy to donate either materials or gifts for use in the completed building.

The Speaker acted as the focal point for offers of gifts:

29th March 1944
Dear Mr Speaker,
In view of the agreement which was reached at your conference last week, to the effect that all decisions regarding offers of donations to the new House of Commons should be deferred until the Select Committee on Rebuilding has reported to the House, and that they should meanwhile be collected in your hands, I beg to enclose herewith copies of the correspondence regarding the only two offers so far received by the Select Committee.
Yours sincerely,[63]

The picture was totally different by 6th February 1951, figures 9.8 and 9.9.

	Donor	Gift	Material
1	Australia	The Speaker's Chair	Black Bean
2	Basutoland	2 Silver gilt ash trays	
3	Bechuanaland Protectorate	1 Silver gilt ash tray	
4	Canada	Table of the House	Canadian oak
5	Ceylon	Sergeant at Arms Chair	Oak
6	States of Guernsey	4 Chairs, 1 Ministers desk	Oak
7	India	1 Entrance door to Chamber	Oak
8	States of Jersey	Minister's writing desk and chair, 1 silver gilt inkstand	Oak
9	Isle of Man	1 Single silver gilt inkstand and 2 silver gilt ash trays for Prime Minister's Conference Room	

57   National Archives FD 1/444.
58   National Archives WORK 11/428.
59   National Archives WORK 11/448.
60   National Archives WORK 11/483.
61   National Archives WORK 11/534.
62   National Archives WORK 11/578.
63   National Archives WORK 11/419.

	Donor	Gift	Material
10	Newfoundland	6 Single chairs for PM's Conference Room	Birch
11	New Zealand	2 Despatch boxes	Pururi
12	Northern Ireland	3 Chamber clocks	
13	Pakistan	1 Entrance door to Chamber	Oak
14	South Africa	3 Chairs for Clerk's table	Stinkwood
15	Southern Rhodesia	2 Silver gilt inkstands and stationary racks for Chamber	
16	Swaziland	1 Silver gilt ash tray	

Figure 9.8. Commonwealth gifts to the new House of Commons.[64]

	Donor	Gift	Material
1	Aden	Member's writing table	Oak
2	Bahamas	Minister's writing desk and chair	Oak
3	Barbados	Minister's writing desk and chair	Oak
4	Bermuda	2 Triple silver gilt inkstands	
5	British Guiana	Set of four triple silver gilt ink stands	
6	British Honduras	Minister's writing desk and chair	Mayflower
7	Cyprus	Member's writing room table	Oak
8	Falkland Islands	1 Silver gilt ash tray	
9	Fiji	1 Silver gilt inkstand	
10	Gambia	2 Silver gilt ash trays	
11	Gibraltar	2 Table lamps	Oak
12	Gold Coast	Minister's writing desk and chair	Mansonia
13	Hong Kong	1 Triple silver gilt inkstand	
14	Jamaica	Bar of the House	Bronze
15	Kenya	Minister's writing desk and chair	Olive
16	Leeward Island	6 Table lamps	Oak
17	Malaya	Minister's desk and armchair	Oak
18	Malta	3 Silver gilt ash trays	
19	Mauritius	Minister's writing desk and chair	Oak
20	Nigeria	Furniture for one Division Lobby	Iroko
21	North Borneo	Interview Room furniture (1 table and 5 chairs)	White Seraya
22	Northern Rhodesia	2 Pairs mace brackets	Bronze

64 National Archives WORK 11/420.

	Donor	Gift	Material
23	Nyasaland	1 Triple silver gilt inkstand and 1 silver gilt ash tray	
24	St Helena	Chairman's chair for Minister's Conference Room	
25	Seychelles	Minister's writing desk and chair	Oak
26	Sierra Leone	Minister's writing desk	African Walnut
27	Singapore	Interview Room furniture 1 table and 5 chairs	Oak
28	Tanganyika	Interview Room furniture 1 table and 5 chairs	Iroko
29	Trinidad	Minister's writing desk and chair	Oak
30	Uganda	Furniture for one Division Lobby	Mvul
31	Windward Islands		
	Dominica	1 Silver gilt inkstand	
	Grenada	1 Silver gilt inkstand	
	St Lucia	1 Silver gilt inkstand	
	St Vincent	1 silver ash tray	

Figure 9.9. Colonial gifts to the New House of Commons.[65]

The press notice written for the opening ceremony documents further details of the gifts and the re-construction and is in the same National Archives folio. Planning for the opening ceremony took place over a number of weeks, the first meeting for which took place on the 20th April 1948.[66]

There are some interesting pictures in the National Archives of both the devastation caused by the bomb and of the dedication ceremony which are worth viewing should the opportunity present itself.[67]

Other parts of Whitehall also needed rebuilding. For example (and figure 9.10):

The Treasury
I attach preliminary sketch plans of the Treasury rebuilding plan scheme, together with drawings indicating the existing plan which also shows the effect of war damage.

The scheme is somewhat complicated as the work may have to be done in two parts. It will probably be necessary for me to meet you to discuss some of the details. The following notes meanwhile are relevant:

1.   The tunnel underneath Whitehall will be built before this rebuilding scheme goes on, and will be constructed of cast iron segments reaching to the area outside the Treasury, a temporary manhole being provided from which the heating pipes will run along the area and across Downing Street. The

65   Ibid.
66   National Archives WORK 11/506.
67   National Archives WORK 69/16.

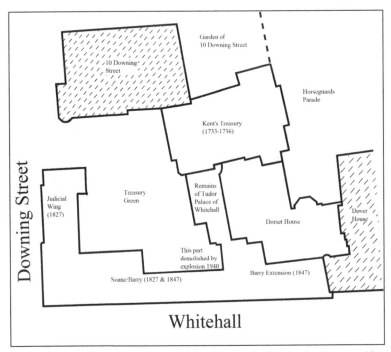

Figure 9.10. The area of Whitehall needing work. (Author's photograph)

     rebuilding scheme includes a trench and continuation of the tunnel from the area. Particulars of this will be obtained for you from the architect concerned.

2.   It is likely that modernisation of services and structural repairs will be undertaken in the Judicial Committee Wing and also in the Kent Treasury simultaneously, but I would like the costs shown separately.

3.   The structural engineer's report on method of construction and condition of the two wings referred to above is still awaited, but it will be passed to you within the next few days. It will indicate how the Whitehall façade is to be shored up whilst re-construction takes place. It will also indicate the extent of repairs and renewals in the old buildings. Modernisation of services in the older parts will create a problem as far as estimating is concerned, especially as no scheme has yet been designed.

4.   On the first floor is Court Number 2, which is really a reinstatement of the existing room at this level, utilising existing panelling and renewing some of the decoration.

5.   The new structure will probably be in reinforced concrete with flat slab floor construction to facilitate removal and re-erection of partitions, but I still await the advice of the Structural Engineers regarding this.

6.   Where connections are made to the existing buildings and where alterations are required in them, a special care must be taken to preserve architectural detail. This especially applies to Dorset House and Kent Treasury.

7. Office accommodation generally should be to normal standards, i.e. hollow block partitions plastered and painted both sides, wood block floors. Staircases will probably have wooden treads with wrought iron balusters. If the Treasury can be evacuated completely I shall hope all the work simultaneously with Number 10 Downing Street starting in 1958. We may be asked, however, what the effect on cost would be if the older parts are re-conditioned later, piece meal fashion after Number 10 and the Treasury have been rebuilt. I should like your observations on the cost from this point of view.

8. The rear elevation will probably be in first-class London stocks, with windows to match existing. You will note that the basement has a degree of protection according to normal standards.

Please let me know if there is any other information you want and when you would like to see me.

F L Rothwell
Superintending Architect
29th February 1956[68]

A diagram of the area was presented with the above, which is also reproduced above. Horse Guards building was also in need of some restoration.

November 1949
Dear Sir,

Horse Guards Building

The Ministry are planning to carry out the repair and restoration of the bomb-damaged block of the Horse Guards during the financial year 1950-1951, so as to have the work completed in time for the 1951 Festival of Britain. The total cost of the work is estimated at £23,000 and this sum is being provided in our draft estimates for 1950-1951. Application has been made for Treasury Authority.

Of this total, however, £7,000 is due to work which it is understood has been requested by the War Department, consisting of lowering the top floor of the building in order to provide sufficient space for a new quarter, and of providing a cloakroom and bathroom for the occupant of the existing quarter, on the ground floor.

This part of the work does not appear to fall within the scope of normal maintenance by the Ministry. It must be considered as an improvement request by the War Department for military purposes. As such, in accordance with the Ministry's agreement with the War Department on the maintenance of historic buildings, it will be work for which the War Department will be financially responsible, although the Ministry will carry it out on a recoverable basis.

I should, therefore, be glad if you would arrange for funds to be made available for this part of the work in the financial year 1950-1951.

Yours faithfully,

68 National Archives CM 23/205.

N Digney[69]

This was not the only London military building needing repair, others included:

1. The Infirmary at the Royal Hospital, Chelsea, to which Sir Winston Churchill received an invitation to attend.

> December 4, 1954
> My Dear General Paget,
> Thank you for your invitation to the inspection of the In-Pensioners on May 28. I value the compliment you have paid me but think that I must decline since I try to spend the week-ends away from London.
>   I am glad to hear that a decision has been reached to rebuild the Infirmary in the grounds of the Royal Hospital and that a start is being made in planning this work.
> Yours v. sincerely,
> W S C[70]

2. The Guards Chapel at Wellington Barracks.

> Guards Chapel
> As you know, the Royal Military Chapel (known as the Guards Chapel) in Wellington Barracks was destroyed during the War. The War Office propose to rebuild it concurrently with the modernisation of Wellington Barracks, which they expect to get round to in some years' time. They have sought the Treasury's agreement in principle, and raised the question of how much of the cost should fall to public funds (certain private funds are available).
>   The Treasury have replied raising a number of questions, and there is in fact scope for some further clarification at the official level. But a number of high personages are interested (including the Duke of Gloucester), both as regards the timing and as regards the cost of the rebuilding, and we understand that it is quite likely that the next step will be pressure on the Treasury at an exalted level.
>   You may therefore like to have this preliminary warning.
> 22nd October 1957.[71]

3. Admiral President's House, Greenwich College.

> First Lord,
> I attach two notes by the Head of GFII about matters which may come up when you visit the RN College, Greenwich, with the Ministry of Works.

69 National Archives WORK 14/2370.
70 National Archives PREM 11/592.
71 National Archives T 225/1265.

The first, marked A, is a full and useful statement of the reasons which could be urged upon the Minister to expedite the commencement of repairs to the war damaged part of the College.

The Admiral President is, of course, very keen that a beginning should be made in 1954/1955. Personally I should doubt whether the Ministry could now find sufficient resources in that year, and if that should appear to be the case the best tactics would be to try to persuade him to make sure that the Treasury allow him to include money for an early start in 1955/1956.

There is one possible pitfall of which you should be aware. During 1954/1955 (round about the end of this calendar year) the Ministry of Works are reckoning to make a start of the repair of the bomb damage in the Admiralty Old Building, which will be followed immediately by the repair of the damage to the South Block ... [72]

Many other commercial London buildings needed repair, including:

a)   The Land Registry building at Lincolns Inn Fields.[73]
b)   No 4. Carlton Gardens, part of the Estates Remaining in Crown Possession after 1940.[74]
c)   Piccadilly: numbers 198-202 and numbers 32-33 Jermyn Street.[75]
d)   Rebuilding of Trinity House.[76]
e)   Rebuilding of war-damaged turret on south-western block in Chancery Lane.[77]

At first sight some of the paperwork for the reconstruction of Coventry Cathedral looks like that of any other major rebuilding programme.

A request has been put into the Ministry of Works by the Coventry Cathedral Reconstruction Committee for authorisation to commence this work in the near future.

An examination of the project as it now stands reveals the following position:

On finance. There is available from the War Damage Commission a sum of between £500,000 and £600,000 at least. Some £100,000 has already been subscribed by the public and the Committee expect another £200,000 at least from overseas, mainly dollar contributions. Finance, therefore, seems assured and this money can only be spent on the Cathedral reconstruction and for no other purpose whatever.

---

72   National Archives ADM 1/25106.
73   National Archives LAR 1/272 and LAR 1/315.
74   National Archives CRES 35/2858.
75   National Archives LRRO 1/4841.
76   National Archives MT 101/59.
77   National Archives PRO 1/1476.

Method of construction

i) Foundations are to be in reinforced concrete with economic use of steel and will be reasonably shallow as rock is near the surface and ground is generally good.

ii) Main Walls are to be in stone for both facings with concrete filling. The stone is already being quarried in North Staffordshire.

iii) Columns and roof members are to be in pre-stressed concrete.

iv) Little softwood will be needed and hardwood will be needed for choir stalls, organ housing etc.

v) No brickwork is anticipated, and therefore, no call for bricks or bricklayers.

Time table. It is anticipated that if the foundation stone is to be laid by a 'Personage' some four months' work would be required before the laying of the stone, and that a further 7-8 months to complete the site preparation and foundations. Thereafter it would take approximately five years to complete the edifice. That is, the whole construction will take approximately six years.

Labour requirements.

i) The intention of the Reconstruction Committee and the architect is to employ a National Civil Engineering Contractor to carry out the site works, foundations and pre-stressed columns and roof work.

ii) The stone wall work will require a firm experienced in masonry and mason's work and it is not unlikely that a well-known firm in the region experienced in this work, who already have connections within the City of Coventry and who are now engaged in cutting the stone in the quarries, will be employed for the erection of these walls.

iii) Based on the above, the first year's work would require about 50 civil engineering labourers, of which the national contractor would undoubtedly bring in a number, together with his own supervisory staff.

iv) During the ensuing five years the labour requirements would approximate to 20 stone masons and 30 civil engineering labourers with, towards the end of the period, a few woodworking tradesmen and painters.

There is already in the region, and within travelling distance of Coventry, some unemployment amongst civil engineering trades and painters.

There is a national shortage of masons but the stone working firm have already received a considerable number of applications from boys wishing to become apprentice masons ... [78]

However, this was not a normal rebuilding programme as the original building, or rather the shell of the original building, was left standing and the new building built to the side of the ruin. This serves as a permanent reminder of the bomb damage to the cathedral and by extension to the rest of Coventry which suffered more than most with air raids.

78 National Archives HLG 79/878.

Figure 9.11. A contemporary picture of Coventry Cathedral. (Author's photograph)

Figure 9.11 is a contemporary picture of the cathedral ruin with the new cathedral off to the left. It stands as a fitting and permanent reminder of the sacrifices and defiance of war.

Appendix I

It can now be revealed – Home Forces MOI[1]

Situation before Dunkirk

During that opening phase of the War which became known as the 'Bore War', or 'Phony War', the Army had of course made plans for repelling an invasion of Great Britain. But the threat did not appear a serious one, and the troops in England, apart from those guarding against sabotage and minor raids were there for training rather than for defence.

Before Dunkirk there were sixteen Infantry Divisions, an Armoured Brigade in Great Britain, and they were there because they were not fit to take their place in the line overseas. Practically the whole of the Regular Army was in the BEF in France, and there formations were Territorials and Militia men. At that time, in the early Spring of 1940, the Territorial Army still suffered severe growing pains for it had been doubled in size the previous year; and the decision a few years before the War to mechanise the Army completely was still in little more than the 'rattle and green flag' stage with the exception of the BEF who had taken the cream of all we had in vehicles and equipment.

There was very little left for the Army at home. Only eight medium tanks mounting a 2-pounder, 120 light tanks mounting a machine gun and about 60 armoured cars. Only 250 25-pounders and about 90 obsolescent 18-pounder guns; only about 100 2-pounder anti-tank guns, in all, not more than one eighth of the equipment needed for the troops available.

All the time the BEF were calling for reinforcement and more equipment – anti-tank guns for instance. An attempt to counter the invasion of Norway came as an added strain; an attempt was made by a few gallant Territorial units who were pitifully short of equipment and still only half trained. Then came Dunkirk, and the BEF came home – without its equipment.

After Dunkirk

In those few days of May and early June 1940, the situation was completely altered. Invasion became an imminent peril and the army was not ready for it. A colossal effort started to prepare for the onslaught which was regarded as certain to come, for

1   National Archives WO 106/2825.

in those days the truth of the maxim that the air battle must be won before the land battle can be started had not been fully driven home.

The Division of the BEF were reformed and immense efforts were made to re-equip them as mobile troops. The strength of the army at home quickly rose to 22 Divisions. But of these, a half had never trained as formations, since they had been handicapped by lack of equipment, protective duties on Vulnerable Points, airfields and so on, and by the new task of building beach defences.

State of Equipment and Vehicles

Of the Divisions from the BEF, which were reformed, four were fully equipped during the summer. Of the remainder, eight Divisions were fairly well equipped, and the rest – 10 of the 22 – were short of many vital items.

But the standard by which we judged them was low. There were for instance serious deficiencies in unit transport despite the fact that all suitable types of civilian vehicles had been requisitioned. For moving troops in threatened areas civilian vehicles of the charabanc type were requisitioned. These were fairly plentiful though drivers for them were short. Nevertheless each mobile division had enough transport to lift one brigade.

Rifle ammunition was held at full scale by the troops but there were now reserves within the formations. Such reserves as were available were kept in central positions with good transport arrangements to supply any sector which might run short at short notice. Stringent economy had to be imposed on the use of ammunition for training and the allocation for rifle and LMG for troops in the United Kingdom worked out at about 2 rounds per man per week. The deficiency in reserves of small arms and ammunition in the Divisions was somewhere in the region of 66 million rounds. Other types of ammunition such as artillery, mortar, anti-tank etc. were similarly scarce.

In September 1940, the army was still short of 146,000 rifles and 10,000 LMG. The majority of the units had to be equipped with the old Lewis gun; Bren guns were in very short supply.

On average there were only enough modern 25-pounder guns, which now formed the basis of artillery fire power, to equip each field regiment with one gun instead of 24. To make good some of the deficiencies obsolete 18-pounder and 4.5 Howitzer guns were issued. Even then the total number of field guns in the hands of the troops was only 710, representing 2/5ths of what was required and of these only some 250 were on issue to training units and would have had to be handed over to the field force if operations started.

There were about 80 infantry tanks mounting a 2-pounder gun in the hands of the troops and the remaining armoured regiments were equipped with obsolete tanks which mounted a medium machine gun and with armoured cars. The Second Armoured Division for example, which had an establishment of 280 light tanks and 260 cruiser tanks, had only 230 light tanks issued to them, and this was the only organised armoured formation in the country.

The shortage was further accentuated by the necessity for reinforcing car troops in the Middle East. There was an ever present difficulty of balancing risks of requirement for equipment in the Middle East and for requirements for Home Defence.

Defence Plan

With these meagre and ill equipped forces, a defence plan was prepared based on four main elements:

1. First on the coast there was to be a 'crust' of resistance.
2. Behind anti-tank 'islands' were designed to cover important points on the Lines of Communication.
3. Thirdly stop lines were prepared by adapting natural obstacles such as rivers and canals, and linking these with anti-tank ditches and other obstacles.
4. Lastly a mobile reserve of the better equipped troops were located in suitable positions to strike at the enemy wherever he penetrated in strength.

Defence of the beach 'crust' was undertaken by Territorial Divisions. Their main preoccupation was the erection of defences which by the end of the summer were progressing well. All possible landing beaches were blocked and wired and anti-tank mines sown. Civilian contractors erected blockhouses which were manned in the main by LDV who subsequently became the Home Guard. But the frontages held by the troops were often absurdly long. There were cases of a platoon of infantry finding itself holding a 10 mile stretch of the coast – that is 3 men to the mile – while in South East England where the threat of invasion was considered greatest one infantry brigade was called upon to hold a front of 25 miles, that is about a platoon and a half to the mile.

Between the coast and the stop lines of anti-tank obstacles were located mobile columns containing armoured fighting vehicles such as Bren Carriers whose task it was to deal with tanks that broke through the 'crust'. Road blocks were erected near blockhouses in places where movement off the road was difficult and stacks of petrol bombs were kept in buildings nearby. For the defence of airfields mobile pillboxes were improvised. They consisted of large diameter concrete pipes mounted vertically on an open lorry which would carry an LMG and its crew. There were also the 'Ironsides' – little boxes of boiler plate on a well-known light car chassis. They would have been death traps in action – but they were the best that could be done in the time.

The mobile reserve at the disposal of GHQ in September 1940 consisted of only 3 infantry divisions, one armoured brigade and a few New Zealand and Australian troops, and were the only troops who were completely mobile.

To overcome the difficulty of communication due to lack of cable, telephone sets and wireless sets, the GPO telephone system had to be largely relied upon. In addition some thousands of civilian wireless sets were issued to units and an army broadcasting station was set up which broadcast information to the units holding the beaches and inland areas.

Camouflage and deception

At a time when men and material are short camouflage is always needed both to preserve what equipment there is intact so that it can be brought into action with the maximum surprise, and also to deceive the enemy as to our actual strength.

Never was the need so great as in 1940. Everyone has seen isolated examples of what camouflage was done at this time; the pillbox outside the garden fence masquerading as a hen house or haystack, the camouflage materials used to cover dumps. The public was also probably mystified by the rash of green stripes and blotches spreading over concrete and corrugated iron, which was usually the outcome of misguided individual enterprise at a time when everybody felt that something must be done against the German air observer. In fact a camouflage officer flying over his area in those days was often horrified to see the out-buildings of an otherwise innocent country house suddenly blossom into a cubist picture of disruptive painting, proclaiming the fact that the army had taken over.

These mistakes were due to lack of training, the urgent necessity to conceal our modest resources, and (probably most important) to the misguided but popular theory that camouflage was magic anyway.

However, as defences grew in the coastal areas and along stop lines, a constant effort was being made to prevent the enemy reading correctly the indications on the ground. He might see a great deal of activity, but should he invade there would be some surprises waiting for him. In fact many of the most successful pieces of work were the least spectacular.

Along the coast displacements for new batteries of heavy guns were being built. At first there were constant failures in trying to hide these guns, because the hiding was so often left until after the construction work was complete. Then it was realised that concealment depended more on the ground chosen for the site, than on elaborate camouflage schemes. Camouflage officers were allowed to attend Siting Boards to help in the choice of sites and to suggest the layouts which the bomb aimer or reconnaissance pilot would find most difficult to locate. With good siting camouflage materials were used with advantage. On certain isolated sites large areas of activity were covered with elaborate overhead covers supported on steel scaffolding; at other sites bungalows, bathing booths, coastguard cottages and so on were used to house and make insignificant all military activity. Before and after construction was complete, the sites had to be viewed from the air and often from the sea, the latter not always a pleasant jaunt in the days of tip-and-turn raider and the magnetic mine.

And so in 1940-41 great efforts were being made in the UK to conceal military activity. All over the country suitable sites were being chosen for strong points, defended localities, Battle Headquarters and so on. Existing installations were being treated to reduce their visibility as targets. The Army was learning to use not only every available piece of cover, but also the patchwork pattern of the English countryside as a background on which it could merge its activity. The layman perhaps gathered some consolation from the Bookstalls and Teashops which did not sell books and tea; and the extra signal boxes which suddenly became needed along some of the railways in Kent although there were no extra signals. But the layman on the ground probably did not appreciate that an AA site or platoon locality which appeared exposed and unconcealed, had in fact been sited in relation to the pattern of the countryside in each a way that the air observer had little chance of stopping it.

At the time the rapidly growing Army had to be trained not to give away well concealed positions by making tell-tale tracks, careless digging and wiring, vehicles badly parked and movement in sight of the enemy.

Denial of resources

There was another side of defence which called for an immense amount of detailed preparation. That was denial of resources. The lesson had been learnt in France how the Panzer division could live and move on the country, and that must be prevented if they came to Great Britain.

The general policy governing denial of resources to the enemy was based on the assumption that the invaders must be beaten back within a week or 10 days. Denial had to be conjured within limits that would avoid our destroying resources to such an extent as to jeopardise our ability to continue the war after the invasion attempt had been defeated. A scorched earth policy was not practical in the United Kingdom. If we destroyed factories and stores in one place we could not replace them by stopping the production in rear areas as they did in Russia. There would be no rear areas in Great Britain. The country is too small for that.

Accordingly the plans were laid for removal of resources from threatened areas so far as transport was available, and for temporary disruption of remaining resources rather than destruction. Stocks of materials which would be useful to the enemy were reduced in the more vulnerable areas. But the plans were complicated by the fact that they could not be allowed to interfere with the preparation of the services to defeat the invasion. There was to be no disruption of the essential services, water, food, light and drainage which must remain for the civil population in areas overrun by the enemy.

Schemes for the denial of resources were started in May 1940 and would have been considerable hindrance to the enemy within a month of their inception, thanks largely to the whole-hearted cooperation of the various Civil Ministries and other authorities concerned and, by no means least, to that of the ordinary man in the street who took all the many emergency measures thrust upon him with astonishing cheerfulness and stoicism. As time went on the schemes became more detailed and by the spring of 1941 we were well on the way to being adequately prepared in this respect.

The following list of facilities and resources which were to be denied gives some indication of the complexity of the problem and of the amount of work involved. There was, moreover, no sort of precedent on which to base this work and everything had to be planned from scratch.

a)   Ports and landing facilities, such as piers.
b)   Merchant vessels in harbours.
c)   Locomotives and rolling stock.
d)   Vessels on inland waters.
e)   Civil motor vehicles.
f)   Agricultural tractors.
g)   Pedal cycles.
h)   Post office telephone exchanges and telegraph offices.
i)   Post office and BBC wireless stations.
j)   Public utility and vital industrial undertakings (excluding electricity, gas and water plants and food processing factories).
k)   Explosives.

l)   Civil food stocks (by distribution to the civil population).

m) Livestock.

n)   Currency.

o)   Papers containing vital information.

p)   Wireless relay exchanges.

q)   Petrol.

Separate schemes were necessary to deny all the above resources, and it is obviously impossible to give even a brief description of them, or of the many difficulties that had to be overcome. As an example the denial of petrol and other similar fuels will be given in outline. This branch of denial was the most complicated of all owing to the many interests involved and the many types of storage and fuels which had to be dealt with.

The German Blitz-Krieg plan of campaign had made one thing abundantly clear. That was that speed was of its essence. Speed in modern war means petrol. The denial of petrol was therefore of first importance. In the UK there was an abundance of petrol, (and other products capable of driving an internal combustion engine) widely distributed and easily accessible. The first essential was to reduce the quantity held in vulnerable areas and to render all stocks remaining there or in other parts of the country difficult to access to the invader or to destroy them when he arrived in sufficient force to make this necessary.

On 20th May 1940 the first GHQ orders were issued by General Sir Walter Kirke, the Commander-in-Chief of the Home Forces. These instructions dealt with the denial of stocks in pumps of the type used by garages and said that in emergency these pumps would be 'smashed with a heavy instrument', ARP personnel and the new-born LDV being responsible for carrying out the destruction. At night and whenever pumps were unattended all of their removable parts would be taken away and hidden. Denial of these convenient and, in the aggregate, very large stocks of petrol was described in the order as being 'of vital urgency'. From this small beginning grew a scheme which at one time covered all holdings in the UK not only of petrol, but of barrels, diesel oil and such possible though unlikely fuels as alcohols, acetone and toluene.

From the middle of 1940 intensive work went on in which GHQ received invaluable assistance in its plan from the other Services, the Ministry of Mines (Petroleum Department), the many other Civil Ministries concerned, and most of all, from the Petroleum Board upon whom fell the heavy burdens of not only reducing stocks of petrol in vulnerable areas, and so carrying out the mass of complicated executive work in connection with the denial of their own immense resources, but also of keeping the fighting services supplied. In addition the Board acted as advisors to GHQ throughout.

Having made rough and ready arrangements to deny pump stocks, the next step was to reduce stocks in the most vulnerable areas. The Petroleum Board assisted in this by closing a large number of their depots immediately and earmarking others for emptying on 'Stand To'. These vulnerable areas became known as the 'Pink Area' – a term which will long be remembered by those who dealt with petrol denial, for within it restrictions on holdings of petrol were more severe than in other parts of the country and denial measures more drastic. The area was defined by GHQ Home Forces. It stretched, after various amendments, around the coast from the South of the Moray Firth to the mouth of the Bristol Channel and varied in depth. The origin of the term 'Pink Area' is not perhaps generally known and has often been questioned. The fact is that pink happened to be the first colour that came to the draftsman's hand when the area was finally agreed and washed in on a map at a conference at which its limits were laid down by GHQ.

On 1st June 1940 the Government, after consultation with GHQ, issued Petroleum (No 3) Order 1940 under Defence Regulation 19B. This gave them the power to control the places at which petrol could be stored, to limit quantities stored and to lay down any other conditions deemed necessary. Under the powers thus taken the drastic thinning out of garages and other pumps began, and those that remained in operation in the 'Pink Area' were only permitted if provided with special 'security fit marks' for their immobilisation. Over 100,000 pumps or 90% of those in the 'Pink Area' were closed down. A share of the profits of retailers remaining open in that area was divided by the Petroleum Board among those who were put out of business.

From June 1940 until the end of 1941 the Petrol Denial Scheme grew until every type of storage, Naval, Military, Air Force and Civil was covered, and would have been denied if necessary by fire, demolition, or in the case of pump stocks immobilisation. Another method of denying stocks was contamination, but the only fuel for which a fairly satisfactory contaminant was ever found was benzole, and even then doubtful value owing to difficulty in thoroughly mixing the required quantity in the time available. Sugar, water, resin and fuel oil, which were all tried, among others, were found to be useless. They would all stop a private car if inserted in the right place in the right quantities, but would not contaminate petrol in bulk. Many contaminants were suggested by members of the public, but the answer was always either that they would not mix intimately with petrol, and remain mixed, or that they were substances already in short supply and for which there were heavy demands.

Conclusion

So in the vital summer months of 1940 the struggle to prepare went on, it was perhaps a blessing in disguise that the resistance in the Low Countries and France had quickly collapsed. If it had come more slowly to the same tragic end, the Germans would have been more ready for an immediate follow up with perhaps 30 or 40 of the 250 divisions of which they disposed at the time, and we should have lost those few months which gave us the opportunity to make up some of the deficiencies of equipment and some of the backwardness in training, and to prepare defences throughout the country. To aid the magnificent efforts of British Industry, we bought weapons from America, including the millions of rifles and many 75mm field guns. Canadian production too came to our aid. Long after the worst danger had receded the preparations for defences went on, until gradually they merged into our own plans and preparations to strike back.

But in 1940/41 it was not a pleasant prospect for those who were in the 'know'. Before the war there was often a joke cracked at the expense of the Territorial Army; 'Thank God' said the scoffers 'for the British Navy'. In the summer of 1940, it wasn't a joke any longer. Then the Army did thank God for the Navy, and for the Air Force too. Let us hope they never have to again.

Appendix II

Report on Marshall Aid[1]

Note by the Chairman of the London Committee

1. President Truman's address to the Congress on 19th December and the European Co-operation Bill (reproduced as appendix ii) mark a new stage in the progress of the European Recovery Programme (ERP). The Paris Report has been accepted as a reasonable starting point in the formulation of proposals for United States aid, and the Bill, which makes provision for aid in the scale suggested by that Report, will, if enacted in its present form, make possible the greater part of the Paris programme.

2. The Bill will no doubt encounter difficulties at some stage, and considerable amendments will probably be made. The Administration hopes that a Bill will be enacted by the end of March, but it may of course be delayed much longer.

3. However, the Administration wants the European Recovery Programme to start on 1st April, and it therefore intends to have bilateral discussions with the recipient countries as soon as the structure of the Bill is clear. These are likely to begin some time during February. The scope of such discussions depend upon the freedom which Congress gives to the Administration, but it may include the amount of aid which we receive by grants and the amount by loans and it will certainly cover the undertakings which we shall be required to give and the other conditions which the Americans will impose.

4. We must be ready by 1st February to enter these negotiations. We shall have to state how much aid we want and how we propose to use it; we shall be required to explain and defend our plans for achieving our own recovery with Marshall aid and for assisting and participating in European recovery.

5. The case is a formidable one to prepare; it cannot be prepared at a few days notice. In order to be ready in time, we must draw up detailed plans in January. But there are other reasons why we must move quickly. It would be useful and it may be necessary for us to discuss certain points with other European participants; Ministers may require to make statements in Parliament soon after the recess; consideration of the Economic Survey for 1948 will be impossible without an appreciation of ERP prospects. Finally, although our economic planning

1   National Archives CAB 134/215.

and overseas negotiations are based upon the assumption that there will be no Marshall aid – an assumption which is absolutely necessary until we are certain of Marshall aid in suitable quantity and with acceptable conditions – it is necessary to know what modifications will be possible or necessary if we receive Marshall aid. Indeed, ERP is so vital to all our economic affairs that in spite of the uncertainties we must get the best idea we can of where we stand.

6. The report in appendix i which was prepared before it had been possible to study the Economic Co-operation Bill and the supporting memoranda shows the framework, into which the detail can fit. This is as far as we can get without the guidance from Ministers. At this stage, we are not asking for decisions on matters of detail, but seek Ministerial approval for:

    a)   Certain major principles which govern the whole lay-out of our economy under ERP.

    b)   A provisional basis for working out our detailed programmes; and

    c)   An indication of the sort of conditions which we should be prepared to accept.

Principles

7. We recommend that in all our ERP planning we should be guided by two major principles (paragraphs 17-26):

    i)   That we must use Marshall aid to get ourselves as fast as possible into a position in which we are not dependent upon outside economic support.

    ii) That we must take the lead among, and co-operate to the fullest extent, with the other participating European countries, in our own interests and in the interests of the programmes as a whole we should take the lead in this co-operation.

8. The first of these is necessary in any event, for the system of annual appropriation means that aid may be cut off at any time; it is also a sound principle upon which to build our negotiating case, for the Americans will require a progressive reduction in the rate of aid; moreover, this will be a sound basis for resisting American pressures which would have the effect of increasing our dollar deficit.

9. The second principle is inherent in the whole concept of ERP, and we should take (or, rather, hold) the initiative rather than be dragged along by American and European pressure. The political advantages of this are considerable; it must be recognised that there will be short-term economic dis-advantages, but these will not be as serious as those which would confront us if there was no ERP at all or if we did not participate in ERP. Any such co-operation with the participating countries would have to take fully into account our Commonwealth interests, and the Commonwealth countries must be kept very fully informed.

Provisional Basis of the Programme

10. We have examined the economic possibilities for the fifteen-month period ending mid-1949 (the first period of ERP) and have drawn up an outline of the level of consumption, raw material and equipment supply, exports and investment which would be consistent with the principles in paragraph 7 above and with the amount of aid which at present appears to be contemplated by the United States Administration, provided that this is mainly in the form of grants (paragraphs 27-60). This would enable us to put a case which would imply food consumption restored to a level broadly similar to that ruling before the cuts were imposed this summer; the present consumption of textiles, tobacco and steel-using consumer goods; increased consumption of furniture and non-steel using consumer goods; restoration of some basic petrol and tourism and a six-page newspaper; some increase in home investment; some restocking of raw materials. Although it is probable that there will be sufficient financial aid to cover such a programme it is by no means certain that supplies will actually be available. It will only be possible if we receive the right amounts of individual commodities. It is a striking fact (which shows how far beyond our means we have been living) that even if we get one-quarter of our imports free under ERP, we shall still be unable to afford to do better than the level of consumption before this summer's cuts. Clearly therefore we cannot afford to cut back the export drive in order to increase consumption.

11. *We recommend* that the outline programme be approved as a provisional basis for planning our case.

Conditions of Aid

12. We shall be required to make commitments both to other participating countries (who will likewise have to make them to us) and to the United States. These will embrace the whole field of commitments made in Paris, both as regards mutual help, including working through a continuing organisation of the participating countries, and as regards specific production and export commitments.

13. *We recommend* that His Majesty's Government should be ready to make commitments on the following lines, which would probably be sufficient if the President's proposals were enacted as they stand:

    i) *Production* – undertakings to use our best endeavours to achieve specific production targets, e.g. for coal.

    ii) *Exports* – commitments to make available for export to the participating countries as a group (but not to individual countries) specific quantities of products e.g. tractors and fertilisers, which were examined in detail in Paris; in particular, to export to them 12½ million tons of coal between now and 30th June 1949, less any shortfall caused by non-availability of United States mining equipment; these commitments to be kept as flexible as possible.

    iii) *Reduction of trade barriers* – Accept the LTO draft charter in relation to general commercial policy; no specific commitment to abolish quantitative restrictions on trade with participants; no present undertaking to join a European customs union.

iv) *Stockpiling* – We should be ready, subject to suitable conditions, to help the United States Government to purchase in the Colonies reasonable quantities of strategic materials for stockpiles at reasonable prices.

v) *Use of Sterling proceeds of sales of ERP goods* – if sterling accruing from sales of goods given us under grant-in-aid were beneficially owned by His Majesty's Government, we should be prepared to accept a scheme whereby the use of these funds were circumscribed by some form of Trust Deed.

vi) *Publicity* – We could agree to publish regularly in the United Kingdom information about the aid received from the United States, and to take reasonable steps to provide United States with information about the use of ERP supplies.

14. The United States Administration may be unable to avoid imposing some restriction upon our freedom to export goods containing raw materials imported under ERP. If this happens, *we recommend* that we should seek to buy our freedom from such obligations on the best terms we can get.

15. If the Congress insists that some part of the aid given must be paid for by raw materials for stockpiles *we recommend* that we should agree to have some part of our repayment obligations applied for the purchase in the Colonies of such material at an agreed rate.

16. *We recommend* that assistance should not be sought at this stage to cover the dollar drain upon our reserves on account of the rest of the sterling area etc. An application on these lines might be necessary, however, if the Colonies dollar surplus were offset against the United Kingdom deficit and the amount of aid reduced accordingly.

17. This report does not cover two important questions, upon which recommendations cannot be made at this stage:

i) *Offshore Purchases* – It is crucially important to us that ERP dollars should be provided to enable us to make purchases of essential food and materials in Canada and Latin America. The President's message makes general provision for this. The nature of the arrangements made is vital for us, both financially and in the safety of our supplies. The United States Administration has been told what arrangement suits us best, and we will report to Ministers as soon as the United States intentions become clear.

ii) *Continuing Organisation* – we are committed to participate in – and, indeed, it would be desirable for us to take the lead in forming – a continuing organisation of the participating European Countries. The United States intentions about the scope and functions of this organisation (and particularly its relation to the Economic Committee for Europe) are not yet clear; but information is being sought. Preliminary discussion may also be necessary with the other European participants before we can make definite recommendations. We will report further to Ministers on this. Nor does the report deal with the organisational questions which will arise, both in London and in Washington and in relation to the European organisation. These questions are under consideration.

18. A further report will be submitted to Ministers when the Bill and the supporting memoranda have been fully examined.
19. The approval of Ministers is requested for the recommendations in paragraphs 7, 11, 13, 14, 15 and 16 above.

RWBC
Treasury Chambers SW1
22nd December 1947

Appendix III

Control of Expenditure after the Defeat in Germany[1]

I am directed by the Lords Commissioners of His Majesty's Treasury to state that during the last few years, when the nation's resources have all been devoted to the prosecution of the war, the main instrument for ensuring that those resources be used in accordance with Government policy has been the system of allocation of manpower and material between competing war purposes. The end of hostilities in Europe calls for a review of the position, and for the issue of fresh instructions to Departments.

For some considerable time to come, pressure on the nation's resources will remain intense. More particularly, while the war against Japan lasts, it will only be possible to meet the more vital of the other competing demands – housing, the repair of war damage, the rebuilding of civil industry, including, in particular, the export trade, and other civil purposes. The first essential, therefore, is to increase to the utmost the total volume of resources available for these purposes by the speedy winding up of all services rendered unnecessary by the end of the war in Europe. In the second place, regard must be had to the total means available, before deciding that services suspended or contracted during the war can be resumed or expanded or that new services can be instituted. In the third place, the present burden of war taxation must be reduced as soon as possible; but this cannot be done unless the present level of expenditure, which is not far short of double the proceeds of taxation even at its present high level, is substantially reduced as quickly as possible.

In furtherance of this policy, I am to inform you that the following measures will be taken:-

   a)   *Service and Supply expenditure.* The size and character of the Forces to be deployed in the Far East will be settled by directives issued by the Prime Minister and the Minister for Defence.

The existing delegations from the Treasury of financial authority will continue so far as they relate to immediate operational needs. It will be for consideration, between officers of the Treasury and of the Department concerned, how far existing delegations for other purposes should be withdrawn or reduced. The Service and Supply Departments should for their part consider how far their delegations to subordinate authorities should now

1   National Archives T 273/326.

239

be restricted.

The programmes of the Supply Departments will be governed by what is necessary to meet the need of the Forces in the field. The Treasury will make such proposals for stricter control as are compatible with conditions from time to time.

b) *All services administered by civil Departments in support of active operations or of passive defence* in connection with the war in Europe are to be brought to an end as soon as possible. My Lords would be glad to receive reports by 30th June 1945 of any such service which cannot be wound up by that date or which Departments may consider should be carried on, possibly in nucleus form, as part of the permanent post-war organisation.

c) *General.* No Department should automatically resume or expand services which have been suspended or contracted at the beginning of, or in the course, the war. Treasury authority must be sought in each case, and also, of course, for the institution of new services.

d) *Establishment matters.* The general principles set out in the preceding paragraphs apply equally in the field of establishments. Savings in manpower are urgently necessary over the whole field of Government employment (including Service and Supply Departments) and all Departments are asked to ensure that reductions in services are followed without delay by reductions in their staffs; for the time being and until further notice. Departments should continue to report actual and expected redundancies to their liaison officers.

During the next few months, when the situation will be changing rapidly, the handing of manpower and staff questions will be facilitated by the submission of reports from Departments on broad lines:

i)   Showing what functions can be discontinued or reduced.

ii) Showing the extent of the resultant savings in manpower, and

iii) Giving forecasts of the total staff which will be employed at given dates in the future.

Any general directions as to the rate of reductions which must be achieved, or as to the general disposition of manpower in Government Departments, will be based on these reports. The detailed form of these reports will be communicated separately to Departments and will be varied to allow for the different circumstances of Departments. Pending the submission of these reports, My Lords rely on Departments to cut out all work that is unnecessary, and to see that there is no waste in the staffs employed.

Wartime arrangements for the delegation of Treasury control of complements and of financial authority on establishment questions vary widely from Department to Department and My Lords will examine with each Department that is in possession of such delegated authority the extent to which that delegation should be withdrawn or modified.

e) *Wartime delegations of financial authority (other than on establishment matters).* Besides the continuance of the delegations to Service and Supply

Departments referred to at a) above, wartime delegations will be continued as regards any activities of civil Departments which are directly part of operational activities in the war against Japan. Moreover, these delegations will be continued for the present as regards certain services whose essential character is not altered by the end of the war in Europe. The chief examples of these are the shipping activities of the Ministry of War Transport under authorised programmes, the commercial operations of the Ministry of Food and of the Ministry of Fuel and Power, and the housing activities of the Ministry of Works. Treasury control cannot be effectively exercised over the very large volume of transactions in these fields, but their Lordships should, of course, continue to be consulted where general policy is involved and where general financial issues arise.

My Lords are prepared to consider other cases in which Departments consider the continuance of wartime delegations to be necessary. Apart from such special cases and except as indicated above, delegations of financial authority to Departments (other than on establishment matters) are withdrawn.

In light of the above, Departments are asked to consider how far in the changed circumstances their internal delegations of authority, e.g. to Regional Officers and Local Authorities, require to be modified if not immediately withdrawn.

f) *The cost of services* at present being financed out of Votes of Credit will continue to be so borne; but the question whether provision for new services during the current financial year should be made from the Vote of Credit or from ordinary Votes will be determined according to the principles laid down in paragraph 3 of Treasury Circular of the 2nd October 1944, on the subject of the Estimates for 1945. The question whether Parliament should be asked for Votes of Credit in 1946-47 cannot, of course, yet be determined.

I am Sir, your obedient servant
E E Bridges

Appendix IV

India's Demobilisation Scheme[1]

Plans for the reconstruction of the Post-war Regular Army in India are a priority requirement in the preparation of any scheme of demobilisation. If no decision can be given now, a hypothetical solution of the problem must be worked to.

In the first place there are matters of policy, which have to be considered to enable a reasonable assumption to be made for the demobilisation plan.

A few are indicated below:

a)   Whether the problem of Imperial Defence will be altered in the future and the repercussion on India of any such change.

b)   The composition, strength and location of strategical reserves.

c)   The strength and location of any detachments which India may be asked to provide, in peacetime, outside her boundaries.

d)   Co-ordination of the role of the Regular Army with any interim army.

e)   The proportion of British Troops which may be required to form part of the post-war army in India.

A. Policy

The complications which affect the reconstruction of the British Regular Army are enhanced in the army in India by the special conditions in that country.

This is still more complicated by the uncertainty of the new constitution.

At present it is only possible to imagine the probable influences which will affect the decisions to be made.

In any case the problem of defence of the North West Frontier will always be present.

B. Subsequent Action

When a working hypothesis for the strength and composition of the post-war Regular Army in India has been agreed upon or assumed, the plans for providing the man power will have to be laid down.

Some of the considerations affecting the problem are set out below:

a)   Provision of King's Commissioned Officers for the Indian Army. What

1   National Archives WO 32/13808.

arrangements can be made to fill the gap existing between the officers of the pre-war army and the entry after the war.

This can only be done by selection from among the ECO European Officers and the ICOs given emergency commissions. To this purpose some sort of committee will have to be constituted on the lines of the Moens Committee. One principle should be maintained. Officers should be distributed amongst battalions so that their seniority does not interfere with others.

It is for serious consideration whether the pre-war system of selecting officers on application by Brigade and Regimental Commanders must not be altered. By this system the popular regiments got the pick of officers and those not so much in the limelight, the remainder. The experience of this war shows the material in many of what may be termed the unfashionable regiments is just as good as that in the others. To get a good level with efficiency the only claim that an officer should have on a unit is a hereditary or family connection. The remainder should be distributed by GHQ without favour or affection.

b) The source of provision for personnel of the Technical branches of the Army

The tendency will be for unit trained personnel to seek civil employment. Owing to competition they are unlikely to get employment but until bitter experience proves it, and destroys the tendency, the only solution would appear to offer special terms to induce men to stay – these should be in the form of increased deferred pay.

c) The personnel for coast defence and anti-aircraft units.

Suggested that these should be manned by Anglo-Indian personnel. As long as 'Class' units exit in the Indian Army there can be no objection to forming Anglo-Indian Units.

d) The future of Auxiliary Forces, both British, Anglo-Indian and Indian.

It would appear that all these forces will have to be amalgamated into one force. Legal complications would have to be worked out. Again there will be no objection to these being 'Class' Units.

e) The provision of instructors for any reconstituted Auxiliary Forces.

f) The reintroduction, or otherwise, of Territorial Units.

This is covered by suggestion d).

g) The broadening of the area of recruitment so as to cover most of India

This is obvious and will entail diminution of the large proportion enlisted in the North as compared with those from the South.

The biggest repercussion will be the economic effect on the Punjab which has, for so long, greatly depended on the pay and pensions drawn from the army.

h) Modernisation and mechanisation will undoubtedly influence our organisation and distribution of the various components of the army. Where in the past, units on an IS role were distributed widely in single unit stations, mechanisation will permit more concentration and also economy in troops.

Comments by Commands tend to suggest that single unit stations give good OsC excellent opportunities for training their units. Large stations are expensive to individuals and with mechanisation make training areas congested.

In view of the possibility of a reduction in the size of the army, apart from any other points of view, concentration would appear to be the right policy.

Appendix V

Report by the Government Organisation Committee on National Registration[1]

Cabinet – Lord President's Committee

1. We have had the future of National Registration under consideration for some time. The setting up of the National Register was an emergency measure, made possible by emergency legislation, and there are evident political objections to its indefinite continuance. We have, in fact, been forcibly reminded of these recently by the publicity which has followed the High Court decision in the Willcock case.

2. We have not gone into the legal difficulties raised by this latter decision, nor have we attempted to assess the weight of the political objections to the continuation of National Registration. We have addressed ourselves to the following questions: do we still need National Registration and, if so, for what purpose; or could we now make do without it?

Use of the National Register

3. In essence the National Registration system secures that for each member of the population there is an identity card and a central record of his personal particulars, both the card and the record bearing a unique code number for each person. It is evident that such a system will be a great convenience for a wide variety of purposes; everyone will have a number by means of which he can be identified in official and other records and an identity card enabling him to establish his identity, while the central record will provide a useful point of reference for anyone requiring the personal particulars of a named individual.

4. We do not propose to detail all the many uses of the system. But certain of them stand out either because security is in question or because administrative efficiency or public financial interests are at stake. We deal with these uses below, and we also mention other main purposes for which it is evident to use National Registration.

    a) National Service. The Ministry of Labour and National Service use the National Registration system to trace national service defaulters. From the central register it is possible to identify those men in any age group who have failed to register for national service, and to supply their current addresses.

1   National Archives CAB 21/3476.

A large number of defaulters are traced in this way; moreover, the operation of the system is undoubtedly a valuable deterrent to the would-be defaulter.

b) Reservists. The Service Departments are at present engaged in checking the addresses of the reservists on their books; the War Office alone have 1,800,000 addresses to check. The purpose of the operation is to make it possible on mobilisation to communicate with reservists individually instead of by proclamation; this may be necessary for security reasons, and in any case will ensure a quicker and more selective recall.

c) Security Service. The Security authorities rely heavily on the National Register in order to obtain dependable evidence as to the identity of people whom they are asked to investigate. The number of these people is large and growing, and the method used ensures discretion since news of the enquiries do not reach the subjects of them.

d) National Health Service. The Health Departments are using the Register as a means of checking inflation in doctors lists – due to duplicate entries, the failure to remove people who have died or transferred to other doctors etc. Such inflation distorts the arrangements for paying doctors, and the Health Departments proposed to user the National Register:
   (i) To remove the present inflation.
   (ii) To prevent the recurrence of inflation by providing a central index in which each individual member of the population is represented by a unique code number.

e) Food Rationing. The National Register provides a valuable supplementary control to prevent the issue of duplicate ration books.

f) Other main uses. The identity card is used to establish the identity of persons withdrawing money from the Post Office Savings Bank, and of applicants for passports and National Assistance.

Efficiency of National Registration

5. It will be seen that for a preponderance of the uses of the National Register it is essential that the addresses in it be up to date. It is, therefore, important to know how long the National Register is likely to continue at its present level of efficiency as a source of up to date addresses.

6. The Register's main source of notifications of address changes is its link with food rationing. Each year seven million notifications are received, and the bulk of these come in during the period of the ration book issue. The prospects of an early end to food rationing are not rosy, and it seems certain that for an indefinite period some foods will continue to be rationed. It follows that National Registration could be maintained indefinitely at its present level of efficiency. This, of course, assumes that the present system of issuing ration books continues. If the system is changed and a postal issue or biennial ration book is introduced (both possibilities have been considered), the result would be some falling off in the efficiency of the National Register.

National Insurance Records

7. If National Registration were discontinued most of the users would have to look to the records of the Ministry of National Insurance to take its place. It is, therefore, important to consider how efficient these records would be for their purposes as compared with the National Register.

8. The National Insurance records contain particulars of the 25 million people who are registered for national insurance, plus 15 million people who are recorded separately in the pensions and family allowance sections. Of the people who do not appear in the records, the vast majority are, therefore, people of pensionable age, married with women and children. For most purposes these exclusions are not the first importance; certainly one can assume that the records will cover most of the people affected by national service or the mobilisation of reservists, and most of those in whom the Security Services are interested (though we understand that a proportion of the latter are over pensionable age).

9. A more serious weakness of the National Insurance records than their incomplete coverage is the fact that the addresses they contain are not so up-to-date as those in the National Register; as evidence of this, we understand that they send 360,000 address queries annually to the National Register. However, no doubt more could be done to improve the arrangements for keeping addresses in National Insurance records up-to-date if it were decided that National Registration must go.

10. Our broad conclusion is that the National Insurance records would provide a possible, though less efficient, substitute for all the important uses of National Registration except for those which are the concern of the Health Departments and the Ministry of Food. For their purposes a central record covering every member of the population is needed, and if this is not available they will no longer be able to apply the checks for which they are now using National Registration.

Views of the Users

11. We now set out the views of the main users Departments on the proposition that National Registration should be discontinued and the records of the Ministry of National Insurance used in place of it wherever necessary and possible.

    (1) The Ministry of Labour and National Service realise that the work of detecting call-up defaulters will be less efficient once National Registration has gone; but they are prepared to make do with the National Insurance records.

    (2) The Service Departments feel strongly that the National Register should be kept in being until they have completed their check of the addresses of reservists. They are satisfied that during this period the National Insurance records will not be a satisfactory substitute.

    (3) The Security Service would strongly deprecate a decision to dispense with the National Register. They regard it as by far the most satisfactory source of reliable evidence of identity, which is so important in the cases they have to handle.

    (4) The Health Departments would prefer to see National Registration continued so as to provide them with an efficient central record for their own purposes;

they do, however, accept that their need alone would not justify the retention of the Register. They are now using it to screen doctor's lists; and they would propose, if and when the National Registration system were wound up, to take over its central records as a central index for the National Health Service.

(5) The Ministry of Food is prepared to dispense with the supplementary check on the issue of food ration books for which they at present use the National Register.

Arguments against retention

12. The arguments for the retention of the National Registration system are all mentioned above. It remains to set out the arguments against it.

13. There is no doubt that National Registration is very convenient for its many users; but it is difficult to maintain that it is indispensable. Certainly in normal times it would be impossible to justify retaining the National Register as well as the National Insurance records; and at present, while the near-emergency conditions may be thought to justify such an arrangement, we have to remember that those same conditions make it necessary to cut out any unnecessary activities. The immediate saving which would result from the ending of National Registration, allowing for the retention of the central records for National Health Service purposes, has been estimated at £500,000 per annum.

14. It may be suggested that National Registration should be retained for the time being, since it would be required if war broke out. But the shift of population on the outbreak of war would be so great that the Government would probably be compelled to re-register the whole population.

Conclusions

15. On the practical issue whether or not the balance of advantage is on the side of retaining or of dispensing with National Registration, we were unable to reach agreement. Opinion was in fact clearly divided between two alternative recommendations to Ministers:

(1) That a decision in principle to dispense with National Registration should be taken now and work started immediately on detailed arrangements to prepare the way for its termination as soon as possible.

(2) That no final decision should be taken on the future of National Registration for the moment; that it should be kept in being for a year and that in the meantime a full report should be prepared for Ministers on the best arrangements which could be made to meet the needs of users in other ways.

But behind this issue there lies an important political issue, which Ministers will wish to consider. A good deal of the criticism of the continuance of the National Register derives from the argument that it was established for the purposes of the national emergency and has been retained for the purposes different from those intended in 1939 without any express decision of Parliament that it should be so used.

16. If, therefore, Ministers decide that the National Register should be retained for

a substantial period, they may wish to consider whether it would be desirable to introduce legislation for its retention on a permanent basis and setting out the purposes for which it should be used.

Signed on behalf of the Committee
Cabinet Office SW1
August 1951

Appendix VI

Limitation of Suppliers in future rationing schemes[1]

1. In the 1939-45 war certain broad measures (outlined briefly in paragraphs 2 to 5) were taken which resulted in:
   a) A saving in transport, manpower and petrol.
   b) Economy in overall stocks needed to enable retailers to honour declared rations.
   c) A simplification of Food Office work in connection with permit procedures.
2. Retailers and establishments (i.e. catering establishments and institutes) were required to nominate their suppliers for the principal rationed and controlled foods. The following restrictions were imposed:
   a) A retailer or an establishment purchasing by wholesale could not nominate more than one supplier for each of the following commodities:
      i) Sugar (a second supplier was, however, permitted for speciality sugars).
      ii) Cooking fats (a second supplier was, however, permitted for vegetarian cooking fats).
      iii) Butter (excluding farm butter).
      iv) Cheese.
      v) Margarine (a second supplier was, however, permitted for vegetarian nut butters).
      Not more than two suppliers for:
      vi) Bacon.
      vii) Tea (if less than 24lb per 4 week period was sold).
      Not more than four suppliers for:
      viii) Tea (if not less than 24lb per week period was sold).
   b) An establishment purchasing from a retailer could not nominate more than one supplier for any one food and could not nominate more than one retailer in respect of commodities in the fats group (viz. butter, margarine and cooking fats).
3. A sector scheme operated with certain exceptions, prohibited a wholesaler, first-hand distributor or manufacturer, from supplying customers outside his own sector. The sectors were constituted as follows:

1   National Archives MAF 313/26.

i)   Sector 1 – London, Eastern, South-Eastern and Southern Regions.

ii)   Sector 2 – South-Western Region.

iii)   Sector 3 – South Wales Region.

iv)   Sector 4 – Midland Region.

v)   Sector 5 – North-Midland Region.

vi)   Sector 6 – North-Western, North Wales and East and West Ridings Regions.

vii)   Sector 7 – Northern Region.

viii)   Sector 8 – Scotland.

ix)   Sector 9 – Northern Ireland.

Transport Division was responsible for the operation of this Scheme.

4. In the case of certain manufactured commodities where the area of distribution was largely dependent upon the place of production the Sector Scheme restrictions were deemed to be inapplicable and were replaced by monitoring schemes operated by the interested commodity divisions. The four main statutory zoning schemes were those of self-raising flour, breakfast cereals, preserves and pickles and sauces.

5. There was also a scheme operated by the Milk Division, governing the rationalisation of collection and distribution of milk supplies.

6. It is anticipated that conditions in a future war may well be such as would warrant measures of far greater stringency than those applied previously. Whilst this Division is not responsible for devising Sector, zoning and rationalisation schemes, it would have responsibility in co-ordinating capacity for determining what restrictions regarding limitation of suppliers ought to be imposed in any future rationing schemes. In this connection it is relevant to recall that in the confidential document entitled 'Food Distribution in the event of a future War – Groceries and Provisions (Wholesale)', which was agreed by both the Independent Wholesaler's representatives and the Ministry in 1953, paragraph 5 states:

Limitation of Suppliers – if the economy in the use of transport is to be effected, it is essential that an agreed basis for limitation of suppliers should be laid down, and it is suggested that retailers with a turnover of less than £150 per week in groceries and provisions should not be permitted to draw supplies from more than five wholesale suppliers, including specialist wholesalers, but excluding manufacturers, whilst the largest retailers should not be allowed more than ten. It must be recognised that some restrictions in the number of suppliers allowed to a wholesaler will be inevitable.

7. As detailed in paragraph 2 a retailer with a minimum trade stipulated in the case of tea, could during the previous scheme, have as many as 15 different suppliers for the principal rationed and controlled foods. It should also be borne in mind that under the points, soap and personal points rationing schemes there was no limitation as to the number of suppliers that a retailer could have. With minor modifications this applied also to establishments.

8. It has been suggested in the document quoted in paragraph 6 that retailers should have from five to ten wholesale suppliers (excluding manufacturers according to turnover in groceries and provisions). This would, however, present certain difficulties, viz:

    a) In equity, there would need to be a sliding scale of suppliers related to turnover – it would obviously be unfair to allow a retailer with £150 turnover five suppliers whilst one with £151 could have ten.

    b) In order to determine the number of suppliers to be allowed it would be necessary either to obtain from retailers a declaration of turnover, which would be of doubtful accuracy, or to examine accounts, in which case, owing to differing accounting years and the time required to produce statements, it would be extremely unlikely that details relating to a specified recent period could in all cases be made available. Examination of accounts, the only reliable criterion would almost certainly be impracticable anyway, in view of the immense amount of detailed work involved.

    c) Further to b) above, it would be necessary carefully to define 'Groceries and Provisions' as this term might well be construed to include points foods in respect of which limitation of suppliers has not been previously applied. If such limitation were to be applied in future, points food suppliers would not necessarily include suppliers of the main rationed/controlled commodities, in which case it would be logical to exclude points foods from the definition.

    d) Whatever method of determining turnover were adopted it would inevitably involve a considerable amount of preliminary work by Food Offices. Such work would of necessity have to be done before initial permits could be prepared and the time taken would therefore represent a delay in implementing formal rationing.

9. It is therefore suggested that simplicity might be achieved and dissatisfaction within the trade avoided if all retailers and establishments were instructed at the material time that they could have only <u>one supplier</u> (retailer, wholesaler, manufacturer or FHD) for each rationed or controlled food (including special varieties), except tea for which retailers only could have two (irrespective of turnover), and not more than five suppliers in all.
    Notes:

    i)   If an overall limitation to five suppliers is deemed practicable for retailers with a turnover of £150 per week (vide para. 6) it is difficult to see why it should not also be practicable in the case of larger retailers who would presumably merely be dealing in larger quantities of the same commodities.

    ii) If National Tea were introduced only one supplier would be needed for tea.

10. It is further suggested that, while nomination of suppliers is not contemplated in the proposed scheme for points, personal points and soap rationing in a future war, similar advantages would nevertheless accrue (mainly concerning transport, manpower and petrol economies) if retailers were restricted to purchasing goods (by transfer slips) from not more than say four suppliers in respect of each of the above schemes. This would be effected either by requiring retailers to nominate

their four suppliers or by stipulating that they may purchase from not more than four suppliers during each ration period (4-week or 8-week as appropriate): the latter arrangement would allow retailers to vary their suppliers so long as they did not exceed the limited number, would give increased flexibility. The number of suppliers would be apparent from the statement on the back of each surrendered deposit slip. The same restriction could be applied also to establishments' points accounts and to institutions' personal points accounts.

11. Although it is accepted that wholesalers' suppliers would also need to be limited it is probable that the main rationed/controlled commodities would again be distributed to wholesalers either by the Ministry or by Ministry sponsored companies in which case no problem would arise. If this were not so, however, it would be necessary to consider what restrictions, if any, would be practicable. Where wholesalers operated points, personal points or soap accounts, consideration would also need to be given to the practicability or otherwise of restricting the number of suppliers in respect of each account.

12. To summarise, the advantages of the restrictions outlined in previous paragraphs would be as follows:
    a) A saving in transport, manpower and petrol.
    b) Economy in stocks required to be held at and above the retail level.
    c) A simplification of the work required to be done by both Food Offices and traders in connection with permit and points etc. account procedures.

The objectives must obviously be to achieve the greatest possible economy and simplification commensurate with supply arrangements that, in the circumstances envisaged, can be no better than adequate: anything more would constitute a luxury that could not be afforded.

Rationing and Welfare Foods Division
20 September 1954

Appendix VII

Railway (London Plan) Committee 1944. Report to the Minister of War Transport 21 January 1946[1]

Summary of conclusions and recommendations
The following summary is an attempt to tabulate the specific conclusions we have reached. For the precise nature of the recommendations, however, and for the arguments on which they are based, reference should in every case be made to the main body of the report.

General Principles
a) As a general proposition, the railways for passenger and goods operation should be electrified, priority being given to completing the electrification of suburban passenger services.
b) Loop working is not a practicable proposition.
c) The underground system should, in general, be separated from main line tracks so far as inter-running is concerned.
d) Deep level stations for suburban traffic carried in standard size rolling stock are possible, provided:
    i) Sliding-door stock is used.
    ii) Services are arranged to localize the handling of heavy luggage and parcels traffic without inconvenience.
e) It is possible to project suburban traffic across London in tunnel.
f) Deep-level stations for long-distance main line traffic are impracticable, but sub-surface terminals (say 20-30 feet below road level) could be operated where conditions are favourable.

Conclusions on proposals in the County of London Plan
a) The deep-level loop from London Bridge to Waterloo, Charing Cross, Cannon Street and back to London Bridge is not recommended.
b) The North Bank Link at deep level, from Clapham Junction to Deptford, is not recommended.
c) The North-South deep line from Snow Hill to Loughborough Junction is

1   National Archives MT 6/2787.

recommended, subject to minor amendment, in the Committee's own proposals.

d) Preliminary consideration of the Northern Arc suggests that it should not be approved.

e) Charing Cross and Cannon Street stations should not be removed until alternative facilities have been provided. The existing prohibition on any improvement to Charing Cross Station should be withdrawn.

Railway Development as related to Housing and Industry

The factors which affect the volume of traffic and the provision of transport in the Greater London area are:

a) **The future population of the area**. It is assumed that this will not change appreciably in magnitude for the next generation.

b) **Its distribution within the area**. The tendency for a wider dispersion of residence will continue.

c) **Travel from home to work**. The satellite town proposals of the Greater London Plan are designed to unite residence with work, and if future development is on these lines, as compared with the suburban sprawl of the past, it should result in the volume of travel between home and work being much less than such a dispersion of the population would otherwise have made it. On the other hand, it is not understood to be the intention that compulsion should be used either to limit residence in satellite towns to those who work there or to restrict their industries to local labour.

d) **Social habits**. As income rises, the demand for transport can be expected to rise more than proportionately.

e) **The magnitude of the rush hour peak**. The prospect of reducing this is not encouraging.

For all these reasons, we conclude that the volume of travel, as measured in passenger journeys and still more in passenger miles, will continue to rise.

Outline of the Committee's proposals

a) In order to provide for the removal of Charing Cross and Cannon Street stations, all suburban services on the Eastern Section of the Southern Railway not terminating at these stations should be put into tunnel.

b) Similarly, suburban services on the Central Section now terminating at London Bridge should be put into tunnel.

c) Suitable provision should be made for a new tunnel for main line trains now terminating at Charing Cross, Cannon Street, London Bridge and Holborn Viaduct.

d) The tunnels should be projected across London so as to secure through running with suburban services of the other main line companies.

e) The tunnels should be of diameter large enough to take standard-size stock. They should be designed for high speed operation, with a limited number of in-town stations, located as near as physical conditions permit to focal points on the existing underground system.

f) In general, these cross-London services should be provided with their own tracks on the surface sections beyond the limits of the new tunnel system.

g) Facilities for handling parcels, newspapers, merchandise and luggage should be provided in the new tunnels only at the stations to be located beneath the present main line terminals.

Proposals designed to facilitate the re-planning of the South Bank

a) The major proposal under this head is for five lines in tunnel all diverging from a new deep level station under the Southern Railway at Tower Bridge Road. There are:

  i) **Route 1**. Via Fenchurch Street and Moorgate connecting there with the existing Northern City line to Finsbury Park and thence with the Alexandra Park and Enfield Town branches of the LNER.

  ii) **Route 2**. Via Bank, Holborn Viaduct, Euston and the LMS line to Watford.

  iii) **Route 3**. Via Bank, Holborn, Tottenham Court Road, Bond Street, Marylebone and the LNER line to High Wycombe and perhaps Aylesbury.

  iv) **Route 4**. Via Cannon Street, Aldwych, Piccadilly Circus, Marble Arch, Paddington, Maida Vale, Cricklewood and the LMS line to St Albans and Harpenden.

  v) **Route 5**. Via Waterloo, Charing Cross, Piccadilly Circus, Marble Arch, Paddington and the GWR suburban system.

b) The proposal in the County of London Plan for a North-South deep level line is incorporated as follows:

  vi) **Route 6**. A line in tunnel for passenger traffic from Loughborough Junction via Elephant and Castle, Waterloo, Ludgate Circus, Holborn Viaduct, Mount Pleasant, King's Cross, and connecting with the LNER suburban system near Finsbury Park.

  vii) **Route 7**. A line in tunnel for freight traffic from Loughborough Junction, following the existing surface route through Blackfriars and Holborn to Farringdon, where it would join the existing 'Widened Lines' and make contact with the main line system to the north.

c) London Bridge Station would have to be moved about half a mile to the south-west and a new station built at Tower Bridge Road, beneath which would be the deep level station from which Routes 1 to 5 would diverge.

d) A new terminal for main line trains should be built at Waterloo Junction and surface trains (i.e. main line traffic) should reach this station from Tower Bridge Road by a partly or wholly new route running to the south of the present viaduct.

Proposals to meet immediate traffic requirements

a) **Route 8**. A new line from East Croydon in tunnel from Norbury via Streatham, Brixton, Stockwell, Vauxhall, Victoria, Hyde Park Corner, Bond Street, Euston, King's Cross and Finsbury Park, beyond which connection would be made with the LNER routes to Hitchin via Potters Bar and via Cuffley. The purpose of this route is:

    i)   To relieve the heavy pressure on the railway between Balham and Victoria.

    ii)   To provide badly needed cross-town communication from Victoria.

b)   **Route 9**. A new line in tunnel from Raynes Park (Where connection would be made with the Southern Railway) via Wimbledon, Clapham Junction, Vauxhall, Millbank, Westminster, Charing Cross, Holborn, St Paul's, Liverpool Street, Dalston and Clapton, where connection would be made with the Chingford Branch of the LNER. The purposes of this route are, among others, to provide relief for the Southern Railway between Raynes Park and Waterloo and, between the West End and Liverpool Street, to provide relief for the LPTB Central Line, which will be overlooked when the schemes included in the 1935/40 programme are complete.

c)   Relief is also needed for the LTPB Northern Line. Route 10 would double the existing tube.

Appendix VIII

Nationalisation – Transport Bill 1946: Memorandum to the general managers[1]

Transport Commission

The Commission is to consist of a chairman and four other members, all of whom shall be appointed by the Minister from among persons appearing to him to have had wide experience and shown capacity in Transport, Industrial, Commercial or Financial matters, in Administration or in the organisation of workers.

The powers of the Commission, which are set out in Clause 2 of the Bill include, amongst other things, power to do anything for the purpose of advancing the skill of persons employed by the Commission or the efficiency of the equipment of the Commission or of the manner in which that equipment is operated, including the provision by the Commission, and the assistance of provision by others, of facilities for training, education and research.

The Executive

Public authorities known as Executives to assist the Commission are to be appointed as follows:

    i)   Railway Executive.
    ii)   Docks and Inland Waterways Executive.
    iii) Road Transport Executive.
    iv) London Transport Executive.
    v)   Hotels Executive.

The Executives shall, as agents of the Commission, exercise such functions of the Commission as are for the time being delegated to them by a scheme made by the Commission and approved by the Minister.

Each Executive shall consist of a chairman and not less than four and not more than eight other members appointed by the Minister, after consultation with the Commission, from among persons who appear to the Minister to have had wide experience and shown capacity in transport, industrial, commercial or financial matters, in administration or in the organisation of workers.

It will be seen from the foregoing that the Bill enables trade union officials to

1   National Archives RAIL 1172/1305.

be appointed as members of the Transport Commission and of the Executives. It is presumed that on appointment they would cease to be trade union officials.

The comments of the Conference on Part VII of the Bill are as follows:

Clause 99

This clause lays a duty on the Commission to satisfy themselves that adequate machinery exists for:

a)   The **settlement** by negotiation of terms and conditions of employment of persons employed by the Commission, with provision for reference to arbitration in default of such settlement in such cases as may be determined by or under the agreements.

b)   The **discussion** of matters affecting the safety, health and welfare of persons employed by the Commission, and of other matters of mutual interest to the Commission and such persons, including efficiency in the operation of the Commission's services.

And where they are not so satisfied it is their duty to seek consultation with any organisation appearing to them to be appropriate for the purpose of concluding such agreements as appear to the parties to be desirable.

Sub-clause (3) declares that the above provisions require to be satisfied separately as respects the persons under the control of <u>each Executive</u> or under the direct control of the Commission itself.

The clause places an obligation on the Commission and the Executives respectively to supply copies of all agreements entered into to the Ministry of Labour and National Service.

Comments:

There is a difference between this clause and clause 101 of the Bill in the wording as to the matters for negotiation. Under sub-clause (a) above reference is made to the 'terms and conditions of employment' while in clause 101 the questions to be dealt with are referred to as 'rates of pay, hours of duty and conditions of service'. It is not clear why this distinction is made as the questions to be dealt with under both clauses are, presumably, intended to be the same, viz., rates of pay, hours of duty and conditions of service of the persons employed by the Commission. The Railway Staff Conference suggest that this should be made clear in the Bill.

The existing provision of the Railways Act for the staff other than police refers to rates of pay, hours of duty and other conditions of service, and the implications of this difference will doubtless be the subject of consideration by the solicitors, including consideration of what are to be regarded as conditions of employment or conditions of service, as the case may be.

The reference to the provision for arbitration of cases 'in default of such settlement in such cases as may be determined by or under the agreements', referred to in sub-clause (a) above is not clear.

Dealing with the clause generally, so far as the staff of the main line railways are concerned there exist at the present time Schemes of Machinery of Negotiation, for dealing with questions relating to rates of pay, hours of duty and conditions of service, but certain modifications would appear to be necessary in those schemes under this clause. For example, the schemes would require to be extended to embrace the staff of the Minor Railway Companies which are not at present covered by the schemes, and under sub-clause (3) of Clause 99 it would appear that separate provision would require to be made for the following sections of staff, which are embraced within the Scheme of Machinery of Negotiation for railway staff:

Salaried and conciliation staff employed at railway-owned docks and on railway-owned canals which would come under the control of the Docks and Inland Waterways Executive.

The workshop staff employed in connection with railway-owned docks and canals would also presumably have to be taken out of the Scheme of Machinery of Negotiation for Railway Shopmen and be provided for under the Docks and Inland Waterways Executive.

For the purposes of their comments the Railway Staff Conference have assumed that the Railway Cartage staff will continue as railway staff and come within the jurisdiction of the Railway Executive.

Clause 100
This clause continues in force, until agreements are reached under the preceding clause, the agreements made under Sections 62 to 66 of the Railways Act 1921 and the London Passenger Transport Act 1933, and provides that it shall not be necessary for there to be separate Councils under Section 63 of the Railways Act but that one Council may be established for two or more of the Railways.

Comments:
The clause appears to provide for the possibility of one set of Sectional Councils for the whole of the railways and the Railways Staff Conference who have no comments to make thereon.

Clause 101
This clause provides for the establishment of a Conference consisting of an equal number of representatives of the Commission and of the members of the Police Forces of the Commission for dealing with the questions of rates of pay, hours of duty and conditions of service of the Commission's police forces. As in the case of the present Machinery for the Main Line Police it provides for the appointment of an independent chairman to give binding decisions in the event of disagreement between the two sides of the Conference.

Comments:
The effect of the clause will be to substitute for the present Scheme of Machinery of Negotiation for Police staff established under the Railways Act 1921, which covers the police staff of the main line railways only, a new scheme which will

include, in addition to the main line police, the police of the London Transport Board and the Dock Authorities who have their own police forces.

Clause 102
This clause authorises the Minister to make regulations for providing pensions, for the continuance, amendment, repeal or revocation of existing pension schemes and for the provisions, including the provision for the winding up of bodies, whether incorporate or not, the continued existence whereof is unnecessary having regard to the regulations.

The regulations are to be so framed as to secure that persons having pension rights are not placed in any worse position by reason of the amendment, repeal, revocation, transfer, extinguishment or winding-up.

Nothing in this section is to be taken to derogate from the power conferred by sub-section (4) of section 69 of the National Insurance Act 1946, to make regulations modifying or winding-up of pension schemes in connection with the passing of this act.

Comments:
The Railways Staff Conference have no comments to make on this clause.

Clause 103
This clause provides that the provisions of the act which direct that obligations and liabilities of a body shall become, as from the date of transfer, obligations and liabilities of the Commission shall apply in relation to customary obligations of the body in relation to pensions, notwithstanding that the body was not under legal obligation in respect of those pensions. Disputes are to be referred to a referee or board of referees. The clause also safeguards the pension rights of individuals and provides that any power which, under statutory provision, rules, trust deeds and other instruments relating to a pension fund, is expressed to be exercisable by a director or officer of any of the bodies specified in the Third Schedule to the Bill, shall, on and after the date of transfer, be exercisable by such person as the Commission may appoint.

Comments:
The words 'customary obligations' used in this clause are different from those used in the Railways Act of 1921 which referred to 'customary practice' and the significance of the change of expression is not clear to the Railways Staff Conference.

Clause 104
This clause provides that a person who:
a)   Was, immediately before the date of transfer, in the employment of any of the bodies mentioned in the Third Schedule to this Act, but has by arrangement

with that body acted continuously as an officer of the Minister since before the end of the year nineteen hundred and forty two, and:

b) Was, immediately before the date of transfer, a participant in any such scheme as is mentioned in the last preceding section, and:

c) Becomes, on the date of transfer, an officer of the Minister, and:

d) Consents that this section shall apply to them.

shall cease to be a participant of the scheme on the date of transfer and shall pay over to the Minister any return of contributions made to him under the scheme.

Comments:

The clause appears to be drafted to meet the position of the people who were transferred to the Ministry of Transport during the war. So far as the railways are concerned it is a limited number and the Railways Staff Conference have no comment to make on the clause.

Clause 105

This clause provides that the Minister shall, by regulations, require the Commission to pay in such cases and to such extent as may be specified in the regulations, compensation:

a) To officers or servants of any person whose undertaking is transferred to the Commission by Part II of this Act, or:

b) To officers or servants of any person whose undertaking or part of whose undertaking is transferred to the Commission by notice of acquisition given under Part III of this Act, or:

c) To officers or servants employed in connection with the Caledonian and Crinan or Holyhead Harbour or by or in connection with the Railways Clearing House.

being officers or servants who suffer loss of employment or loss or diminution of emoluments or pension rights by reason of the transfer.

The regulations made under this clause:

a) May prescribe the procedure to be followed in making claims for compensation, and the manner in which and the persons by whom the question whether any or what compensation is payable is to be determined, and:

b) May in particular contain provisions enabling appeals from any determination as to whether any or what compensation is payable to be brought, in such cases and subject to such conditions as may be prescribed by the regulations, to a referee or board of referees appointed by the Minister of Labour and National Service.

The decision of the referee or board of referees is to be final.

The regulations shall not prejudice the rights of any person under the Third Schedule to the Railway Act 1921.

Comments:

The compensation provisions of the Railway Act 1921 are more comprehensive than the provisions of this clause.

Further, this clause gives no indications as to the basis on which compensation will be assessed but provides for regulations to be made on the subject.

The Railways Staff Conference consider that the grounds for compensation should be as comprehensive as those provided for in the Railways Act and that the basis on which compensation will be assessed should be included in the Bill.

Clause 124

This clause contains the following definitions amongst others:

i)   **Pension** in relation to a person, means a pension whether contributory or not, of any kind whatsoever payable to him, and includes a gratuity so payable and a return of contributions to a pension fund, with or without interest thereon or any other addition thereto.

ii) **Pension fund** means a fund established for the purposes of paying a pension.

iii) **Pension rights** includes, in relation to any person, all forms of right to or eligibility for the present or future payment of a pension, and any expectation of the accruer of a pension under any customary practice.

iv) **Pension scheme** includes any form of arrangements for the payment of pensions, whether subsisting by virtue of the Act of Parliament, trust, contract or otherwise.

Comments:

The Railways Staff Conference have no comments to make on this clause.

Bibliography

Archive Documents

National Archives: ADM 1/16621, ADM 1/17779, ADM 1/25106, ADM 116/5264, ADM 116/5324, ADM 116/5533, AIR 2/8678, AIR 49/384, AIR 77/271, AN 35/20, AN 7/139, AST 7/1007, AST 7/1098, AST 7/1129, AST 7/1148, AST 7/1154, AST 7/1165, AST 7/1167, AST 7/1195, AST 7/1206, AST 7/1213, AST 7/1394, AST 7/857, AST 7/913, AVIA 22/1207, AVIA 22/465, BD 18/1492, BD 18/32, BD 2/1, BK 2/126, BT 177/1315, BT 255/263, BT 258/1231, BT 64/1482, BT 64/1500, BT 64/1939, BT 64/2976, CAB 122/1181, CAB 122/1278, CAB 122/1278, CAB 124/841, CAB 134/215, CAB 134/215/20, CAB 21/3476, CAB 78/33, CM 23/205, CO 968/189, COAL 35/1, CRES 35/2858, DO 35/1133, DSIR 27/39, DSIR 4/642, ED 146/2, ED 146/21, ED 147/366, ED 147/371, ED 147/384, ED 147/387, ED 147/393, ED 147/420, ED 147/55, ED 147/73, ED 147/85, ED 151/90, ED 160/154, ED 166/230, ED 166/231, ED 169/11, ED 169/35, ED 169/66, ED 220/9, ED 42/12, ED 42/18, ED 42/2, FCO 141/2800, FD 1/444, FD 1/5422, FD 1/5438, FD 1/5460, FO 1051/323, FO 371/44647, FO 371/44648, FO 371/46367, FO 371/51753, FO 371/81763, FO 371/95216, FO 372/4358, FO 372/4361, FO 372/4362, HLG 71/1114, HLG 79/263, HLG 79/878, HO 186/2483, HO 187/1090, HO 213/1829, HO 334/229, HO 45/25320, IR 34/1141, IR 34/1162, IR 34/1165, IR 34/1168, IR 34/1170, IR 34/1171, IR 34/1173, IR 34/1174, IR 34/1176, IR 34/1177, IR 34/1179, IR 34/1183, IR 34/1184, IR 34/1188, IR 36/107, IR 40/12420, IR 40/13472, LAB 10/1219, LAB 12/495, LAB 12/497, LAB 12/680, LAB 25/208, LAB 26/273, LAB 6/2, LAB 9/178, LAB 9/203, LAR 1/272, LAR 1/315, LRRO 1/4841, MAF 154/365, MAF 156/262, MAF 223/97, MAF 313/2, MAF 313/26, MAF 313/3, MAF 313/4, MAF 313/5, MAF 79/63, MAF 79/78, MAF 84/202, MAF 84/204, MAF 99/1124, MAF 99/1246, MEPO 2/6429, MH 10/156, MH 10/160, MH 101/34, MH 133/369, MH 133/449, MH 154/341, MH 174/23, MH 52/491, MH 55/2023, MH 77/149, MH 77/220, MH 79/547, MH 79/552, MH 79/621, MH 79/623, MH 89/158, MT 101/59, MT 39/463, MT 47/223, MT 55/237, MT 55/239, MT 6/2765, MT 6/2767, MT 6/2787, MT 6/2791, MT 6/2800, MT 6/2822, MT 9/4849, PIN 15/3703, PIN 16/24, PIN 18/67, PIN 19/80, PIN 22/62, PIN 23/144, PIN 7/292, PIN 7/311, PIN 73/1, POWE 25/147, POWE 26/1290, POWE 28/11, POWE 28/29, POWE 28/67, POWE 28/74, POWE 33/1370, POWE 33/1429, POWE 33/1437, POWE 38/13, PREM 11/592, PREM 8/75, PREM 8/77, PRO 1/1476, RAIL 1172/1305, T 161/1248, T 161/1249, T 161/1277, T 213/11, T 213/9, T 216/15, T 225/1265, T 230/152, T 233/1032, T 233/49, T 273/326, T 223/79, WO 106/2825, WO 32/10461, WO 32/10559, WO 32/10561, WO 32/10564, WO 32/12242, WO 32/13808, WO 32/9762, WORK 11/419, WORK 11/420, WORK 11/428, WORK 11/448, WORK 11/449, WORK 11/483, WORK 11/506, WORK

11/534, WORK 11/578, WORK 4/2370, WORK 19/1152, WORK 21/204, WORK 69/16.

Printed Books

Rogers, David, *Men Amidst the Madness: British Technology Development in World War II*, (Solihull: Helion and Company, 2014).

Rogers, David, *Top Secret British Boffins in WW I*, (Solihull: Helion and Company, 2013). *Who was Who 1961-1970*, (London: A. & C. Black Limited, 1967).

Royal Society Publications

Biographical Memoirs of Fellows of the Royal Society Vol 16 1970.

Biographical Memoirs of Fellows of the Royal Society Vol 29 1983.

Obituary Notices of Fellows of the Royal Society Vol 8 1952-1953.

Journals

London Gazette 18 February 1966, issue 43904.

Websites

British Parliament website, *About Parliament – Living Heritage* <http://www.parliament.uk/about/living-heritage/transformingsociety/private-lives/yourcountry/overview/conscriptionww2/>. (Accessed June 2014).

British Parliament, *About Parliament* <http://www.parliament.uk/about/living-heritage/transformingsociety/private-lives/yourcountry/key-dates-/1914-1960/>. (Accessed June 2014).

Cardiff University School of Medicine, *home page* < http://medicine.cf.ac.uk/>. (Accessed July 2014)

Government Legislation, <http://www.legislation.gov.uk/ukpga/Geo6/11-12/29/part/II/crossheading/the-national-assistance-board/enacted>. (Accessed June 2014)

Government Legislation, <http://www.legislation.gov.uk/ukpga/Geo6/11-12/29/part/II/crossheading/the-national-assistance-board/enacted>. (Accessed June 2014).

National Archives, <http://discovery.nationalarchives.gov.uk/SearchUI/details?uri=C2721>. (Accessed May 2014).

National Archives, <http://www.nationalarchives.gov.uk/cabinetpapers/themes/beveridge-report-child-benefit>. (Accessed June 2014).

National Archives, <http://www.nationalarchives.gov.uk/education/topics/attlee-beveridge-report-aims-vision.htm>. (Accessed June 2014).

National Archives, <http://www.nationalarchives.gov.uk/pathways/citizenship/brave_new_world/welfare.htm>. (Accessed June 2014).

Oxford Dictionary on line, *definition of welfare state* <http://www.oxforddictionaries.com/definition/english/welfare-state>. (Accessed June 2014)

Royal Society, *Collections* <http://royalsociety.org/library/collections/>. (Accessed May 2014).

Royal Society, *Collections* <http://royalsociety.org/library/collections/>. (Accessed June 2014).

United States Holocaust Memorial Museum, Learn about the holocaust <http://www.ushmm.org/wlc/en/article.php?ModuleId=10005685>. (Accessed July 2014).

Index

Air Ministry, 26, 29, 42, 51, 52, 56, 57, 79, 190

Alexander, Field Marshall, 18, 19, 20, 21, 22, 24, 42

Anderson, Sir John, 72

Appleton, Sir Edward FRS, 144

Approved Societies, 169, 179-181

Army Council, 42, 43, 45, 59

Army Reserve, 50

Assistance Board, 79, 165-167, 173, 175-177

Attlee, Clement, 55

Bellamy, Dr David, 129

Beveridge, Sir William, 164-166, 172

Board of Education, 196

Board of Trade, 37, 59, 107, 114, 116, 120, 197

Bomb Damage, viii, 186, 197, 199, 200, 202, 209, 211, 223, 224

Branson, Richard, 39

Bridge, 26, 180, 201, 202, 204, 206, 215, 254-256

British Coking Industry, 145

Buckingham Palace, 28, 161, 186, 214, 215

Building Research Station, 212

Burrough, Admiral, 24

Butler, R A B, 92, 99, 209

Cabinet Office, 155, 249

Cabinet, 21-23, 26, 30, 33, 46, 51, 55, 58, 80, 99, 155, 168, 171, 245, 249

Cardiff University, 152, 265

Central Advisory Council, 93, 95

Central Medical War Committee, 68, 69

Central Pharmaceutical War Committee, 71

Chamber of Commerce, 188, 196

Chamberlain, Neville, 72

Channel Islands, 108

Chiefs of Staff, 18, 21, 23, 24, 44, 83

Churchill, Sir Winston, 5, 23, 24, 33, 34, 40, 54, 222

City and Guilds, 106

Civil Defence Camouflage Establishment, 186, 187

Civil Nursing Reserve, 70

Class A Release, 50, 54, 59, 62, 69

Class B release, ix, 46, 51, 54, 55, 62, 63, 70

Clothing coupons, x, 59, 61, 114, 116, 118, 120

Coal Board, 141-144, 146

Coal Commission, 141, 142

Coal Industry, i, 140-142

Coal Mines, 104

Commission for Protection and Restitution of Cultural Material, 99

Conference of Allied Ministers of Education, 98, 99

Coningham, Air Marshal, 24

Conscientious Objectors, vii, 72, 86, 88, 89

Consumer Rationing Order, 107

Corn Exchange, 213

Coupons, vii, ix, x, 56, 59, 61, 107, 108, 112, 114, 116-120, 125-128, 131, 132, 134, 135

Coventry Cathedral, 39, 223

Croft Committee, 54

Curtis, William Edward FRS, 186

Dale, His Honour Judge Edgar T, 156

Defence Committee, 83

Defence Regulations, 32

Defence works, 206

Demobilisation Scheme, viii, 46, 64, 242

Department of Health, 155, 158

Department of Scientific and Industrial Research (DSIR), 144, 199, 212

Dependents Allowance, 79

Education Act, i, vii, xii, 92, 93, 95-98, 209
Eisenhower, General, 18-22, 42
European Recovery Programme (ERP), 234-237

Family Allowances Act, 165
Folkestone Harbour, 207
Food Books, 61
Food Transport, 123
French soldiers, 66

Gower Committee, 156
Guards Chapel, 222
Guttmann Sir Ludwig FRS, i, x, 16, 160-162

His Majesty The King, 23, 27, 28, 31-33, 41-45,
    146, 167, 176, 187, 203, 204, 214, 215, 242,
    256
Home Forces, viii, 226
Home Secretary, 20-22, 25, 26
Horse Guards, 26, 221
House of Commons, 22, 23, 33, 54, 61, 115, 217

Identity card, 15, 67, 245, 246
India, viii, 22, 42, 43, 63, 64, 120, 217, 242, 243
Inglis, Sir Charles FRS, 146, 203, 204
Inter-departmental Committee on Heathrow,
    205
Iron and Steel, 136, 137
Ismay, General, 23, 24

Kirk, Admiral, 24

Leeds College of Technology, 105
Local Education Authority, 92
London Plan, viii, 146, 203, 254-256

Marshall Aid, viii, 234, 235
Marylebone Cricket Club, 102
Mellanby, Sir Edward FRS, 121-123
Merchant seaman, 119
Military Training Act, 72, 75
Minister of Defence, 83
Minister of Fuel and Power, 142, 144
Minister of Health, 32, 68, 70, 157, 168, 172

Minister of Information, 31
Minister of Labour, 46, 53, 61, 70, 71, 86, 89, 102,
    155, 158, 262
Minister of National Insurance, 167, 169, 184
Minister of Reconstruction, 31
Minister of War Transport, viii, 146, 254
Ministry of Agriculture, 109
Ministry of Food, 61, 109-111, 114, 125, 126,
    129, 130, 241, 248
Ministry of Fuel and Power, 26, 134, 135, 138,
    142
Ministry of Health, 32, 55, 68, 70, 71, 84, 150,
    154, 155, 158, 180
Ministry of Labour and National Service, 54, 84,
    89, 90, 179, 245, 247
Ministry of Labour, 30, 37, 54, 61, 73, 84, 88-90,
    179, 183, 201, 245, 247, 259
Ministry of National Insurance, 169, 170, 174,
    175, 179, 183, 247
Ministry of Pensions, 32, 45, 79, 177, 178
Ministry of Supply, 37, 136
Ministry of Transport, 131, 170, 201, 203, 262
Ministry of Works, 28, 145, 188, 193, 215, 223
Mobile Labour Force, 194
Montgomery, Field Marshal, 40
Morrison, Herbert, 31
Motor Spirit, 131, 132, 134

National Assistance Act, 165, 166, 175, 178
National Assistance, viii, 73, 79, 165-167, 172-
    178, 183
National Coal Board, 141-144
National Debt Commissioners, 141
National Federation of Old Age Pensions
    Associations, 176
National Health Service, i, viii, 122, 150, 151, 154,
    155, 157, 159, 165, 172, 248
National Health Services Act, 150, 154, 165
National Hospital Service Reserve, 157, 158
National Insurance Act, 165, 166, 168, 170, 261
National Insurance Bill, 179, 181
National Insurance, viii, 165-172, 174-176, 178,
    179, 181, 183, 184, 247, 248, 261
National Maritime Board, 169

National Register, 245-248
National Registration, viii, 80, 111, 245-248
National Service Grants, ix, 79, 80
National Service Hostels Corporation, 90
National Service Personnel, 87, 88
National Services Act, 72
National Tea, 252
National Union of Mineworkers, 142

Old Age Pensions Act, 175
Olympic Games, 103, 162

Paralympic Games, viii, 16, 158, 163
Pedigree Breeders, 125
Pensions, 32, 45, 66, 79, 147, 155, 165, 173, 175-179, 182, 243, 247
Petrol Rationing Scheme, 130, 131
Petroleum Board, 131, 231, 232
Polish airmen, 66
Poor Law, 165, 166
Port warehouses, 197
Portsmouth, 190
President, 21, 25, 42, 44, 83, 89, 155, 222, 223, 234, 236, 237, 245
Prime Minister, 21-25, 27, 29, 31, 32, 43, 55, 72, 84, 217, 239
Pyke, Dr Magnus, 129

Ration Book, x, 108, 110, 124, 125, 129, 133, 246
Rationing Schemes, viii, 250, 251
Reconstruction Committee, 223, 224
Rehabilitation, 93, 100, 101, 137, 158, 159, 161, 162, 179, 188
Release Book, ix, 49, 52
Requisitioned Land, 148
Reservists, 86, 246
Road Haulage Association, 138
Roberts Commission, 100
Royal Army Service Corps (RASC), 50
Royal Electrical and Mechanical Engineers (REME), 50, 56, 78
Royal Institute of British Architects, 191
Russia, 34

Salford, 210, 211
Shinwell, Emanuel, 142
Southampton, 188
Special Repair Service Camp, 193
St Paul's, 26, 28
Stalin, Marshal, 25
Standing Cancer and Radiotherapy Advisory Committee, 153
Standing Pharmaceutical Advisory Committee, 152
Stoke Mandeville Hospital, 16, 159, 162, 163
Supply Departments, 29, 239, 240
Supreme Commanders, 43
Supreme Headquarters of the Allied Expeditionary Forces, 101

Tedder, Air Chief Marshal, 24
Town and Country Planning Act, 210
Trafalgar Square, 27
Transport Act, 138, 139, 260
Transport Bill, viii, 147, 258
Treasury Chambers, 30, 238
Treasury, 27, 29-31, 56, 79, 129, 130, 136, 137, 141, 142, 167, 173, 219-223, 238-241
Truman, President, 25, 234

Unemployability Supplement, 184
Unemployment Insurance Act, 171
Unemployment Insurance, 167, 168, 171, 183
United Nations Relief and Rehabilitation Administration, 100
United Nations, 27, 99, 100, 122
United States, 19, 22, 34, 35, 42, 44, 100, 101, 171, 186, 234, 236, 237, 265

VE Day, vii, 15, 18-24, 27, 28, 31-34, 42
VJ Day, vii, ix, 35, 36, 53, 100, 187
Voluntary Schools, 209

Walker Committee, 56
War Cabinet, 21-23, 30, 46, 51, 58
War Damage Act, 187, 192, 208
War Damage Commission, viii, 186, 187, 191, 192, 195, 207, 213, 214, 223

War Debris, 190
War Gratuity, 56-58
War Office, 36, 42, 45, 56, 57, 59, 71, 222, 246
War Service Grants, 79, 80
Welfare (Foods) Schemes, 112, 113
Welfare State, i, viii, x, 164-166, 172, 180, 265
Wilhelmina, Queen, 41
Windsor Castle, 27
Women's Voluntary Services, 107
Woolton, Lord, 31

Lightning Source UK Ltd.
Milton Keynes UK
UKOW06f1616150216

268396UK00005B/223/P